KEEPING
THE
LOVE
YOU FIND

A Guide for Singles

KEEPING
THE
LOVE
YOU FIND

A Guide for Singles

HARVILLE HENDRIX, PH.D.

POCKET BOOKS
New York London Toronto Sydney Tokyo Singapore

TO ALL MY CHILDREN

Hunter, Leah, Kimberly, Kathryn, Mara, and Josh

and the success of their future marriages

POCKET BOOKS, a division of Simon & Schuster Inc.
1230 Avenue of the Americas, New York, NY 10020

Hendrix, Harville.
    Keeping the love you find / Harville Hendrix.
        p.   cm.
    Includes bibliographical references and index.
    ISBN: 0-671-73419-9 : $22.00
        1. Interpersonal relations.   2. Love.   3. Single people.
    I. Title.
HQ801.H46   1992
306.7—dc20   91-32329
                                                    CIP

DESIGN: Stanley S. Drate/Folio Graphics Co. Inc.

First Pocket Books hardcover printing February 1992

10   9   8   7   6   5   4   3   2   1

Printed in the U.S.A.

Contents

Part I

BEING HUMAN, BEING SINGLE

v

Part IV

_____

THE JOURNEY OF PARTNERSHIP

Part V

BECOMING A CONSCIOUS SINGLE

Special Acknowledgment

to
Laura Torbet

I want to express my deep appreciation to Laura Torbet. Laura is an author in her own right and an accomplished editor and writer. Working with her over the past eighteen months, I have come to know her as a person as well as an artist. She is intelligent, resourceful, patient, tireless, and well organized. She takes initiative and is completely responsible—as well as fun. Working with her has been extremely satisfying and instructive.

But I want to make my debt to her specific. Laura is responsible for the design, organization, and flow of the work. Starting with some chapter drafts and notes, and embellishing with hours of tape-recorded interviews and conversations, she has helped me bring this long-gestating book to birth. I especially appreciate her patience with the many additions of ideas and processes I made along the way, her patient reworking of chapters to incorporate emergent ideas, and the many revisions this required. Without her expertise as a writer, her dedication to the project, and her enthusiasm, the book would not have been written for a long time. Thank you, Laura.

Acknowledgments

Writing a book is always a joint venture. Every writer is dependent upon the research and ideas of others. I am indebted to the giants in the mental-health field: Sigmund Freud and Carl Jung for their understanding of the unconscious; Eric Berne, Harry Stack Sullivan, and Martin Buber, for their insights into the interpersonal; Erik Erikson and Margaret Mahler for their contributions to my understanding of the developmental process; John Pierakos for insights into human energy systems; and B. F. Skinner, for my understanding of behavioral reinforcement. In addition, I am embedded in the Western spiritual tradition upon which I am dependent for my understanding of transcendence.

Closer to home, I would like to thank the staff at the Institute for Relationship Therapy—Nancy Jones, Audrey Davis, Lory Lazrus, and Mark McColl—for managing the details of the Institute so I could have time to write. Appreciation is also due to the hundreds of singles and couples from whom I have gleaned most of my ideas, and the students in my training program who have given me valuable feedback on my theories and therapeutic processes. Barney Karpfinger, my agent, deserves special mention for his support. I also want to thank Leslie Wells, for her early feedback on the manuscript while she was an editor at Pocket Books, and Claire Zion, who took it over in process and brought it to completion. I especially appreciate her thoughtful and helpful critiques and enthusiasm.

But my deepest appreciation goes to my wife, Helen, for her patience during the past eighteen months as she shared me with the computer. She endured endless discussions about the project, sharing her ideas with me, supporting and participating in my vision of healthy intimate relationships while taking on more than her share of family duties. In short, she has been unconditionally supportive of me in this enterprise. Last, I want to thank Leah and Hunter, my youngest children, for their inspiration, their enjoyment of having a dad who is a writer, and for their patience with me when I could not stop and play with them during the final phases of the work.

Introduction

I don't know your personal history, but I suspect that, like most single adults in this country, you are no stranger to the pain and disillusionment of love gone awry. Perhaps you want very much to fall in love and marry, but you never seem to meet the right person. Or, when you do, it doesn't last: your love is not returned, or the one you love doesn't want to be tied down. Maybe you are divorced—perhaps not for the first time. Or you are separated, caught in the tangled emotional and financial throes of dividing the spoils—and the children—of a marriage that didn't make it. As a gay or lesbian, you may find it hard to create and sustain a committed relationship in a society that doesn't recognize nonheterosexual marriage. If you are widowed, you can't imagine how to find love anew if it means going to singles bars or placing ads in the personals column.

Maybe your love life has been a series of one-night—or three-night—stands: either they're not right, or you're not right, but the result is the same—on to the next. Perhaps it's gotten to the point where you date just to have someone to go to the movies with, or to sleep with, but you never seem to fall in love, or you get bored quickly, and the idea of staying in a relationship is scary. If you're involved with someone now, you may be wondering whether it will last, but already you can see that your partner is not the person you thought he or she was; it's bound to end soon, and you will be alone, again.

For singles today, the spectrum of experience is broad, but confusion and despair about finding lasting love run deep. Marriage and commitment seem both elusive and perilous, fraught with potential for hurt and heartbreak. It's not surprising that many single people become frantic about finding a mate, any mate. Others, too discouraged to try again, give up the search for lasting love and, like wounded animals, retreat to their caves to lick their wounds. They turn their attention to making the most of their single lives, their work and friends, their homes and hobbies, resigning themselves to casual, occasional relationships, or to none at all. I sympathize with them, for it is understandable to feel that the next time won't be very different from the last, and that they may be better off alone. And yet . . . most of us still harbor the dream of lasting love. We still hope that it will happen to us.

I believe that dream is possible for just about anyone who chooses to pursue it—whether you have never married, are divorced or widowed, gay or lesbian, young or old—and I believe that its fulfill-ment is vital to our wholeness. It is the goal of *Keeping the Love You Find* to show you how you can realize that dream. [NOTE: I want to acknowledge that while most of the material in this book pertains as well to homosexual singles, and it is my hope that gays and lesbians will find it useful, it is addressed more directly to heterosexual singles.]

A PERSONAL NOTE

For over ten years I have worked with couples in troubled mar-riages. It is often discouraging and heartbreaking work. The partners are angry, disillusioned, and in pain. They feel betrayed by their mates—and by love itself. Caught in a vortex of intense emotions and entrenched behavior, they can't understand how their joy evap-orated, how their love turned to dust. I am often discouraged, too, because I know that in order for them to heal their marriages, there is much to learn—about themselves and about relationships. But too often they are overwhelmed by their day-to-day conflicts, and it is too late, and too hard—no matter how badly they want to make it right again—for the long, arduous process of reeducation and re-loving.

I saw this in my own first marriage. Although I was a pastoral counselor myself, years of therapy and the best of intentions couldn't seem to put it back together again. Now I recognize that the ingredients of lasting love remained a mystery to us, and to the professionals we worked with; we just didn't have the information and skills vital to the survival of our partnership. My devastation over the failure of that marriage, which we tried so hard to rescue, led me to devote my studies and my professional life to uncovering the true nature, and the deeper purpose, of relationships. It was during this period that I developed the theories and practice of Imago Relationship Therapy, which is the foundation for this book. Now, happily, I am in a marriage that works very differently, but sometimes I wonder what would have happened *if only I'd known then what I now know about relationships*, not only for myself, but for the couples who I counseled with such frustrating results.

It's that feeling of "if only . . ." that inspired me to write *Keeping the Love You Find*. Whatever your history, whatever your heartbreak, I believe that as a single person you have an advantage over those who are married and trying to solve their problems in the throes of day-to-day crisis and hurt. You are in an ideal position to learn what you need to know and what you can do to greatly improve your chances for finding, and keeping, love. I do not mean to diminish your doubt and anguish, but I believe you are fortunate to be single in a culture that offers you the wherewithal and the opportunity to know yourself and your needs, to learn how to live on your own, to experiment with sex, relationships, and careers before you marry. Not only that, but if you don't get it right the first time, you're allowed second, and even third and fourth, chances to get it right.

This book is not like other singles books. It is not about how to snare the perfect mate, because the perfect mate is a myth. And it is certainly not about the joys of being single, for while I respect those who choose to remain single in these difficult times, I don't believe that you can fully grow and become whole except in a committed relationship. This book is about *relationships*; in particular, it is about what you can do *now*, as a single person, to prepare for lasting love.

I believe in the transforming power of love. And I believe that just about anyone, no matter how discouraged by past failures, or how troubled his or her history, can find and keep love. In 1988 I wrote a book called *Getting the Love You Want: A Guide for Couples*, which was about repairing damaged relationships. *Keeping the Love You Find* is about *preventing* them. So much of the heartbreak of love could be avoided if we would postpone marriage until we learn what relationships are really about, and until we uncover the hidden land mines we bring to our partnerships. I think you will find that the program outlined in this book opens the door to growth and change, and to an awareness of the tremendous potential for healing and happiness inherent in the modern love marriage.

However, I don't have any quick cures for your relationship blues. You may find that the message of this book is discouraging at times, because while I'm idealistic about love, I'm hard-nosed about what

makes it work. But I assure you that if you do the work, you will see
results. You will know yourself better, you will understand what
relationships are really about, and you will be able to work on the
things in yourself that need to be changed in order to have the
partnership you yearn for. You will be able to break the repetitive
patterns of past relationships; you will change the kind of person to
whom you are attracted (and who eventually frustrates you); and
you will be in a better position to attract someone who is willing and
able to work to achieve a deep and lasting love. The severity of your
partnership conflicts will be lessened, and you will have the tools to
deal more effectively with what does come up.

HOW THE BOOK WORKS

Keeping the Love You Find is presented in five sections. Part I looks
at who we are as singles and as human beings, what it is that we
long for from life, and how our relationships can be the path to the
fulfillment of our deepest yearnings.

The purpose of Parts II and III is to reeducate us about ourselves,
to show how the experiences of childhood brought us to where we
find ourselves today. Part II talks about how we were nurtured; Part
III is about our socialization. Because how we were socialized with
regard to gender and sexuality has such a powerful influence on our
relationships, I have devoted a whole chapter to this topic. As you
read these sections and complete the exercises, it will become clear
how your particular childhood experiences charted the course you
now follow. You will see that who we fall in love with, and how we
behave in our relationships, is a direct outgrowth of what came
before.

The dynamics of partnership is the subject of Part IV, which
begins with your discovering what kind of partner your childhood
has prepared you to fall in love with. In all likelihood, you will find
the description of what I call the "unconscious" relationship all too
familiar, from its romantic beginning in mystery and joy, through
the long siege of disillusionment and anger, struggle and disappointment, to its ending in mystery and pain. On a more hopeful note,
we will chart the course of the kind of intentional, truly intimate
relationship that we want, a "conscious" relationship, in which
couples understand and accept the challenge of keeping the love
they find.

Part V is the nuts-and-bolts section, an intensive training course
in which you practice the skills and work on the behavior changes
necessary to become a "conscious single," in preparation for a

conscious partnership. In the final chapter I will give you a preview of the prize for the hard work of a conscious relationship: real love.

Love is hard—life is hard—but it's the only game in town. It's a high-stakes game, because how well you play determines how you will thrive and grow. You might as well learn to play it as well as possible, as soon as possible. I believe that *Keeping the Love You Find* tells you what you need to know to do just that.

PART

I

BEING HUMAN, BEING SINGLE

1

What's Wrong with Being Single?

Everything that lives, lives not alone nor
for itself.

—WILLIAM BLAKE

For the first time in our cultural history, being single is considered
by some to be a preferred life-style. It's easy to see why. Carefree
singles breeze through cola commercials with adorable partners,
wearing great clothes, having a fabulous time. No doubt they have
interesting careers, and apartments filled with the latest appliances
and high-tech sound equipment. After dining out in trendy restau-
rants, they come home and have wild sex (of course!)—and there are
no kids or dirty laundry to deal with.

An appealing scenario . . . but it's not the whole picture. I heard
quite a different story from the singles who attended my workshops,
many of whom had recycled through singlehood several times. They
were there because the single life—even if it included the nice clothes
and dream dates—wasn't making them happy, and they were wondering if there wasn't more to life, if they were ever going to find
someone they really loved who would love them in return and with
whom they would live happily ever after.

3

Now, why is that? Why, when in our society, finally, it is possible to live a good life alone, to live with a lover, to have sex with numerous partners, or even to have children outside of marriage, when marriage often seems like just the first step toward divorce, do most single people still want to marry? And why, for that matter, are those who are divorced or widowed so anxious to reenlist? To me the answer is very simple: we have an unconscious yearning for partnership, which is essential for our fulfillment; without it we can never feel whole. In this book I want to show you why our desire for a committed relationship is so powerful. I'll explain why you haven't had such a relationship (or why the attempts you've made have failed) and how you can. But first I want to talk about the issues singles are facing today. In particular I want to address the widespread lack of understanding about the deeper purpose of relationships, which I feel is at the heart of the confusion and pain felt so acutely by singles today.

Singledom: A Neglected Rite of Passage

Much can be said in favor of the single life, and this thirty-year-old New York ad-copy writer says it well:

"I have had a great time since coming to the city after graduation. I started out in a Greenwich Village walk-up with my old college roommate; we were scraping by on our entry-level wages. We learned how to iron our shirts and we cooked on a two-burner hotplate. In the evenings we'd check out free local entertainment and poetry readings, and cadge the free food at local bars during 'Happy Hour.' I met all kinds of people, many of them pretty strange by Midwestern-college standards. Now I have my own place in a high-rise on the Upper East Side with a modern kitchen—even a microwave. I've dated a lot off and on, many different women, usually nothing serious, but one who I lived with for almost two years (and who broke my heart). I've been to Europe twice and last year I camped and hitchhiked my way across Canada. I've been studying t'ai chi for two years and been in therapy for one. I'm terrified of getting married—it doesn't seem to me like I see many terrific marriages—but I've noticed that I'm beginning to lose interest in just having someone to go out with on a Saturday night, or even just another sexual adventure—and I never thought I'd say that. My girlfriend and I are about to move in together, and now it feels like it might be time to settle down."

I'd say this young man has had the ideal single life. His single period has been a *stage*, not an end in itself. Although it has been a period of relatively footloose independence, he has had to take care of his day-to-day living and be responsible for his own welfare. His time and his money are his own, and he's made his own choices about career, friends, and travel. He's experimented with different life-styles and with sex and dating, and pursued newfound interests and hobbies. He's sown his wild oats, and along the way had various relationships with women, at least one of them a relatively serious living arrangement. There have been good times and bad. He has established an identity separate from the collective/familial matrix from which he emerged. Through all of this, he has developed a strong sense of who he is, what he wants, and how to get it. It seems to me that his single years have provided him with education, experience, and an expanded awareness of the world. He is ready to move on without regrets.

I wish I could say that this man's story was typical. Unfortunately, many singles manage to bungle this valuable opportunity for independence and self-knowledge. It's not surprising, for despite the freedoms, choices, and wherewithal singles have today, many of them haven't a clue about how to make the most of their single years. But how should they know? Until recently there was no such thing as singledom as we know it—it was merely a bridge between the childhood bed and the marriage bed, to be crossed as quickly and uneventfully as possible. It's no wonder that, free to live in new and exploratory and self-defining ways, young men and women play out traditional scripts, or grapple in confusion with murky new gender roles and relationship dynamics.

Typically, the tales I hear are of women whose entire focus during their single years is staking out a mate, and not just any mate, but one who meets an exhaustive list of specifications. Predictably, they are disappointed that this paragon hasn't made an appearance, or, if he has, that he's not dying to tie the knot. I talk to young men, trained on a parallel track (same teachers, different lessons!) who devote these same years single-mindedly to having as good a time as possible, chalking up sexual conquests while they move through the appropriate career ranks as fast as possible. Complaining that all their dates want from them is a marriage proposal, they avoid for as long as they can the kind of intimacy that they will have to face when the pressure builds on them to knuckle under to grown-up demands. You'd think men and women came from different planets, they are so at cross-purposes.

Those who go against the social grain have their own set of problems. Young women intent on establishing careers feel at risk in postponing marriage, knowing that their statistical chances of marrying decline precipitously the longer they wait. Women still have the stigma of old-maidhood to contend with. "Does anyone notice," laments Mary Anne Meyer in an essay on the *New York Times* Op-Ed page, "the paradox of a society that says no matter how much success a woman achieves, she hasn't really made it until she says 'I do'?"[1] Young men who are *not* focused on advancing their careers, or who try and explore nontraditional gender paths, also feel they pay a price; they worry that their eligibility and desirability are compromised.

Appearances to the contrary, these are difficult times for singles. A glance at the wealth of newspaper and magazine offerings for singles tells the story. First there are all the products and services aimed at bringing singles together: the Club Med vacations, the single-gourmet clubs, the singles-only condominiums; the books on how to meet men, or to pick up women, on learning what the opposite sex is really like and what they want; the personals ads in which singles enumerate the qualities they want—and offer—in a mate. Then there are the offerings aimed at singles for whom none of the above seems to be working: therapists specializing in the depression and loneliness of singles, support groups for the "temporarily single," dating services that promise to deliver where others have failed, books on women who love too much and on men who hate women. Singles feel caught between a rock and a hard place, unwilling to go backward to a traditional relationship, unprepared to move forward to the new, under pressure both to settle down and to live it up. What, as they say, is wrong with this picture?

REDEFINING SINGLENESS

In *Childhood and Society*,[2] the famed psychoanalyst Erik Erikson talks about the moratorium period observed in most primitive societies, in which the individual is allowed, even expected, to have a period of irresponsible dependency before settling down with a mate, having children, and becoming a contributing member of the community.

In our culture, those fortunate enough to go to college have, by default, such a moratorium. Even so, many college students marry soon after graduation, before they've had a chance to try their wings. Though the increasing numbers of students going to college have raised the average age of first marriages in recent years, many young people still marry directly out of high school. Those who get the opportunity to fly solo for a while do so without a clear map of where they're going, or where to land.

A BETTER WAY

We need to redefine singleness, to update the rules, and to educate singles as to the purpose and benefits of this vital transition. I suggest that the best way to accomplish this is to institute a modernized version of Erikson's moratorium. In our society we hold up to young people a model of early decision and commitment as to life's path, and then we end up with burned-out executives and displaced homemakers thirty years down the line.

Not that all early marriages are disastrous, by any means. Those who have had a healthy family life, who have used college or their early work years to explore and establish a sense of self, and who have made good partner choices, have what it takes for a successful marriage, despite their youth. But these are fortunate circumstances. To my mind, most people should wait to marry until they're well into their twenties. During this period between childhood/school and marriage, singles would be *expected* to try on the world and its goods and services for size. There would be no pressure to marry; in fact there would be pressure *not* to marry. For that matter, there would be pressure not to fixate on career, but rather to explore all areas of life. Singleness would be recognized as a vital stage of the journey to maturation, a time to learn about who we are, to learn responsibility and self-sufficiency, to identify our true desires, and to confront our inner strengths and demons, a time to make changes in the things that stymie our pleasure and progress in life, to learn how to connect and communicate on all levels. It would be sorely needed relationship training.

If it were to become the norm for singles to delay marriage until they had made this journey, many of the problems that sabotage relationships would not arise. To be sure, certain deep issues only appear, and can only be resolved, in a committed, day-by-day partnership. But some of the underbrush could be cleared away. Fundamental issues of selfhood would have been dealt with, so that they would not be an additional burden on marriage. Partners would know themselves better; they would be more comfortable with intimacy, and ready to take on the responsibilities of marriage. Knowing more about what they truly want from life, they would not face so many surprises later on. Such singles would be more able to cope with the powerful psychological confrontations that are intrinsic to marriage, and more aware of its tremendous spiritual potential. Besides, what's the rush? At twenty-eight or thirty or thirty-two, there is still plenty of time to have a couple of kids, to move ahead with a career that has been freely chosen.

IT'S NEVER TOO LATE TO BE SINGLE

Given the limited life expectancy of marriage today, being single is not just for the young. Thirty-, forty-, and sixty-something singlehood can be particularly difficult for those who married early and innocent, who thought they'd managed to avoid confronting their loneliness and dependence. All too often mid-life singledom is compounded by fears of aging or entering the job market for the first time, by the difficulties of raising children alone, by financial straits.

But a moratorium on mate hunting can be an invaluable opportunity for self-discovery at any age. Even forced, unwanted singleness can be a blessing in disguise, a time for healing and reestablishing one's priorities and sense of oneself. I've heard numerous tales from divorced people who dreaded being on their own, even if their marriages were loveless and painful, who dreaded "dating" and reentering careers, but who found to their relief that their new lives were a wonderful balm, a time to heal and to reconnect with themselves.

A middle-aged woman who had great foreboding about the loneliness and change of life-style that leaving her marriage portended was pleasantly surprised:

"I would find myself singing around the house; I relished the most elementary things, like eating a meal alone (and eating exactly what I wanted and when I wanted, no matter how unorthodox). I took baths, browsed through magazines, stayed up half the night working. For a long time I had no desire or need to find a mate; it was as though I had to put myself back together, to find out who I was and what I really liked, in every area. In some ways it was tremendously painful, but my growing sense of myself and my ability to go it alone were a revelation to me. Of course, there came the time when things just seemed so easy on my own that I feared any involvement that would upset my equilibrium. And now I worry that at my age I won't find a partner. But that's another story."

Brian, a driven, headstrong man who divorced in his fifties, told me that after an initial splurge of dating and doing everything to avoid going home to his empty apartment, he found out that what he really liked to do was bake bread, stay up late and play the piano (which he hadn't touched since he was twenty), go in late to the office, and take camping trips to exotic fishing areas—all of which were radical changes from what he thought his life was about. "Why did it take me so long to figure this out?" he said. "And couldn't I have had all this, and my marriage, too?" Many divorced or widowed people—especially if they can get past what one man characterized as his period of "panic and promiscuity"—do with their singleness what they should have done *before* they married the first time: live alone, find their own rhythms, date a variety of people, go into therapy, develop new friends and interests, learn how to live with and care for themselves.

FOREVER SINGLE

For increasing numbers of people, however, singleness is not just an interlude between relationships, but a permanent life choice. Some consider it a sacrifice necessary to pursue demanding creative or career goals, while for others it is a rebellion against expected gender roles or responsibilities, and for yet others a decision to avoid either the pain or the intimacy they've experienced in past relationships. (In a separate category are those whose singleness is a part of their religious vows, and their devotion to a life of service. In this case, there is a cultural validation for singleness. But even Roman Catholic nuns, who have chosen singleness and celibacy, take vows of "marriage" to Jesus.)

I have a friend who has chosen to remain single. A dedicated composer, he is a semi-hermit who works erratic hours and lives a simple life, content getting by on the $15–20,000 income that his work generates. He fears that marriage would obligate him not only to increase his income, but to change his habits and whole way of life at the expense of his true love, music. "I live in a ramshackle cabin with a leaky roof. There's no TV, I've got no health insurance, and I haven't left the state in three years. Do I sound like an eligible bachelor to you?"

Ingrid, a dedicated research chemist, says she is happy with her life but angry at the choice she feels she's had to make.

> "Men in my position have wives to take care of them, to cope with the daily chores and logistics and distractions, and to be of support. Not only is it hard for a woman like me to find a man who would understand or tolerate my immersion in my work, but in most cases I would be expected to give this up in order to have the privileges of marriage. At least nowadays I can have a lover without getting too much flak—though for some people it's a problem that my current lover is so much

younger than I—again, a choice that would go unnoticed if I were a man."

In a somewhat different category are those who are single by default. They may have come to terms with living a single life, and to making the best of it—which many do well. But on some level, in choosing to be single they have given up their dream of a relationship, often because they have been badly hurt in the past. As Edna Ferber quipped, "Being an old maid is like death by drowning, not an altogether unpleasant sensation after you cease to struggle."

For some, of course, the choice to remain single is but a rationalization of their inability to deal with the demands of a relationship: "I need my space," "I never found the right person," "My work consumes all my energy." Often those who choose singleness have run repeatedly into the same problems and pains. They feel that their troubled childhoods have left them with scars that wreak devastation in each successive relationship. Wounds are reopened and not healed; again and again they find themselves in the same stuck place. And so they decide, perhaps rightly, that they are better off alone. They choose to make the best of the situation, in a cultural climate that at least tolerates their singleness.

I see the coming years as happier ones for those who choose to remain single, and more productive ones for those who see singlehood as a stage in their growth, a passage en route to marriage. I applaud the growing acceptance of singleness, and hope that it becomes even less stigmatized. But as you have no doubt guessed, I see singleness in a limited framework, as an opportunity to find and establish oneself, at whatever stage of life. Mostly, given my own experience, my view of human nature, and my experience with singles, I see *what's wrong* with being single. Presumably, you're reading this book because you don't think it's so hot either, even if you're currently enjoying your single life. Presumably your desire is to be in a lasting relationship, and presumably that hasn't come to pass yet.

WE'VE GOTTA HAVE IT

Singles often tell me they feel there's something wrong with them because they're so needy of a relationship. Sometimes, they say, they get to the point where they just hope that someone—anyone, practically—will come along and fall in love with them, and they'll get married and everything will work out fine. This seems immature and desperate, but such "it's my only chance" marriages occur all too frequently, with disastrous results. People who marry without honoring the mandate of their singleness are, in a way, just postponing their single years until after they divorce—unless they get lucky, or work very hard in their marriages, or stay in dead-end relationships.

I don't want to judge too harshly, though, because in most cases something more complex is going on here—not just a desperation to get married, or a desire to fill up an empty life. That neediness is symptomatic of a profound but unrecognized desire in the unconscious, a manifestation of the human need for wholeness and connection and, specifically, for a safe, intimate, enlivening partnership. I am saying that in order to feel whole, to feel fully alive, fully human, and to heal the wounds we carry from childhood, *we've gotta have it*. This sounds pretty dramatic, but I believe it is profoundly true. It is not just a matter of desperate singles. Our human nature and needs, no matter how we rationalize or adapt, cannot be denied.

Just think about how we use the term single—it doesn't at all mean what the word implies. We define singles *in relationship to their relationships:* divorced, widowed, separated, engaged, bachelors or spinsters—some version of *not married*. On the surface, this may seem to reflect our society's bias toward marriage; in fact, it reveals our unconscious acknowledgment of our essential relational nature. We have only to recall how alive and at peace with the world we feel when we are in love and connected to another, how disconnected and out of sorts we feel when such a connection is missing, to see the truth of this.

Health statistics reveal our innate need for relationship. People who are single over long periods of time tend to suffer from depression to one degree or another; they have weakened immune systems and so are more vulnerable to disease and have a shorter life expectancy. They are also less efficient in the workplace, and less able to weather crisis or disappointment. It is practically a commonplace for a widowed person to go into decline, to become ill and even die within a year or so of a spouse's death—whether the marriage was a happy one or not. And numerous studies have demonstrated the withering effect of neglect or lack of affection on babies.[3]

In short, we need relationships, and in particular we need the kind of committed long-term love relationships that allow us to heal and grow. To my way of thinking, perpetual singleness stunts growth, for it denies the fundamental needs of the unconscious. I believe that singleness is meant to be a stage, not a permanent way of life. There are certain things that we can only accomplish, spiritually and psychologically, in a committed dyadic relationship. I don't want singles criticized. They have been left dangling in the breeze by a culture that doesn't understand, or support, the purpose of singleness in modern times. Singles are coping with serious problems without the tools to deal with them. I want singleness to be accepted and, moreover, to be understood and encouraged in its proper context. At the same time, I want to put an end to the idea that it is a choice equal in value to marriage. It isn't. In choosing to remain single we are accepting a cap on our development and ignoring the directives of the unconscious at our peril. We are meant to be coupled.

THE PROBLEM WITH SINGLES

So I sympathize with those who so fervently want to find, and keep, love. But it can be frustrating dealing with singles, for often I find them woefully ignorant in their expectations and behavior with regard to relationships. Brought up by the old rules and playing by the new, they want to be intimate with others before they understand what intimacy is, and before they've been intimate with themselves.

For years, when I was a minister, I worked with singles in church groups. It never ceased to amaze me that without fail during the course of any meeting several of the assembled multitude—surrounded as they were by one hundred to two hundred attractive potential mates—would go on about how there was no one out there for them or they were never going to meet the right person. No one seemed to fill the bill. Flanked by apparently eligible candidates, they could find no one who interested them.

Another recurrent pattern was that I would get questions that began, "What if the person I meet *won't* . . . ," followed by a variety of thinly veiled complaints: " . . . be open," " . . . call back," " . . . have sex," " . . . be honest," " . . . marry me," " . . . pay for dinner." It struck me that these people were sorely lacking in basic communication and relationship skills—or why would they be asking such questions? And would it even help if I gave them the answers: "Fred won't marry you because he's having a good time being single." "Mona won't have sex with you because she thinks that's all you want from her." "Irwin senses how needy you are, and he feels threatened by that, so he won't be calling again." "Alan won't pay for dinner because he doesn't like being thought of as a meal ticket and you have to reassure him that you really care for him."

For a long time I was puzzled as to why these attractive people were having such an inexplicable lack of success in their love lives, until one day I was talking to the minister who ran the singles program in a large congregation nearby. He admitted that he was having the same problems. "You know," he said to me, "what I've concluded is that many singles just aren't mature—they're not connected to reality, they don't know themselves, they haven't the capacity to take on responsibilities, and they have fantasy-world ideas about love. They're either running to or running from marriage, but they are in the dark as to what it's really about. They have adult privileges and adult possessions, but they haven't reached adulthood, and that's why they are chronically single."

At first I resisted what he was saying, but that term *chronically single* stuck with me. Now, it's hard to generalize about singledom, but at its core these days is a massive group that could certainly be classified as chronically single—the bachelor who never settles down, the woman whose dates never call back or who never finds the airtight Mr. Right, the single who seems always to have career goals that require postponing marriage. Even those who have had a series of failed marriages are in a way *chronically single*, doing intermittent stints in relationships in the course of their fundamental singleness.

When I was doing singles workshops, I found that singles expected to find some magic answer to their accursed matelessness, hoping that I would tell them what to do, where to go, what to say, so that they would find a mate—fast. Or they hoped that Ms. Right would be sitting next to them, when it seemed obvious to me that they wouldn't recognize true love if it were sitting in their laps. They would still be wondering if there wasn't *still* someone better, and wouldn't know how to proceed to the next stages of intimacy and commitment. One young woman actually said to me, "Well, I love Joel, but he's only a trainee at the bank, and he's not interested in theater or going to museums. What will happen if I tell Joel I'll marry him and *then* I meet someone better?"

So many singles concentrate all their efforts on perfecting the outside trappings and strategies of singleness, in order to stand up to the scrutiny of the mating game, while their inner selves remain unexamined and neglected. They want to find the perfect partner, get married, and *then* worry about being happily married. They reject prospective partners, finding them defective in one way or another, not realizing that the fault is in themselves, the rejectors. The irony is that nearly 50 percent of those who marry before they unpack and examine their childhood baggage, before they get some relationship training, are all but doomed to rejoin the ranks of the single the hard way—via divorce. What they don't understand is that nothing will change until *they* change. They won't meet a healthier, more mature lover until they are healthier and more mature, until they've done their homework and preparation.

FINDING A LOVE TO KEEP

Although this book is not about *finding* a mate, I am well aware of the problems that singles face in meeting prospective partners. Shyness, fear, ambivalence, and past dating disasters can be powerful inhibitors when we go out to seek a partner. Believe me, I have heard many horrifying stories of rejection, embarrassment—even danger—from discouraged singles, and I can appreciate the impulse to stay home to read a book and hope that you'll bump into your beloved-to-be on the way to work. But the inescapable truth is that in order to have a relationship, you do have to put yourself in a position to meet people. This means that you have to expose yourself. I don't mean that you should parade your wares in the town square at high noon, but that you should give yourself as many options as possible by enlarging your pool of potential mates. No one ever met his or her partner sitting at home waiting for UPS to deliver a dream mate. You need to explore every avenue—singles retreats, church groups and special-interest clubs for singles, classes and activities geared to singles sponsored by organizations such as the Learning Annex. Don't rule out the better dating services or placing personals ads in publications that you feel would attract the kind of person you seek.

In addition to physically putting yourself out there, I encourage you to enlarge your pool of choices by expanding the criteria by which you judge them. The narrower and more detailed your checklist of specifications, the more circumscribed your idea of an acceptable date, the more limited your choices. Unwittingly you are dismissing thousands of prospective partners before they've had a chance to win your heart. Expose yourself to dates who look, act, and think differently from what you're used to. Even if you don't believe you'll find your partner this way, you will enlarge *yourself*, and that will enlarge your pool of partners.

I also want to talk for a moment about the issue of self-sabotage that I have noted with many singles. This in part manifests itself in not getting out to meet partners, or severely limiting the criteria for choosing one's potential mate. But it often extends to behavior that is sure to turn off prospective partners. A friend of mine who recently remarried mentioned to me that many women he had dated during his single years would "shoot themselves in the foot." When I asked him to elaborate, he listed several behaviors: talking negatively about their previous dates or relationships; disparaging their looks or intelligence; generally expressing negative attitudes right away, especially about the opposite sex; finding something about him to criticize in the first few minutes; being late and making up an excuse on the first date; blaming the failure of past relationships entirely on their partners; sending messages of availability, sexual or otherwise, and then reacting with shaming, or leaving, when he responded to the message. "Now I wonder if I was doing the same things," he remarked.

Watch out for self-defeating behavior. The capsule recipe for meeting your mate is to be positive, be honest, be available and open to meeting new people, and be yourself with as much self-confidence as you can muster.

The reason I don't have more to say on this subject is that I believe this is all you can do. It is useless to try and nail down the "right" person. Only your unconscious can do that, and you probably won't be too thrilled with what it comes up with. The only thing you can consciously do with regard to your partner choice is to pick someone who is self-aware and who is willing to do the work necessary for lasting love.

YOUR MISSION: BE PREPARED

So, you're asking, how *is* this book going to help me find lasting love? Let me answer that with a metaphor. I like to compare marriage to a rafting trip down the Colorado River. You have a choice about taking the journey, but you cannot avoid the rapids along the way. However, you can learn what to expect, and if you practice on the smaller rapids, you won't drown in the big ones. What I want to present here is a map, so you won't get lost along the way, or be shocked when the white water appears. I also want to provide you with the right equipment: some essential skills to help you run the rapids.

In other words, what you are doing is *preparing for a journey*—the journey of marriage. Preparedness is a precondition of any successful journey, and your single years are the time to do this. I want to be clear, though, that while your safety and well-being on this journey will depend upon the thoroughness of your preparation, you cannot avoid its perils.

We all have what we are capable of having right now, given who we are inherently and our personal history. Paradoxically, what we have become as a result of our environment's response to us—and vice versa—is the reason we do not have what we want and envision to be our birthright. Stubbornly, we want what we need without having to change who we are, but that is impossible, for what we need is ourselves—our lost wholeness—which is attainable only through changing what we have become.

I do not want to promise too much. This preparation—your awareness and your willingness to educate and change yourself—is all you can do as a single person. You can begin the process of becoming whole while you are single, but you cannot fully heal your wounds or fully recover your wholeness without a partner. You can regain your missing self only through the journey of intimate relationship, which activates your lost originality, and you can prepare for the journey only by changing your character defenses and maladaptive behavior.

In other words, you cannot have the prize—real love—without the journey. Even then, the journey of marriage is not a vacation, with a tour guide who does all the work. You will be on your own, for each partnership is unique. But now you are going to study the terrain, and acquire the right stuff, so that you will be able to improvise successfully in almost any situation.

Forget the Mating Game!

It is not your fault that you have not found lasting love, but it is your responsibility to do what needs to be done to find it. If you have had repeated problems with relationships, it's not something to feel bad about; it's something to understand and to do something constructive about. The answers to your problems are not "out there" with the right apartment or car or dress, but in your acknowledging your freedom and power to grow within yourself, in your intention to make changes, to take responsibility for what is happening in your life—in short, to undertake the journey toward your own maturation.

If you are serious about having a full and lasting love relationship, you have to get serious about being single. There are essentially four things you must do to prepare yourself before your partner comes along and you embark on the journey of marriage: 1) Educate yourself about relationships; 2) Educate yourself about yourself; 3) Train yourself in the skills of relationships; and 4) Do what you can to change the behaviors and character defenses that are keeping you from keeping the love you find.

This is your mission as a single person. Believe me, if you do this, you will have no problem in finding a mate, and in all likelihood that mate will be more able to make a commitment and less likely to frustrate you than the person you will pick (or who will pick you) before you do your homework.

What I am proposing is that you impose a moratorium on making a commitment to a relationship for the time it takes you to do the work outlined in this book. I urge you to step back from the mate search for now. That doesn't mean you shouldn't date, or live with someone. On the contrary, current relationships are ideal training grounds for the real thing. But postpone marriage, and by all means have your "affairs" before you marry. Get your singlehood right this time, not after another heartbreaking breakup or divorce. *Becoming a "conscious single" is the preparation for the journey of marriage.*

2

What's Really Going On in Your Relationships?

Marriage is sought and kept alive by a
deep yearning to know another and be
known by another.

—JOHN PIERRAKOS

In preparation for any journey, it helps to know the lay of the land
in which you'll be traveling. In this context, that means learning
about yourself, and about relationships—yours, and relationships in
general. Most of this chapter is devoted to a Self-Knowledge Questionnaire, and a series of exercises aimed at pinpointing the patterns
of your past relationships. But first I want to talk briefly about the
underlying dynamics of relationships from a psychological and historical perspective. Many of these topics will be discussed in more
detail throughout the book, but I want at least to touch on them
here, because our failure to understand what is really going on when
singles can't find partners, or when relationships are in trouble, is
behind much of our current confusion.

Many singles cling to fantasies about love and marriage. But
fantasies are devastating, individually and societally. Confused, unhappy singles become confused, unhappy married couples, except

that two people's problems are more than double trouble, and the stakes get higher. This especially concerns me if there are children, because the damage is passed along to innocent victims. The social fabric of our country is unraveling before our eyes, and the disintegration is directly traceable to the crisis in the family, specifically to the quality of marriages—the nest from which children come. Underlying the crisis is a critical overlooked fact: *the long-stagnant institution of marriage has undergone a revolution in the last century.* But our minds and our hearts have not kept up with this change. Because we have not reoriented ourselves to the revised agenda of marriage, we're making a mess of it. Let's look at how this change has come about.

WHAT'S *REALLY* GOING ON IN RELATIONSHIPS?

The thing that we need to understand is that marriage is not—or, to be precise, is no longer—a rigid institution, but a psychological process that correlates to the evolution of the collective human psyche. By this I mean that changes in marriage, and our expectations of marriage, have to do with evolutionary changes in ourselves as a culture and as a species.

The combination of love and marriage is a phenomenon of very recent history—and it's a volatile mix. In times past, it was love and adultery that went together "like a horse and carriage." Marriages were arranged; wives were bought or traded.[1] Such marriages were typically passionless, but stable; their primary agenda was the continuity of the family and community, the perpetuation of property rights. Only infrequently, and usually accidentally, was romantic love connected with the marriage partner.

The first change in this pattern came about in the sixteenth century when European scholars rediscovered the literature of ancient Greece, which described a democratic system in which the *individual* had rights, a radical concept in a world in which the individual hadn't even existed except as part of the collective. Still, the spillover into the arena of marriage was slight until the late eighteenth century, with the emergence of democracy in America and the destruction of the monarchic system in England and France. These political changes brought with them the emergence of the idea that the individual could decide his own destiny. The rights of the individual came to include the right to marry the person of one's choice, thus radically transforming marriage from a sociopolitical institution to a psychological and spiritual process. For the first time in history the energy of attraction between men and women was directed into and contained within the structure of marriage. This radical idea precipitated tremendous upheaval in the institution of marriage. For while the purpose and process of marriage had changed, the structure had not: the traditional marriage was still the house in which the romantic marriage lived. Too, because individual rights referred to men and not women, the foundation of equality necessary for a transformative marriage was still lacking.

ENTER THE UNCONSCIOUS

There was an additional complication to the "new" marriage. Coincident with the recognition of individual rights came a belief that human beings were inherently rational, could make logical choices, and were in total charge of their destiny. But that elevated assumption was soon enough challenged by the discovery by Sigmund Freud that underneath our apparent but illusory rationality was a sea of chaotic instincts that influenced and often undermined our choices. It was quite a shock. Here was the new individual, reveling in his freedom from the collective and in his view of himself as, above all, rational and autonomous, confronted by the notion that a large part of his hard-won free will was illusory. He began to understand that choices presumably made on the basis of logic were in fact swayed by emotion and by unconscious predispositions and directives. Thus a door to understanding the transition from passionless, stable marriages to marriages of passion and volatility was opened.

The bottom line is that the choice of a love partner, though entirely personal, is in fact made by some part of the individual that is *not in his right mind.* Even though we now get to choose our partners, there is still some kind of parallel to the arranged marriage, in the sense that as the arranged marriage had a specific purpose, so does our unconscious select a partner to suit its particular needs. The problem is that most of us don't recognize this, and we behave as though we are making a logical, analytical choice, which will lead to a logical, straightforward marriage. Wrong! Wrong! It is true that we now marry for love, and that we expect romantic fulfillment in marriage. And it is right that we marry for love. But love—or marriage, for that matter—is not what we think it is. Whatever we may think, and however careful our checklist, what is going on in mate selection is not love, but need. Love, if it appears at all, appears in marriage, as a result of our commitment to healing our partner.[2]

The Imago: Our Ghost Partner

Now we arrive at the heart of the matter. Our "free" choice of a mate is, in the end, a product of our unconscious, which has an agenda of its own. And what the unconscious wants is to become whole and to heal the wounds of childhood. To this end, it is carrying around its own detailed picture of a proper match, searching not for the right stats, but for the right chemistry. And what is that chemistry? Nothing more than our unconscious attraction to someone who we feel will meet our particular emotional needs. Specifically, that need is to cover the "shortfall" of childhood by having our mates fill in the psychological gaps left by our imperfect childhood caretakers. How do we go about that? By falling madly in love with someone who has both the positive *and the negative* traits of our imperfect parents, someone who fits an image that we carry deep inside us, and for whose embodiment we are unconsciously searching.

I call this buried parental image the *Imago,* after the Latin word for "image." It is forged in the interaction between how we attempted to get our childhood needs met and how our caretakers responded to those needs, and etched on a template in our unconscious. What we unconsciously want is to get what we didn't get in childhood from someone who is like the people who didn't give us what we needed in the first place. When we meet an Imago match, that chemical reaction occurs, and love ignites. All other bets, all other ideas about what we want in a mate, are off. We feel alive and whole, confident that we have met the person who will make everything all right.

Unfortunately, since we've almost surely chosen someone with negative traits similar to those of the parents who wounded us in the first place, the chance of a more positive outcome this time around are slim indeed. In fact, most people who have had serial relationships report that despite their best intentions they manage to find the same problems each time around.

We are doomed to failure both in finding and keeping love as long as we fail to bring the conduct of our mate search in line with the realities of our unconscious needs and our evolutionary heritage. But most of us don't know how to do that, because our society hasn't recognized the tremendous psychic shift inherent in the modern love marriage. Marriages and relationships have changed because *we* have changed. Yet because we haven't articulated and codified that change, we're still playing by the old rules. It's a serious oversight. The failure of our society to recognize the problem and upgrade our understanding to match our psychic evolution portends serious trouble for our civilization.

THE PRICE OF IGNORANCE

Our ignorance has already had drastic consequences. Because we were operating in the dark, not knowing what to expect or hope for, untrained and unprepared for the new marriage, the intense energy of romantic love began to break apart the rigid and unaccommodating structure of marriage. Yet until the 1950s, after the upheaval of World War II, divorce was not undertaken lightly and was considered essentially a moral (read *im*moral) decision. Because of the great shame and censoriousness attached to it, many unhappy marriages stayed together, and romantic love again switched out of marriages and into affairs.

But eventually the widespread frustration with marriage led to a lessening of the power of morality or religion to hold things together. Divorce became a *permitted* exit from an unhappy marriage. While formerly divorces were granted only on grounds of infidelity or abuse, incompatibility became an accepted out.

Marital therapy wasn't even around until 1930 or so; but even professionals were still unaware of the psychological underpinnings of troubled marriages, so therapy did little to stem the tide of divorce. Until recently most marital therapists operated primarily as "deal makers," encouraging couples to solve their problems regarding in-laws, sex, money, infidelity, child rearing (which themselves are only red herrings for the underlying problems) on a contractual basis—"you do this for me and I'll do that for you."[3]

Widespread divorce, following the Second World War, wrought havoc. The structure of the family began breaking down under the crushing number of divorces. With the burgeoning number of second, and third, marriages, themselves misguided answers to the marriage crisis, the step-family emerged. Now single-parent families and "blended" families of every stripe are considered the norm, primarily because we have become disillusioned with the possibility for happy marriages. All are adaptations to the problem of marital failure, an attempt to normalize cultural realities that have come about because of our lack of understanding of the underlying agenda of marriage. We have bought the idea that unhappy people should not have to stay in unhappy marriages. We have given credence to the idea that when trouble comes you should just change partners, when the truth is that the *way* you are living with that person must be changed. It's all backward. Rather than getting rid of the partner and keeping the problem, you should get rid of the problem so that you can keep the partner. What has happened is that in trying to make things easier, and more tolerant, we have lost sight of our own real needs and desires. I am all for such a tolerant attitude toward "families of choice," but ultimately, it's not helpful.

Until we recognize the unconscious agenda of mate selection and marriage, and cooperate with that agenda in the conduct of our relationships, our social problems will continue to grow out of hand, and our individual lives will suffer. If we could get this situation under control, if there could be a nationwide recognition of the need to reeducate ourselves about relationships, marriages would survive and prosper, our children would be healthier, and we wouldn't need 80 percent of the remedial programs now dealing with the end products of unloved children—whether they be drugs, violence, incest, child abuse, high dropout rates, thievery, alcoholism, or teenage pregnancy.

Heaven knows divorce is not the answer; we now have a whole generation of people who have found that out the hard way. We are learning, too, that no matter how easy we make it, the children of divorce carry lasting scars that go unnoticed.[4] Divorce may allow people to escape from bad marriages, but until we take steps to ensure good marriages, to facilitate individual happiness and fulfillment, until we learn what we're about, we will continue to have desperate singles, joyless marriages, troubled children, and a society becoming more dysfunctional by the decade.

DOING IT DIFFERENTLY

The irony is that it doesn't have to be this way. We have every opportunity, individually and societally, to have powerful, transforming marriages, and to have those marriages transform our society. The modern romantic marriage is an evolutionary gift to the psyche, with unique potential for healing our childhood wounds and facilitating our spiritual growth. Somehow we have gotten the misguided idea that you have to leave a marriage in order to grow and change. But we are now discovering that powerful healing is possible *through* marriage—that marriage is not so much a rigid institution as it is the framework within which a dynamic process takes place. *Marriage itself, properly understood, is the therapy we need to grow and become whole*, to return to our innate joyful state.

We've just got to learn to get our relationships right. And, not to pull any punches about it, when I talk about relationships, I am talking about marriage. As I see it, committed relationships, live-in relationships, all of the many variants of singledom today are excellent training grounds for marriage, but they are not a substitute. The ingredients necessary for full growth and healing—attention, concentration, security, time, deepest intimacy, and the full mirroring of ourselves through our partner—are possible only in marriage. The elements that activate the chemistry of growth—the tension of complementary character defenses, symmetrical wounds, unconscious attraction—appear only in marriage. It is through the commitment to accept and heal the other's wounds, to provide a safe haven for the partner to experience his or her wholeness *over a lifetime,* that we are able to recapture our original wholeness. We cannot heal ourselves, and we cannot heal in open-ended, precarious relationships. So we must educate, prepare, and train ourselves for the journey of a conscious marriage.

EXERCISE 2A   ▪   ▪   ▪   ▪   ▪

Self-Knowledge Inventory

Before we can know another intimately, we must first know ourselves. But many of us never stop to decode who we are, what we think and feel. The purpose of the following questionnaire is not to determine any hard-and-fast answers, but to give you a chance to articulate, and to see in writing, your view of yourself and some of the critical issues in your life.

Since the object of this exercise is to try and catch the subconscious unawares and find out what's *really* on your mind, try not to analyze your responses. Write down the first thing that comes to you as quickly as possible. Feel free to write as much as you want; use these questions to trigger any further thoughts and feelings you may want to explore.

NOTE: The exercises in Parts I to IV are geared toward collecting information about yourself that you will use to make changes in Part V. You will find that they require a substantial commitment of time and energy to complete properly. Obviously, the more careful thought and attention you give to them, the more you will learn about yourself. Accurate and specific information will help you to develop a program of self-change in Part V. These exercises are an important part of preparing to keep the love you find.

While you may prefer to read through the book before doing the exercises, there are two reasons why I recommend that you do the exercises in this chapter before moving on. One, the information you unearth here will enrich your reading of the rest of the book; two, your responses will be more useful to your later work if they are spontaneous and uninfluenced by what you are going to learn about relationships.

Complete the following sentences with the first thing that comes to mind:

1. My goal in life is _____
   _____.

2. The thing that gives me the most satisfaction is _____
   _____.

3. My childhood was _____
   _____.

4. I think sex is _____
   _____.

5. When I make love, I prefer _____
   _____.

6. My deepest fear is _____ .

7. My deepest need is _____ .

8. My most frequent feeling is _____ .

9. The thing I hate most is _____ .

10. I worry most about _____ .

11. My goals for a primary relationship are _____
    _____.

12. My reasons for wanting a primary relationship are _____
    _____.

13. I think my relationships have been _____
    _____.

14. Three things about myself I want to change are:
    a. _____
    b. _____
    c. _____

15. I fantasize about _____ .

16. I feel anger when _____ .

17. I think I am _____ .

18. My highest value is _____ .

19. I think spending money on _____ is foolish and wasteful.

20. A nude body is _____ .

21. My most frequent pleasure is _____ .

22. I am happiest when _____ .

23. When a man makes love, he should _____ .

24. Your body should always be _____ .

25. To me, work is _____ .

26. In general, I view life as _____ .

27. When I go to a party, I _____ .

28. Women's bodies are _____ .

29. My idea of a dream career is _____ .

30. The person I admire most is _____ .

31. To me, death _____ .

32. I think war is _____ .

33. I have no use for people who _____ .

34. I am afraid of _____ .

35. When someone is rude to me, I _____ .

36. I can't understand people who believe _____ .

37. Men's bodies are _____ .

38. In general, I think my strengths are _____

_____ .

39. After making love, a man _____ .

40. My weaknesses are _____

_____ .

41. My view of money is _____ .

42. To me, children are _____ .

43. Parents are _____ .

44. Married life is _____ .

45. I am envious of _____ .

46. I wish _____ .

47. My dream vacation is _____ .

48. I have the most fun _____ .

49. I take great pleasure in _____ .

50. My favorite sport is _____ .

51. What disgusts me _____ .

52. I think retirement _____ .

53. Many of my dreams are about _____ .

54. When I am afraid, I _____ .

55. When I see couples kissing in public, I _____ .

56. Regarding a man's orgasm, a woman _____ .

57. When I fall in love, I _____ .

58. When I have spare time, I like to _____ .

59. I can't stand it when a man _____ .

60. I think touching _____ .

61. Religion for me _____ .

62. Child rearing, in my mind, _____ .

63. I think God _____ .

64. What I want when I get sick is _____ .

65. I can't stand it when a woman _____ .

66. Discipline _____ .

67. The thing that bothers me most about my body is _____ .

68. When I die, I _____ .

69. What hurts me most _____ .

70. My parents _____ .

71. I've never told anyone that I like _____ .

72. In a long marriage, sex _____ .

73. I like sex when _____ .

74. Politics is _____ .

75. Orgasms are _____ .

76. The worst thing in life is _____ .

77. The best thing in life is _____ .

78. The way I feel about separate vacations is _____ .

79. The first thing I notice about someone is _____ .

80. I think marriage is _____ .

81. My most shameful secret is _____ .

82. In an argument, I _____ .

83. To me intimacy means _____ .

84. Divorce is _____ .

85. When I disagree with someone, I _____ .

86. The thing that I fear most about marriage is _____ .

87. In-laws should _____ .

88. The thing I hate most is _____ .

89. What I like most about myself is _____ .

90. The opposite sex is _____ .

91. When someone is angry, I _____ .

92. Women are _____ .

93. Men are _____ .

94. The best thing about the opposite sex is _____ .

95. When I am angry, I _____ .

96. Talking about sex feels _____ .

97. The worst thing about the opposite sex is _____ .

98. What I hate most in anyone is _____ .

99. What I admire most in other people is _____ .

100. When I am my best self, I am _____ .

101. When I am my worst self, I am _____ .

102. People should _____ .

103. When I grow old _____ .

104. My worst experience in life was _____ .

105. Love is _____ .

106. To me, dating _____ .

107. "Till death do us part" means _____ .

108. Falling in love is _____ .

As a way of digesting and organizing the information you've just revealed to yourself, use your responses to write an essay about yourself, grouping the information by topics such as "goals," "sex," "fears," "relationships," etc. This essay will serve as valuable baseline information about your current beliefs when you begin to address the self-change exercises in Part V.

Learning from Past Relationships

The second phase of information gathering has to do with your relationships up to now. Past relationships, though they may be reminders of pain or failure, are a valuable window into the issues, wounds, and conflicts that we must address if we are to make better partner choices and cope better with relationship problems in the future. Every past liaison began in love, and hope. If we can look unblinkingly at the past, and honestly acknowledge what went wrong, what our unmet expectations were, and if we can be objective about the nature of our past partners, we have an ideal opportunity to see who we are, why we made the choices we've made, and how we behave in relationships. With this knowledge, we can begin to see the patterns that repeat themselves so devastatingly; we see where growth and change are needed; we understand the nature of the wound that needs healing; and we can prepare ourselves to do better the next time around.

What follows is a series of exercises designed to mine past relationships for the gold they can unearth about our needs and dynamics in partnership. In my couples workshops, I have partners do variations of these exercises. But for them there are drawbacks. Couples are often in the thick of conflict, and it is hard for them to be objective. Though their memories are fresh, their problems are present and ongoing; they are also more enmeshed in anger and confusion. You have the advantage of a certain degree of emotional distance or detachment (not that you may not have raw and painful memories), and you can evaluate and compare the accumulated data from multiple relationships, and take a longer view of your situation.

Plan to do this work when you have time to fully relax and allow yourself to reexperience what happened. What I want you to do first is identify all the important relationships in your past. By this I mean those that have been emotionally powerful—whether a high-school crush, a college sweetheart, a live-in lover, a long-term dating situation, or a marriage. Relationships that were casual, or that for whatever reason never tugged at your heartstrings, don't count. On the other hand, you may want to include a nonromantic relationship—with a coworker, a friend, a teacher—if it felt emotionally charged and conflicted to you. There may have been many such relationships in your life, or there may have been only one or two (for our purposes here, I suggest you limit yourself to four or five).

E X E R C I S E 2 B ■   ■   ■   ■   ■

Imago Preview

1. Use an 8½-by-11-inch piece of paper, turned sideways. Make a column for each of your past relationships, placing the name of one ex-partner at the top of each column.

Close your eyes, take several deep breaths, relax, and think back to the first relationship. For a few minutes I want you to think about when you first met this person, how s/he looked, what you said to each other, what you did. Try and mentally put yourself back into those past situations. Allow yourself to feel their effect deeply, and to remember deeply their emotional impact. Try and recall what the early stages of your romance were like, how you spent your time together, what it was like the first time you made love.

Now I want you to think about the first time you noticed something wrong, or something you didn't like about your partner. What was it, and what did you do—did you ignore it, or deny that it was happening, were you shocked? Can you recall the transition from intense romantic love to "settling in" to a day-to-day relationship? Can you identify the problems and the things that went wrong? Can you remember how you tried to solve your problems, or restore your earlier feelings? And how did the relationship end? You may just want to think through what happened, or you may want to write some of this down. The idea is to remember as vividly as possible that past situation.

2. With all these memories available now, list in the first column all the traits, both positive and negative, that you would use to describe that person. Use adjectives such as kind, mean, warm, manipulative, generous, stingy, boring, charismatic, etc.

3. When you have finished, go back and put a plus sign (+) next to each trait you consider positive and a minus sign (−) next to the negative traits.

4. Study the list again, and on the left side of the column rank the positive traits in order, placing a "1" next to the traits you liked most, a "2" next to the next-best traits, and so on. On the right side of the column, rank the negative traits in the same manner, giving a "1" to the worst traits, a "2" to the next-worst traits, etc.

5. Repeat steps 1, 2, and 3 for each ex-partner.

6. Go back and put a circle around the positive traits that are common to all (or most, if you've had many) ex-partners. Underline the negative traits they have in common.

7. On a new sheet of paper, draw a circle and divide it in half horizontally. On the top half of the circle, write in all the positive traits that you ranked 1 or 2 for any (or many) of your ex-loves. Draw a circle around any that you circled in step 6. On the bottom half of the circle, enter the negative traits ranked 1 and 2, and underline those you underlined in step 6.

You should now have a preview picture of your Imago, the kind of person to whom you are unconsciously drawn.

E X E R C I S E   2 C   ■   ■   ■   ■   ■

Relationship Frustrations

1. At the top of a horizontal sheet of paper write the name of one of your ex-partners. Divide the paper into five columns. Label Column A, FRUSTRATION; Column B, FEELING; Column C, THOUGHT; Column D, REACTION; and Column E, FEAR.

2. In Column A list the frustrations you had with this person. A frustration is a behavior that caused you some discomfort, pain, or frustration. For example: "S/he would make an appointment with me and then be consistently late without calling me." "When s/he hugged me, s/he would not squeeze me tight." "When I asked her/him a question, s/he tended to give me indirect answers." "Sometimes s/he would criticize me in front of my friends." "S/he often spoke to me in an angry tone of voice." You should avoid pejorative adjectives like "lazy," "stingy," "mean," "angry," "withholding," "unreliable." Instead use sentences that describe *behaviors* that made you form this opinion.

3. In Column B indicate the feeling you had with each frustration. Feelings should be stated in one word, such as "angry," "frightened," "shamed," etc. If you write a sentence, you are describing your thought process. For example, comments like "I felt he didn't appreciate me" or "It made me feel like she was using me" analyze your thoughts about your being with this person. What you are trying to pinpoint in Column B is the *feeling* you had when you had that thought. For example: "When s/he did not call when s/he was late, I thought I was not respected and that made me feel *angry*."

4. Column C is the place to record your thoughts. For instance, in Column 1, you may have written "S/he would make an appointment with me and then be late without calling," and in Column 2 you may have written that the behavior made you feel "angry." In Column C you might write "I am not respected," or "I feel unloved." The complete thought is thus: "S/he would make an appointment with me and be late without calling, and I would feel angry and think that s/he did not respect me."

5. In Column D write your reaction. This is a description of your behavior when you feel "angry and not respected." An example might be: "I sulk," or "I call my mother and tell her how inconsiderate you are," or "I begin to feel depressed and have a drink."

6. Column E, "Fear," is the most difficult. You may need to think some about the hidden fear that the "frustration" in Column A arouses. Your "reaction" hides this fear from yourself—that is the function of a reaction. For instance, your partner's lateness may arouse a fear of being "abandoned." Or you may have fears that s/he is with someone else. The complete sentence that fills all the columns might go something like this: "S/he would make an appointment with me and then be late without calling, and I would feel angry and feel that I was not respected and would react by feeling depressed and having a drink, because I feared that I was abandoned."

7. Repeat steps 1–6 for each of your ex-partners.

8. Divide a new sheet of paper, turned horizontally, into six columns. Label the first five columns identical to step 1. Label the sixth column "Desire."

9. Study the frustration lists you've made for each ex-partner and identify similar, recurring frustrations. You may find, for example, that you have several frustrations around the issue of lateness, or not keeping agreements, or being criticized. Take each group of similar frustrations and summarize them in one sentence or phrase

that includes the essence of each. For example, if you have recurring frustrations around lateness, you might summarize them by stating, "When my partners are unreliable about time, I feel angry." Similarly, cluster the responses around that issue in Columns B through E. The final sentence might read like this: "When my partners are unreliable, I feel angry and think I am not respected or important, and I usually react with depression and drink to hide my fear of abandonment." Finally, in the column labeled "Desire," write what you want, which, if you had it, would cancel the frustration in Column A. For example, "I would like my partner to try harder to be on time, and if s/he is going to be more than ten minutes late, I would like her/him to call." Repeat this summation for each recurrent frustration.

You now have a picture of the problems and frustrations that tend to recur in your relationships, and an idea of what would remedy those frustrations.

E X E R C I S E 2 D ▪ ▪ ▪ ▪ ▪

Your Unconscious Relationship

Complete the following sentences using the material from the preceding exercises. (You may want to copy out these phrases onto a sheet of paper, or make a photocopy of these pages, so that you can fill in the information.)

I tend to be drawn to a person who is _____

_____

(complete the sentence with the negative traits in the bottom of the circle in Exercise 2B, #7, page 31)

. . . with whom I feel _____

_____

(fill in the summary of negative feelings from Exercise 2C, #9, Column B, page 32)

. . . because s/he frustrates me by _____

_____

(fill in the summary of frustrations from Exercise 2C, #9, Column A, page 32)

I wish this person were always _____

_____

(fill in with the positive traits from the top of the circle in Exercise 2B, #7, page 31)

. . . so that I could have _____

_____

(complete this sentence with the list of desires from Exercise 2C, #9, Column F, page 32)

When I do not get these desires met, I think _____

_____

(fill in the summary of thoughts from Exercise 2C, #9, Column C, page 32)

. . . and react by _____

_____

(enter the summary of reactions from Exercise 2C, #9, Column D, page 32)

. . . and experience my deepest fears, which are _____

_____

(Finish this sentence with the summary of your fears from Exercise 2C, #9, Column E, page 32. These fears describe your childhood wound as you reexperience it in your relationships.)

You now have a picture of your "unconscious relationship."

Now you have vital information about your partner choices and relationship issues. We will work more with this data later. But keep what you learned from these exercises in mind as you read the following chapters, where you will no doubt recognize some of the roots of your relationship history.

3

The Human Journey

There is one common flow; one common breathing,
All things are in sympathy.

—HIPPOCRATES

Most of this book is devoted to our psychosocial journey: how our childhood experiences affect partner choice, how in our primary love relationships we are reenacting archaic childhood injuries, and how we can begin the process of change while we are single that will speed the healing process after marriage. But in this chapter I want to talk about the two phases of the human voyage that take place before we are born, what I call our cosmic origins and evolutionary heritage. You may wonder how this will help you in your preparations for lasting love, but I can assure you that it will. You are much larger than your personal experience, and your context is much greater than the network of your relationships.

To fully understand what happens in relationships, it is important to grasp what kind of creature you are, and what you have inherited from your broader human ancestry. Our life since birth, and our conscious awareness, is only part of the story. To fully grasp who we are and what motivates us, we have to go beneath the surface and

35

look at the unconscious, at our instinctual nature, at the way our brain works, and at our subterranean connections to other beings. To make sense of the intense, oceanic emotions of love, to understand our often bizarre and unfathomable dreams, our heartbreak and longing, we have to step back from our day-to-day existence and place our understanding of relationships in the larger context of our human nature.

The Cosmic Journey: Yearning for Connection

Does it ring a bell when I say that we all share an inarticulate longing for something that we cannot quite put our fingers on? Have you ever had a moment, in the midst of your daily rounds, when suddenly, inexplicably, a wave of happiness or joy wells up in you, a sense that all's right with the world?

Such moments arrive unbidden, perhaps as we drive down a dark road at night, as we glance up to see the sun glinting off a city skyline. Something "comes over us" as we sit watching the sunset, or catch a whiff of fresh-mown grass, or even as we're most deeply engrossed in some mundane task. Often in these moments there is a loss of boundaries, a timelessness, when we escape for a moment the rigid strictures of our brain and body. The moment passes, maddeningly unexplainable and irreproducible, and we are left mystified. Yet there is something dimly familiar about such moments, a feeling that we are in touch with our *real* selves, which imparts to these transient moments a special poignancy, and makes us yearn to recapture the feelings they evoke.

Mysterious and elusive as such moments are, I think they tell us something important about who we are as human beings, and about the parts of us that are hidden behind the veil of our day-to-day reality, which has profound impact on our relationships. *For just as our relationship troubles do not originate with our difficulty in finding the right partner or with the moment of our first spat, neither can what happens to us as children fully explain the inchoate, tidal emotions of falling in love or the pain we feel at its loss.* We have to look elsewhere for an explanation.

I think that the quality of these moments out of time gives us a valuable window to understanding our hidden hope in relationships. From what well do these feelings spring, surprising us with their intensity? What memory are they struggling to revive? I believe these feelings arise from our forgotten connection to memories of a time before birth, from the period we spent in our mother's womb, and even before, when we felt totally and safely connected not only to

an all-giving mother but, beyond that, to everything and to everyone. I believe this memory is the source of the primary and universal
human longing, and the unstated hope of love.

This idea fits well with what we know of fetal experience. Floating
tranquilly in the mother's womb, the fetus is fed, protected, and
soothed by the beat of the mother's heart; everything is provided
effortlessly, instantly. The fetus has no concept of itself, of past or
future, no awareness that it is separate from others. Even for a while
after birth the infant still lives idyllically in a world in which it
recognizes no difference between itself and those around it.

But isn't this notion of our timeless connection to everything a bit
farfetched? Aren't we crossing into mumbo-jumbo territory here? I
don't think so.

CLUES TO OUR CONNECTEDNESS

The question of our essential connectedness to the larger universe
has consumed the attention of investigators in many fields, from
science and religion to psychology and philosophy. Modern physics
posits the idea that everything in the universe is essentially pulsating
energy that happens to reconstitute itself as particular configurations
of matter at particular times—specifically, at the moment of observation, i.e., the moment our consciousness happens to concretize it.
Matter, in this sense, is but a medium through which we observe
patterns and densities of energy. Underneath the appearance of a
material world, we are all joined in an energetic dance.

James Lovelock's widely credited "Gaia" theory carries the anal-
ogy further, claiming that the entire earth is one large, living,
pulsating organism, of which oceans, trees, humans, and telephones
are merely smaller, interdependent cells, the flesh and blood and
organs and nerve endings of which all together make up the pulsing
life of the whole, and to the health and functioning of which each
part contributes. William James put it this way:

"We with our lives are like islands in the sea, like the trees in
the forest. The maple and the pine may whisper to each other
with their leaves . . . But the trees also commingle their roots
in the darkest underground, and the islands also hang together through the ocean's bottom. Just so there is a continuum of cosmic consciousness, against which our individuality
builds but accidental fences . . . Our normal consciousness is
circumscribed for adaptation to our external environment, but
the fence is weak in spots, and fitful influences from beyond

leak in, showing the otherwise unverifiable human connection."[1]

Alternative forms of medicine such as acupuncture, homeopathy, biofeedback, and therapeutic touch all assume access to energy fields—electrical, magnetic, mental, psychic—beyond the seemingly arbitrary bounds of our bodies. That we are inextricably entangled with the universe is evidenced by studies that show how our "internal" clocks are affected by circadian cycles: what is jet lag, after all, other than our getting out of sync with the planetary clock? The rhythms of our bodies (composed, like the earth, of more than 70 percent water) are swayed by the moon and tides, and sensitive to magnetic fields both local and global.

Seemingly paranormal phenomena such as telepathy, clairvoyance, and precognition seem to confirm our timeless union. Many of us pooh-pooh psychic powers, rationalists that we are, weary of storefront tea-leaf readers and New Age dogma. Yet few of us have not had unexplainable experiences of our own, whether suddenly and surely knowing who was at the other end of a ringing phone, or having a dream that foreshadowed reality. Dowsers who find water with forked twigs, clairvoyants who predict earthquakes or who lead police to missing persons guided by a piece of their clothing or jewelry, and psychics who tell archaeologists where to dig up lost civilizations are all tuning in to a timeless collective awareness in which we are all, always, one. Historian Arnold Toynbee had several startling retro-cognitive episodes, during which he "saw" the suicide of a Roman rebel in 80 B.C., and shared the Spaniards' first sight of the Aztec capital Tenochtitlan. At one point, he wrote, he found himself "in communion, not just with this or that episode in history, but with all that had been, and was, and was to come. In that instant I was directly aware of the passage of History gently flowing through me in a mighty current, and of my own life welling like a wave in the flow of this vast tide."

Psychologist Carl Jung adds clues to the nature of our connectedness with his theory that we all share a collective unconscious. In this view, our cumulative human experiences coalesce over time around certain archetypes, or repeated patterns of human striving and behavior. The archetypes are the stuff of myth by which we live—hero and villain, earth mother and seductress. As much a part of what we inherit as our animal instincts and our hair color, these universal archetypes are an unconscious influence on our behavior and responses, even as our own thoughts and actions influence their mutation and add to their collective force.

The concept of an original state of relaxed joyfulness cuts across religious and cultural lines in the depiction of paradise: as heaven, the Elysian fields, nirvana, El Dorado, the Garden of Eden. All symbolize primordial perfection, a golden age of peace and joy, a perfect communion in nature among man and beast, bird and forest, an idyllic picture of timeless immortality. And then, according to myth, there is a disturbance, a fall from grace, a cataclysm. We are driven from the garden, and thereafter search in vain for paradise and our spiritual unity.

But we do not have to fall back on myth or magic or science for evidence that we yearn for peacefulness, for relaxed joyfulness. Modern manifestations come across my desk daily, in the form of articles, workshops, pills, processes, and products promising relief from stress. I have to conclude from the deluge of books and self-help tapes on finding joy and happiness, on stress reduction and eliciting "peak experiences," on massage and meditation, that this is a profound drive, and that behind the expressed wish for relief from stress there is something missing that we all want.

WE WANT IT BACK

What it all boils down to is that our inchoate longing for connectedness, and those moments when we pierce the veil of our everyday existence, stem from a hazy memory that at one time we were not separate, but connected to everything, and particularly to all other humans, in a way that felt safe and supporting. And our fundamental yearning is to transcend the barriers that now separate us from our awareness of this connection.

There is something in the psyche that knows that things are not as they should be. We don't hope or long for something imaginary. That buried intimation of a pan-existent human essence, when we contact it, feels absolutely normal and objectively real. We yearn for our original wholeness, for that dimly remembered state of relaxed joyfulness, because we *did* experience it, if only briefly, in the womb. We just can't identify its source. Theologian Martin Buber expressed it well when he said that "birth is the moment when we begin to forget."

It feels so *right* to me that all of life is a struggle to remember this idyllic preexistent state. We are essentially pulsating energy that has been disturbed; our desire is to overcome this disturbance and restore the natural pulsation that is our essence. We're not trying to find something we never had, we're trying to get something *back*, to recapture what was lost. Though we be unaware of it, our secret goal in relationships is not some movie-screen fantasy of love, but rather a drive to recover the state of relaxed joy that is our birthright.

The Evolutionary Journey: Yearning for Aliveness

I've spent a good deal of time presenting evidence for our original state of relaxed joyfulness and connection, because I want you to be fully aware of this powerful hidden influence in our relationships. But there are other, equally powerful drives that we bring to our journey here on earth. While our cosmic origins are present at birth in the form of intuitions of our original wholeness, we also arrive with the history of our species encoded in our genes, the cumulative bounty of our *evolutionary* journey. It's a heritage going back to the first beings that walked upright, and culminating in the eye color and mathematical aptitude passed along by our parents. Imprinted in our genes, latticed through our unconscious, are the drives, the instincts, and the genetic memory forged over aeons. Thirty years of living in Manhattan or Milan can temper or obscure our intrinsic human nature, but they cannot erase it.

NEW MIND, OLD BRAIN

It is our grand, highly evolved brain that separates us upright humanoids from the lower orders. We like to think of our brain as that part of us which digests, organizes, and analyzes the mountains of diverse information we take in. We use our brain to plan, strategize, invent, create, make decisions. It's not surprising that we identify with the brain—we see it as who we are, our consciousness, our center. Well, that is true, as far as it goes. The cerebral cortex—which I call the "new" brain—does do all those wonderful things. But that is, literally, only the half of it. Beneath the convoluted dome familiar from anatomical charts is what I term the "old" brain, which has a profound impact on our behavior in relationships, and that's quite a different story.

There are two parts to the old brain. The brain stem, sometimes referred to as the "reptilian" brain (which shows you how far back it goes), is the brain's primitive inner core. It controls vital physical systems, from reproduction and sleep to blood circulation and muscle response. It's where the action is. Cradling the brain stem is the limbic system, a mammalian addition, the seat of primitive, powerful emotions linking the autonomous functions of the brain stem and the cerebral cortex. The old brain—the brain stem and limbic system—is our survival brain.

Unlike the new brain, which takes in and processes the data of the external world, the instinctual old brain is aware of what's beyond its boundaries only through sensation and feeling. Simple and primitive, it makes broad distinctions related to its safety and survival mainly via the images, symbols, and thoughts relayed to it via the new brain. Eternally concerned with survival, the old brain recognizes certain patterns that it has learned to associate with "love," "loss," "anger," or "danger." It is unable to make subtle distinctions according to circumstance; its knee-jerk reactions are deeply ingrained, and blown way out of proportion to the stimulus. All threats are life threatening; the slightest frown signals total rejection.

Most important to understand about the old brain is that *it exists outside of time:* it makes no distinctions as to why or where or when something happened. Your old brain cannot tell the difference between the stimulus it received thirty years ago when your mother didn't come when you cried and the one it received today when your partner called from work an hour late, canceling your date for the evening. As a baby you may have responded to feeling abandoned by sucking your thumb and cooing to yourself; today you respond to the situation by eating a dozen cookies and, tuning out your anxiety, watching some mindless TV movie until your partner makes amends. In both cases the feelings, and the response, are the same. The response is instinctual; the old brain is doing what it has been conditioned to do in order to survive.

It's easy to believe, when we live in high-rises, drive fast cars, buy our food and clothing ready-made, and "choose" who we will marry, that we are masters of our primal, instinctual natures. We are fooling ourselves, however rational or intellectual we may think we are, however finely tuned our cerebral cortexes. The old and new brain interact in a complex system of checks and balances, a dance of instinct and emotion tempering intellect and reason. We are only human, after all. The new brain cannot hope to overpower the old brain; it is its servant.

Be we humans are unique in our self-awareness: we *know* that we think. Our forebrain, part of the "new" brain, is conscious of the contents of the cortex. It is the means by which we observe ourselves (and even observe ourselves observing ourselves), enabling us to see the interplay of images, thoughts, and symbols. It is the medium of self-change through which we can acknowledge the power of the old brain and cooperate with it.

THE BASIC DRIVES: SAFETY FIRST

Now I want to turn to the subject of our basic drives. It seems that the fundamental instinct of human consciousness in its biological form is to distinguish between safety and danger. This distinction is so significant that scientists now postulate that we have developed an additional neural pathway that warns us of danger, a shortcut that bypasses the cerebral cortex.[2]

The trauma of birth is for every sentient being the first hint of danger, the first clue that paradise is lost. For a brief time after birth, we're still adjusting to the change of scene and haven't yet caught on that the party is over. It is a shocking discovery; thereafter every stimulus is judged in terms of survival: Is it dangerous? Will I die? Any disruption of our state of relaxed joyfulness is a potential threat, be it a twig snapping in the forest, the appearance of a potential predator, a storm. Or, closer to home—an unanswered cry, a toy we can't have, a harsh look from the boss, a casual criticism from our lover. Whatever the provocation, the response always takes one of four forms: to fight, to flee, to freeze passively, or to submit defensively. In other words, we either explode or constrict our energy. These four adaptations to the perception of danger, legacy of our primitive reptilian brain, are encoded in our psycho-neural system, immune to logic. Think of how you respond when something goes wrong in your partnerships: wary of danger, prepared to defend yourself in one way or another, you either fight back, run away, cower quietly and hope the problem will go away, or helplessly give in to what you cannot control.

Once a sense of safety, of survival, is assured, mammalian activity pretty much falls into six categories. We mate, we nurture the offspring of our mating, we work, eat, and sleep, and we play.[3] Though we humans embellish all these activities considerably, that's pretty much all we do, and even these instinctive drives are profoundly influenced by our sense of safety or danger.

EXPRESSING FULL ALIVENESS

Nonetheless, we humans are complex creatures, far removed from the salamander or even the ape. Judging from our desperate search for goods and goals, fame and fortune, love and laughs, it is not enough just to be alive and safe: we want more. Joseph Campbell defined for me what it is we so intensely strive for when he said that while it has always been believed that the fundamental search of human beings is for the meaning of life, what we are actually searching for, yearning for, is a *feeling of aliveness*. It was one of those ideas that catalyzed my own musings and intuitions. I've expanded Campbell's thinking to the hypothesis that we are born with three instinctual directives: we want first to stay alive, but beyond that, we want to *feel fully alive,* and we want to *express* that aliveness.

Every child, before self-consciousness sets in, acts spontaneously, with total abandon and full involvement. If you spend any time around children, you know this. Everything interests them, they whirl until they're dizzy, run until they fall, paint wildly, sing unselfconsciously. We all felt like that once: we felt alive, we expressed it. But then life's realities inevitably intruded: our parents didn't always respond to our cry; the bottle was too hot or cold; we fell out of bed; there was screaming; there weren't enough hugs; a new little sister came along too soon; we were laughed at. We became afraid, and we lost our sense of being fully alive, which we can only feel when we're safe, not when we're scared, vulnerable, threatened, defensive, inadequate. And we carried these feelings, and our ways of coping with them, to our relationships.

A feeling of aliveness is what we're after with our cars and condos and boats and gourmet food, our designer clothes and recreational sex and skin flicks and skydiving, our deafening music and jogging and walks on the beach and TV and movies. Materialism, hedonism, greed, self-centeredness—all the hallmarks of the American way— are getting a bad name these days. Well, heaven knows it's nothing to brag about, but I can only have sympathy for what all this compulsive activity really represents, which is that we live in a world, and in relationships, that don't allow us to feel truly alive. And if we don't feel alive, we feel like we're going to *die.* So we *do* something, *buy* something, *binge* on something, take drugs, drink, run twenty miles, get laid, turn up the music.

Most of us don't acknowledge how vulnerable we are to feelings that our safety or survival is threatened. After all, we're sophisticates, we no longer live in caves. But the primitive nature of these feelings is glaringly evident in the apparent triviality of our hair-trigger reactions. Just a smile, or a frown, can change our perception that the world is safe or dangerous. Think how safe and confident you feel in the presence of someone who likes you and affirms you as you are, as opposed to someone who is disapproving or critical, and you can see the tremendous power of our primitive instincts, and thus of our love relationships, to sustain or destroy us. I have only to look at my own marriage to be aware of the power of the old brain. When Helen and I are having an argument and things aren't good, I feel small and scrunched down. The world seems threatening; my brain feels befogged; simple tasks are daunting. When things are going well, I feel natural, like *myself*. Life is good, and all the creatures of the world are my friends. And I am a grown man, a supposedly rational man, a mental-health professional, for heaven's sake.

The drive to express our full aliveness is not just a nice idea, it's something powerful and fundamental in us. We want to relax, to walk around without our defenses up, to be ourselves. We spend so much of our lives trying to find, or to create, meaning in our lives, when what we truly want is to feel the fullness of our own experience, to feel the pulsation of our aliveness. For so many years I doggedly, intellectually addressed questions of life's meaning, and now I realize that's what you do when you don't *feel* fully alive. Our purposes and goals are a substitute, a sublimation for feeling alive and joyful. Now that I have more of this feeling in my life, I can see what I was up to.

We saw in Russia and Eastern Europe what happens when people are given safety, the chance to do more than just exist. The gates burst open; people felt newly alive, and they expressed it. (Of course, just as with falling in love, those feelings can be sustained only with hard work and trust, and there is bound to be disappointment and disillusionment along the way.) The reaction is the same everywhere safety and the freedom to express one's aliveness is allowed to flourish, be it in a kindergarten class, a corporation, a nation, or a marriage. All of the art and poetry of love, a body of work that would fill one hundred Taj Mahals, is about expressing that feeling of aliveness, or mourning its loss.

In Quest of Full Aliveness

It is the recapturing of our sense of relaxed joyfulness, and a feeling of aliveness, that we seek in relationships. When we fall in love, we reawaken memories of that idyllic state of connection and joy with which we've lost contact. Memories of our original wholeness and essential connectedness come flooding back to us, and we credit our awakened aliveness to our beloved. It is *he* who makes us feel like dancing, *she* who inspires us to poetry, who's responsible for our loving the world, for our snapping out of boredom or depression or anger.

We connect our reawakened feelings to our beloved because he or she unconsciously reminds us of the first people with whom we associate those feelings—our caretakers. And this is why disappointment is inevitable. For it is merely coincidence that we associate our parents with that state of relaxed aliveness: they just happened to be on the scene when, at birth and for a while after, we still had that oceanic feeling of joyful connection. The love object—our parents then, our beloved now, whether nurturing or neglectful—is not the source of those feelings. In fact, it was the deficiencies in our nurturing that originally stifled our sense of joyful aliveness and cosmic union, as it is the shortcomings of our beloved that dampen those feelings now.

What's going on is that, because we live associationally, the old brain doesn't recognize that the caretaker, and now the lover, was never the reason for those feelings to begin with. All it recognizes is a pattern, a set of coordinates, that it correlates to that original condition we were born into. The underlying pain with our caretakers, and later our mates, is that they are not prolonging, or facilitating the recovery of, our original state of relaxed joyfulness. It's an impossible task, more so since they are unaware of your expectations (and they unconsciously have the same impossible expectation of *you*). Angry, critical, despairing, we blame our lovers for their failure to sustain our newfound state of joyful vitality, while at the same time we stay bonded to them in the hope that they will still come through somehow. Our struggle with our partners is in part a dysfunctional attempt to restore an original state that is at once personal and cosmic.

This depressing scenario would seem to portend badly for relationships. In fact, when I first realized that this was why people were so powerfully disappointed in love and so angry at their partners, I began to despair, not only of marriage, but of marital therapy as a sensible vocation. But then I realized that the situation wasn't so gloomy. The fact that falling in love *does* restore our feelings of aliveness and union seems to me proof that relationships are the key to recapturing our wholeness. Understanding what we unconsciously seek, we can use our partnerships to facilitate the reclaiming of our lost vitality and connection.

I believe that this process of recovering our wholeness through the journey of relationship is part of nature's grand design: to complete and restore itself through us. Perhaps nature's purpose in evolving the frontal lobe was to enable us to observe ourselves and correct the imbalances that are destroying us and the planet we live on. Only we humans can see our place in the seamless tapestry of being. Our awareness that we are a node of consciousness in a field of consciousness that encompasses all life forms, and all of the cosmos, is the foundation of our innate spirituality.

WE CAN'T DO IT ALONE

In order to feel fully alive and to recapture our joyfulness, we have to reintegrate the unconscious, instinctual, associational old brain with our clever new brain. But we cannot *think* our way to aliveness. We cannot recapture joyfulness through our cerebral cortex, smart as it is; the old brain is not altered by the cognitive process. It is altered only by concrete experience. We must restore the split-off and denied parts of ourselves that we lost in childhood, and heal the numbness and pain and perceived threats to survival that dampen our feeling of aliveness and filter out our awareness of our connection to others and to the cosmos. The most effective way I know of to accomplish that is through our love relationships.

People disappointed in love don't want to hear that they *need* a relationship to heal. They want to feel that they can be autonomous, and restore their spiritual wholeness on their own, if their caretakers, or their mates, aren't up to the task. But this is a delusion. While there is much you can accomplish on your own, especially with regard to modifying your character defenses, you can't go the whole way to healing without a partner.

The idea that we need the help of others for our fulfillment is unpopular because it challenges the primacy of the individual.[4] The sovereignty of the individual is, rightly, a cornerstone of democracy. The tension between the individual and the collective, the individual and the dyad, the family and society, produces the chemistry of the evolutionary process, in terms of growth as well as in the development of new social and political systems. But there is no individual not in a context, not in a relationship of some sort, and not in a *dependent* relationship.

We hold dear the idea that we are unique individuals with fixed qualities. But even the personality is largely a function of context, with a fluid, molten core. I am not saying that we are chameleonlike, but we adapt to our circumstances and environment. This, too, we see clearly in the dance that couples do, moving toward and away from each other, exaggerating and modifying their supposedly fixed traits in the face of their partners' own mutations.

COMMITMENT TO WHOLENESS

Finding and keeping love is not just a romantic idea; it's crucial to our intact survival. We are irrevocably committed to relationships as the context in which to experience our true nature. Relationships pave the way for us to recapture our wholeness by correcting the distortions of caretaking and socialization that distanced us from our original selves. It is in unconditionally loving our partner, making it safe for them to open to love, letting that love sink in over time so that trust can build, that allows their fullness to come back into being, so they can feel their oneness, their totality. The radical position I'm taking is that *love is the answer*. It is the love we give that heals our partner, and the love we receive that heals us. But it is only in loving that we truly change the rigid parts of ourselves. It is because a committed partnership (far more effectively than the traditional paths of religion or psychotherapy) can bring us back to our original connectedness that I say that marriage is a spiritual path. It is nature's repair process.

Now you are going to move ahead to the nitty-gritty of scrutinizing your childhood, identifying its malfunctions and shortcomings and their repercussions in your relationships, and readjusting your beliefs and behavior. But as you do this, I want you to keep in mind this larger picture, that the fundamental—but unconscious and instinctual—drive in your relationship is to restore your original sense of relaxed joyfulness, and to feel and express aliveness. Looked at in this context, seemingly trivial incidents and issues that send you into a tailspin take on a higher coloring. Your deep hurt, and your longings, will make more sense. The particulars of your childhood, or your partnerships, have left specific wounds that must be healed in order to recapture your wholeness, and that is the task of relationship. But the particulars are the trees; this is the forest from which they sprang. You long to feel reconnected; your drive is to feel fully alive. A conscious relationship is not your *goal*. Not at all; it is the *path*.

PART III

THE IMAGO PUZZLE I: CHILDHOOD NURTURING

4

Growing Pains: Uncovering the Wounds of Childhood

> Those who forget the past are condemned
> to repeat it.
>
> —CARLOS SANTAYANA

Walking to work one day, fascinated as always by the people on the streets of New York, I was struck by how few people appeared happy or relaxed. Nearly everyone seemed to be carrying a burden that broadcast itself in their expression, their stride, their body language: careworn old women stooped by loss and loneliness; middle-aged men with grim, guarded faces off to their jobs, carrying lunch boxes or briefcases; melancholy, defiant teenagers, purpose-less on a summer morning; exhausted, anxious mothers bringing their children to day care—even their young children already bore signs of the losses and tragedies their lives had dealt them. The occasional vibrant or content passerby was an almost jarring exception. I wondered what showed in my own face.

Taken aback by the apparent pain and injury all around me, I thought about how we all came to this moment in life, wearing on our sleeves the toll exacted by disappointment and sorrow, the wear and tear of anger and loss and fear. Yet each of us started life relaxed

51

and whole and joyful. Without quite realizing what I was doing, I began to picture each person coming toward me as a child, tried to pierce the shell of defeat, depression, or barely suppressed anger to the intact and unbroken infant. Seeing the buried inner child, and understanding why we build our defensive armor, I could feel empathy for even the most repulsive and angry of them, and for myself.

Having surveyed our cosmic origins and the legacy of our evolutionary past, we now come closer to home, to our psychosocial histories. It is your own lost, wounded child that we will seek in these next chapters. To prepare ourselves for the journey of an intimate relationship, we must look for clues in our personal pasts. Looking back on childhood, we can answer critical questions: What do we want from a relationship?˙Why do we choose a particular partner? What kind of relationship are we likely to have? Why do most of us experience so much frustration, pain, and failure in our relationships in contrast to the joy, pleasure, and contentment we hoped to have? The answers to these questions are the raw material from which we can fashion understanding and change, and those answers lie hidden in childhood memories.

The rest of the book is about the impact of those memories on our relationships, and about our whole psychosocial journey here on earth, which begins at birth. This section and Part III are about childhood, the crucible of our current circumstances. Each chapter examines some aspect of how we were nurtured, how we were socialized, and how we were affected by the ambience of our home lives and our parents' marriage. I want to show you how these experiences produce, for each of us (and for you in particular), a specific "wound," in which the seamless fabric of our existence is ruptured, and how we clumsily try to repair the damage. We reweave a tangled web, a false self that fills the void of emptiness, covering our true nature with protective devices to shield us from further injury. Understanding the nature of your wound is the key to your healing, for it has affected all your behavior, your decisions, and your life choices, especially in the arena of intimate relationships. It is the healing of our wounds that we seek, consciously or not, in committed relationships.

THE LIFELONG PURSUIT OF WHOLENESS

Recapturing our wholeness and our sense of full aliveness is no trivial matter. Our woundedness, the result of needs not met, threatens our survival. With the stress of birth and in every subsequent instance that a need is not met in early childhood, we lose another particle of our essential wholeness; the seamless fabric of existence is ruptured. The old brain experiences this disturbance as a "danger" to our existence and sounds an alarm. Because its sole concern is keeping us alive, it begins a compulsive, lifelong mission to restore that lost sense of relaxed joyfulness—to turn off the alarm.

The early childhood years from birth to the age of six are the most critical, for it is here, in a timely, age-appropriate way, that we must accomplish the tasks necessary to become secure, competent, whole selves. We will be looking at these early years, as well as middle childhood and adolescence, to see how we fared during this crucial time and to determine the adaptive behavior we've carried into adulthood. The sad truth is that most of us, to one degree or another, do not get in our formative years what we need in the way of love and security and self-acknowledgment. Whatever is not resolved at one stage, though, gets passed along to the next for healing. During our lifetime, the psyche presents its issues for resolution over and over again.

Inevitably, the project of self-completion gets taken to our adult relationships. We present our wounds and burdens to our intimate others and expect them to undo the damage created by deficient nurturing. "Hi, honey," we say, "I'm home. It's your job to make everything all right." If we understand what's going on here, we stand a chance of finding joy and wholeness. But most of us don't know, and we're unhappier than ever. Failing to resolve the issues in our relationships, all our frustration and disappointment comes to a head in the mid-life crisis, a desperate neo-adolescent last-ditch attempt of the psyche to restore itself. The fifty-year-old man has an affair with his secretary, or quits his job, leaving two kids stranded in college. His wife declares her independence from housework, starts wearing miniskirts, and enters law school. But here the changes are so age-inappropriate and disruptive that they break up people's worlds, and their families. Healthy children don't have mid-life crises.

BECOMING A DETECTIVE

You may think that when I speak of childhood wounds I am referring to serious psychological damage, such as physical or emotional abuse, alcoholism, incest, or the trauma of a parent's death. For all too many people today, this is the unfortunate reality of family life, and I will discuss these issues in Chapter 8. But, in truth, all of us, no matter how stable and nurturing our home lives may have been, are wounded. For we were born dependent, insatiable, complicated creatures, to fallible parents with their own needs and problems. Even with the best of intentions, there are myriad opportunities for things to go wrong. And the things that go *wrong* have more impact on our development than those that go right, as we are well aware. It's the one time in a thousand that we *missed* the train that we acutely remember, the time that we *burned* the roast, the occasion when our partner *forgot* to kiss us good-bye, the time that the baby *fell* when our attention faltered for a moment.

The potential for mistakes, for wrong moves, is infinite. After all, our perfect and peaceful stint in the womb, where everything was provided promptly, perfectly, and naturally is a tough act to follow. Failure is, to some degree, inevitable. But it's the degree and type of failure that constitute the idiosyncratic details of our wound. Now, I'm not talking about traumatic events. I'm talking about what can go wrong in responding to the ordinary, day-by-day, hour-by-hour needs of the infant. Because as infants we cannot understand or control what happens to us, every little thing that goes wrong is experienced at the primitive old-brain level as having absolute significance in terms of survival.

We develop defenses against the inadequacies of our childhoods over which we have no control, and we drag them along with us wherever we go, whomever we're with. These are our coping mechanisms, which, through repetition, harden into character defenses that continue throughout life to obey the original mandate: to ensure our survival. They are the only way we know to protect us in what we perceive as threatening situations. If we cling to our partners, if we recoil from affection, if we crawl into a shell at the first sign of criticism, if we stage scenes to get attention, you can be sure that this behavior can be traced right back to our feeble defenses against wounds suffered in the first years of our lives. As long as we remain unaware of our defense mechanisms and their causes, our frustration will continue. Only when we can trace our childhood wounds to their source, and see the effect they have produced in the present, can we effect change in the future.

I urge you to approach these chapters on nurture and socialization as though you were a detective unraveling a mystery. What you are tracking down are clues to your own wounding—the details of time and place and circumstance, of who said what, and did what, to whom. You are trying to locate your true self in the tangle of your adaptations, and to diagnose the trouble. If you can follow the trail from your childhood to your present situation—or, more likely, from the present backward to childhood—you will have the ingredients for understanding and change that will serve you in your current or future relationships.

Throughout this section, I will be describing various categorical responses children develop to their early environment. I will also describe how each of these responses translates as adult behavior, so that you can see the relationship between cause and effect, which will enable you to identify yourself at a deep level in regard to your woundedness and character structure. I want you to see for yourself how the system works, to have the mystery unravel in a graphic way as a result of this process. I want you to say, "Aha, that's why I have a hard time saying no," "That's why Alice's tears make me angry," or "So that's why I chose Kevin." I want you to be aware of how the constant repetition of certain patterns or messages ended up reinforcing your beliefs about yourself, your partners, and the world you live in. As you read through this section, keep in mind that the information you are gathering is going to provide insight into your past relationships, and the raw materials for retraining and repair in preparation for the more whole and self-aware relationship you will have in the future.

At this point, you may be saying to yourself, but this is so hard, so tedious, so painful. Well, yes, it is all that. The path is long and there are demons along the way, and it would be nice if there were a pill you could take, or a machine to wash the psyche clean. Alas, there are no miracle cures. But I assure you that you have control over your healing, and the pain and effort of doing this work surely can't be worse than what you've suffered in difficult, dead-end relationships. Your psyche wants to survive and live fully; it wants to know that it is not going to die or suffer needlessly. It is just asking to be shown the way, and it will gladly follow. This work is the way.

At intervals throughout Parts II and III, you will find exercises that will help you clarify where and how you were wounded with regard to the way you were nurtured and socialized, and with regard to any grievous dysfunction in your family. At the beginning of Part IV, when you've gathered all your raw data, we're going to begin to solve this case. We will form a picture of your Imago, that unconscious by-product of your childhood experiences, the inner image formed by the confluence of childhood experience that powerfully influences your partner choice. With an Imago partner, someone whose character structure approximates your inner image of the significant other, you re-find the ambience of your childhood, and recreate the context in which you were wounded, in the hope that this time around, with this person who is the-same-but-different,

you can be healed. Knowing ahead of time what kind of partner you
will choose will prepare you for the conflicts in store, and give you
clues about the personal issues you can be working with before that
partner comes along.

DIFFERENT STROKES: NATURE VS. NURTURE

The mind, as I've mentioned, is not a blank slate when we arrive
on this planet. It is already imprinted, encoded with the genetic
instincts and drives that unite us all everywhere—our human nature.
Every infant takes the same road through the stages of development,
on a predictable timetable, with allowances for the idiosyncrasies of
individual circumstance, genetic makeup, and temperament. There
are variations, there are parameters, but most of us do not deviate
wildly from the norm. We all come from the same litter; our old
brains, especially, are cut from the same cloth. You did not forge a
new trail in the way you responded to your environment; in the
most literal sense, you are a creature of habit forged over millennia.
In your personal existence, you have reacted to your circumstances
pretty much as all babies and children do. If you were lucky, you
inherited temperament—and parents—that spared you devastating
wounds.

To be sure, I am making generalizations about human behavior
in this discussion of childhood development, when in actuality each
of us puts our own "spin" on what life presents us. There are myriad
variables in the way individual children respond to their circumstances; it is dangerous to make blanket statements about cause and
effect. Which brings us to the subject of "nature versus nurture,"
the ongoing controversy about the impact of our genetic inheritance
relative to that of our environment. Some theorists feel strongly that
inherited temperament is dominant, citing studies of identical twins
who, though separated at birth, nevertheless demonstrated strik-
ingly similar behavior when compared later in life, despite disparate
circumstances. Recent studies have shown unexpected genetic links
to behavior long considered environmentally induced—shyness, for
instance, or a tendency to be conservative in one's politics and dress.
Contradictory studies have shown that we are overwhelmingly a
product of our environment. But it's rarely so cut and dried. Most of
us know situations in which *one* child survived an alcoholic or
abusive family relatively intact, *one* child in a family of five never
recovered from the parents' divorce. To me it is a moot argument.

Heredity and environment are not dualities, distinct parallels of
unrelated entities. Rather they are two ends of a polarity, a unity (as

are mind and body); we all fall somewhere along the continuum.[1] We are all both closed and open. There are windows in the mind, and the size of those windows determines the influence of the environment on the inherent structure. As I see it, the mind is a permeable organism with an internal structure, like a computer disc. What comes in has to be formatted in the language of the software before we can "read" it. Each of us is born with different levels of sensitivity, or resilience to life's blows, a quality referred to in some studies as "hardiness."

The term *ego strength* also describes this—the ability to maintain one's view of oneself in the face of outside influences and messages, especially those which conflict (or which, to use the psychological term, are ego-dystonic). Ego strength is always a function of an inherent disposition amplified or dampened by environment.

I see such differences in my own children, Hunter and Leah, who are only two years apart. Hunter is just not terribly sensitive or reactive. He doesn't see the outside world in the clarity and detail that Leah does. She walks down the street, noticing everything, affected by everything. If you ask Hunter, "How was your walk?" he'll tell you what he was thinking about. He's contained, an introvert, not terribly responsive to sounds; he doesn't jump in fright when something drops. You could put him in a psychologically toxic environment, and he'd turn out to be neurotic, but he'd get by. Leah is much more vulnerable and reactive to her surroundings, with a more volatile sensory system, so she is more easily hurt and frightened, sensitive to stresses. In a harsh or depriving environment, she would develop a more serious personality disorder.

Here's a simple example. The other night I returned from running an errand. Hunter was in the hall and I told him I was glad that I'd gotten back in time to see him before he went to bed. "Oh, you were gone?" was his response; my absence hadn't even registered. Leah came running out, full of concern: "Daddy, where were you? I didn't hear you go out." To some extent, how you have fared as a result of your childhood is the luck of the dice, your inborn tolerance or resistance to environmental stressors. Even so, everyone needs a safe and loving environment; everything grows better in a warm climate with lots of water.

The Stages of Development: Finding the Weak Link

Figure A shows the six stages of child and adolescent development that concern us here—Attachment, Exploration, Identity, Competence, Concern, and Intimacy—and their approximate timetable.

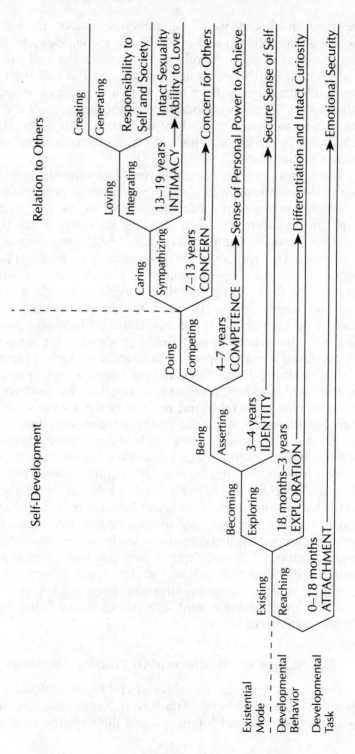

FIGURE A
The Psychosocial Journey of the Self

Self-Development

Relation to Others

	Creating
	Generating
	Responsibility to Self and Society
Loving	Intact Sexuality → Ability to Love
Integrating	
13–19 years INTIMACY → Concern for Others	
Caring	
Sympathizing	
7–13 years CONCERN → Sense of Personal Power to Achieve	
Doing	
Competing	
4–7 years COMPETENCE → Secure Sense of Self	
Being	
Asserting	
3–4 years IDENTITY → Differentiation and Intact Curiosity	
Becoming	
Exploring	
18 months–3 years EXPLORATION	
Existing	
Reaching	
0–18 months ATTACHMENT → Emotional Security	

Existential Mode
Developmental Behavior
Developmental Task

Each phase has its own agenda, its own tasks to perform.[2] Though all of life is, in some sense, a development process, the first four to six years, when we are most dependent, receptive, and malleable, have a profound effect on the rest of our lives.[3]

As Figure A demonstrates, each stage is built upon the preceding one; each is the foundation for accomplishing the task of the next stage. Too, each stage has its own timetable. At the end of each phase, another task emerges whether the preceding task was completed or not. So how we negotiate the hurdles of each stage determines how freely and capably we can move on to the next.

At each stage, there is a norm with a healthy outcome. But if at any point along the way something goes wrong with the way we are nurtured, we instinctively find a way to compensate for what is lacking, in order to survive. But it is a defensive move, and in our desperation and ignorance we develop a maladaptive way of coping with the task at hand. It leaves a weak spot in our development. Lacking in vital skills, and weakened in confidence, we resort to inadequate responses which accumulate like scar tissue around the central core of our wound. Like Sisyphus, we end up pushing a big stone uphill wherever we go, limiting our ability to live and relate in adult life.

Since inevitably our caretakers were to some degree less than perfect at all stages (remember that standard of perfect bliss set in the womb!), we all carry forward some degree of maladaptive response from all stages. *We are all wounded, to some extent, at every stage of development. But there is almost always one stage in which we really got "stuck."* This may have to do with our inherent temperament and how we responded to a particular problem; more likely, it is the result of the way our caretakers handled a particular stage. Their own needs and adaptations may have made some phases harder for them to cope with than others: parents who dote on a newborn infant may feel threatened when he starts to move out into the world, or may be too rigid to mirror the child's fantasies as he tries to establish his identity. They may be uneasy with the juvenile's attachment to his peer group, or the adolescent's venture into sexuality. It can happen that the parents are less available at a particular stage: they are arguing, there is a newborn sibling, an illness, or a cross-country move.

Whatever the case, the major task left uncompleted, or improperly completed, at this stage will have followed us through life, and will turn out to be the core issue around which our current problems turn. Unless some later life experience has broken the maladaptive pattern—a drastic change in the parents' lives such as a positive new relationship (in the case of a single parent), significantly increased time and energy for the child, a major shift in the way the parents treat the child during adolescence—those primitive old-brain adaptations are still with us. Moreover, the accumulating coping mechanisms have a "snowball" effect. The earlier in life we get "stuck," the more inadequately we handle subsequent stages, and the more debris and maladaptive behavior accumulate around the core problem.

THE ADULT CHILD: WHY IS IT IMPORTANT TO KNOW WHERE WE GOT STUCK?

How does our coping behavior translate in adult life, and how does it show up in relationships? Here is where the Imago comes into play. First and foremost, like heat-seeking missiles, we will almost certainly find partners who treat us, in critical ways, much as our caretakers did, and we will use the same childish ploys to deal with them—and end up just as frustrated. We will reenact those old childhood scenarios, and reopen the old wounds that we had bandaged over with our defenses, which we had so hoped to heal when we first fell in love. Alternately, when our spouses fail us as our parents did, and if our childhood reactions produce no effect, we (having no other model of dealing with life than the example our parents provided) will treat our partners the way our parents treated us. That will reopen our partners' childhood wounds and s/he will respond to us much as s/he reacted to his or her parents when s/he was a child.

Say, for instance, your parents criticized you for making a mistake when you were little, like spilling the milk or not getting all A's in school, and you felt guilty and cried and had the recurring thought that you "couldn't do anything right." You will tend to react the same way if your partner finds fault with you for dropping your clothes on the floor or not making enough money. On the other hand, when your partner "makes a mess" or performs at a lower level than you expect, you will tend to criticize your partner as your parents criticized you.

Furthermore, the way things seem to work is that we tend to choose partners who became stuck in the *same* or *adjacent* stage as we did. However, our partners will have adapted to those early frustrations with the *opposite* coping mechanisms, or ways of handling the situation. For example, if you responded to being ignored by jumping through hoops to get attention, your partner may have "solved" the same problem by becoming a loner who doesn't need people.

Gabriel recalls a doting mother whose overprotectiveness felt smothering. Because every attempt to separate from her was met with restraint, he developed a private world of fantasy, which he indulged alone in his bedroom. His mother might prevent him from physically exploring his world, but she could not control his inner life. In contrast, Marion, to whom Gabriel was engaged, felt her parents were never there for her: her mother was preoccupied with her little brother; her father often traveled for business. It seemed that no matter what she did, she could not get their attention. If she went out to play, her mother was on the phone or "tired" or feeding Timmy when she returned for "refueling." She vividly remembers how much she enjoyed drawing pictures in her room; but then she would bring them to her mother, only to have her say, "Not now, Marion, can't you see I'm busy?" Gabriel and Marion were both wounded at the stage of Exploration, but in opposite ways. Gabriel was unable to separate from his mother because she was so possessive, while Marion could not separate because she was afraid no one would be there when she returned. When Gabriel approached his mother, he had to meet her needs; when Marion came to her mother, she could not get her own needs met.

The traits that are dominant in one partner are recessive in the other, but they are fluid. If one partner changes, and their recessive character emerges, the other responds in kind. In the situation above, if Marion were to find that she needn't be so demanding of Gabriel's attention, Gabriel would need to emerge from his shell and seek her out. Each partner yearns for the character adaptations their partner provides them. Marion fears abandonment, but she desperately craves the kind of privacy and independence she sees in Gabriel. Gabriel fears the closeness and contact he so fervently craves.

You can see how important it is for you to recognize your personal quicksand if you hope to change the outcome of your future relationships. Now we will examine each stage of development. As I describe how each stage looks, how our caretakers behave and how we respond, and how the repercussions manifest themselves in the form of so-called adult behavior, you will see clearly how we develop adaptive defenses, and what the potential for damage is. You will be able to pinpoint the stage at which you got "stuck" and be able to use this information as a model, a predictor

5

Attachment and Exploration: Getting Securely Connected

> The freedom to bring into the adult
> relation the deepest elements of infantile
> object-relations is a condition of growth.
>
> H. V. DICKS

Attachment: The Struggle to Exist

Birth is, to put it mildly, a rude awakening. Noise, pain, bright light, heat and cold, *separation* from the warm, safe womb. No wonder newborns yowl. For awhile, the baby remains in a semi-autistic state, half-aware of the change in his environment, intermittently responsive to his new surroundings, as though caught between sleep and waking. If the journey to birth and expulsion was relatively smooth, he exists in his original, primordial state of total relaxation and pleasure. The fabric of existence remains seamless and unbroken.

The sense that things have changed dawns slowly. All lines of supply have been cut off, and the infant emits his first signal of distress about this condition and begins a rooting, grasping search for contact. Finding the mother and succeeding in getting the nipple in his mouth, the alarm subsides and the original relaxed state is restored. The first and most important task of a human being has begun: *Attachment*.[1]

When the newborn utters his first cry and reaches for the mother's warmth and the nipple, the psychosocial journey is activated. The infant has a vital agenda—to close that gulf of separation that opened up so threateningly at birth, and securely reattach himself to the nurturing, protective source of his survival. He is responding to his internal mandate to exist.

That's a tall order, as any exhausted, befuddled parent will attest. All the varied and constant needs that were handled automatically in the womb must now be taken care of manually—food must be provided, diapers changed, a certain level of physical contact maintained, in a calm environment, on a demand basis, around the clock. As long as everything rolls along perfectly, and all needs are promptly and appropriately fulfilled, all is fine, and the infant seems happy as a clam, basking in the warmth and comfort of an environment that feels every bit as friendly as the one he came from. He grasps and sucks and cries and as long as someone is there who knows just what to do, the baby reestablishes his sense that the world is safe, that he is in no danger in this strange land. However, the seamless fabric of existence was temporarily disturbed, and the disturbance has left traces. It is slowly dawning on him that he is a separate creature, and he now knows the difference between pleasure and pain.[2]

It is easy to suppose, from his sucking, grasping, and crying, that what the infant needs most to survive is food, and that if he is fed regularly, all is well. But that is not the case. What babies need even more to survive is physical and emotional contact; they need a reliable source of love and comfort. A now famous study conducted by psychologist Harry Harlow took newborn infant monkeys and put them with two "surrogate mothers," one constructed of wire, the other of soft terry cloth. The infant monkeys became more attached to the terry-cloth "mother," cuddling up with her, running to her when they were frightened—even when the wire "mother" was the only one able to provide food.[3]

Getting attached remains the infant's primary agenda for about the first eighteen months of life. If all goes well, and the infant's signals are properly received and responded to, and he is fed and held and changed and talked to, he develops the sense that he is a separate being in a safe world with the power and wherewithal to get what he needs. He is "securely attached." It doesn't seem like much, but it's critical. The sense of security established at this stage sets the tone of the rest of our journey through life. It is the foundation of our response to life's perils and pleasures.[4]

Fortunately, that's pretty much how it works out for about half of us. Somehow, with all the demands, the missed signals, the personal problems and distractions and crises, the week of the flu, and the imperfectly fulfilled wishes, the love and good intentions of many parents prevail. Their children feel securely connected. Their caretaking, on a day-in and day-out basis, is, in psychologist D. H. Winnicott's phrase, "good enough."

ADAPTING TO DEFICIT NURTURING: COPING MECHANISMS

But what about those children whose parents were "not good enough," who were "not there" emotionally or physically with enough consistency and warmth for secure attachment to take place? Estimates suggest that one-third to one-half of all children fall into this category. For them there is no assurance of a response when their needs surface. Such infants are what is labeled "insecurely" or "anxiously" attached. The seamless fabric of their existence has torn; they have lost contact with their original joyful state.[5]

Here is where the problems—i.e., the maladaptive coping mechanisms—take root. Infants yearn for that essential state of relaxed joy that they have lost, and they try to restore it by adapting as best they can to their inadequate nurturing. In response to the caretaker's nurturing effectiveness, the infant creates an internal image of the caretaker, which I call the Imago, and a self-image, which includes his view of himself in the context of his situation or "world." This internal image of his inner and outer world, often split between "good" and "bad" traits of self and other, then influences the child's behavior, in turn, toward the parents, and determines which coping mechanism he will develop. Depending on how his caretakers respond to his needs, that coping mechanism, at each stage of development, will polarize, taking one of two forms. One infant copes by *diminishing* his affect in the world, the other copes by *exaggerating* his responses, thus replicating the ancient evolutionary legacy of constricting or exploding energy in response to threatening stimuli. I characterize these two responses as the *Minimizer* and the *Maximizer*, describing two poles of character organization found in most male/female pairing. I want to talk more about this phenomenon, for it describes something that it is important for each of us to identify in ourselves. But first let's look at how this response manifests itself in the Attachment stage.

THE CLINGING CHILD: FEAR OF ABANDONMENT

In response to deficit nurturing at the Attachment stage, the infant adapts either by clinging or detaching.

If the caretaker is inconsistent—appropriately warm sometimes, but emotionally cold or absent at others—her child will develop a compulsive clinging response. Such caretakers may be preoccupied, self-centered, angry, or busy; their moods and their timetables fluctuate. They are unpredictable. Perhaps they are uncomfortable with their caretaker role and try to follow some rigid formula they've read about in books, providing the necessary services, but on their own schedule or whim. They may pick the infant up and feed him regularly, but not when *he* cries or fusses for attention. Clearly the child's needs are a burden to this parent. Unable to establish a basic trust that his needs will be met, the child senses that only his incessant demands will keep him alive.

In response to unreliable or inconsistent nurturing, the infant's old brain sounds an alarm, signaling that he is in danger. Because his mother does come through sometimes, the infant keeps trying, feeling that if he can just figure out what to do—cry loud enough or long enough, or respond in a certain way—everything will work out. Thus is established the pattern of stress, inconsistent response, exaggeration, and doubt that creates an anxious child. A clinging child has a highly ambivalent relationship to his mother. Tormented by her unpredictable availability, he is simultaneously addicted to getting her attention and finding a way to get her to respond; at the same time he is angry that his needs aren't being met. He spends half his time crying and holding on, to keep his unpredictable mother by his side, the other half being rejecting, pushing his mother away, even as she is being affectionate. The infant is in a dilemma because the object of pain and pleasure is the same. The first layer of his Imago now includes good and bad elements, thus laying the foundation for a split image of the caretaker. He is experiencing rage, terror, and grief, alternating with unpredictable satisfaction. Because he cannot live in an inconsistently supportive environment and tolerate for long the consequent negative feelings its insecurity stimulates, he develops an ambivalent defensive structure, alternately clinging and pushing away, to ward off these incapacitating feelings. Experiencing some of his needs satisfied and others frustrated, he begins to develop an ambivalent (good/bad) attitude toward himself.

THE ADULT: A CLINGER

As with wounds at all stages, if his situation does not change in later childhood or adolescence, the child will experience a developmental arrest. His defenses will become cemented into his character and show up as his basic personality in adult life. He becomes what I call a Clinger. Hidden behind a fabricated self, his infantile needs are still alive, and these, together with his learned protections, will influence his choice of a partner, his expectations of that partner, and the way he will relate to get his needs met. The core complaint of his relationships will be: "You are never there for me."

Alma, the mother of two children from a previous marriage, came to see me with her fiancé, Will, an entrepreneur in the computer-software business. During the weekends, when they were constantly together, she was happy and content, and she described Will as warm and loving most of the time. But he was often preoccupied with the problems of his struggling business, especially on Sunday nights before the upcoming work week. Extremely sensitive to abandonment feelings, Alma would feel his withdrawal and sink into a mild depression as soon as he turned his attention to his work. "Every time things are good between us, you go away," she'd wail, reflecting the memory of the "bad" or inconsistent childhood caretaker. Or she would cry and come to him asking for reassurance of his love, and question whether he really wanted to get married. When he was able to comfort her, she would snap back into her happy, sexy self and suggest they go to bed and make love, recapturing momentarily the "good" aspects of the childhood caretaker. Other times she was inconsolable, and would go into a tantrum, screaming her constant complaint: "You are never around when I need you." Fearful of intense feelings, his own and hers, Will would withdraw further, and Alma would stomp off to bed and ask him to sleep in another room. When Will went off to work the next day, Alma would panic, and call him at the office by 10:30 to ask what he was doing. If he had time to talk, she was gratified, but if he was busy and emotionally unavailable, she would hang up on him. Then he would call her back and comfort her until she was calm, but she always asked him to call her again at lunchtime before she would let him get off the phone. When he called her at lunch, she would be emotionally remote or state that she was too busy to talk, leaving him in a constant state of confusion about what she wanted from him.

This is classic Clinger (and Maximizer) behavior. Alma, trapped in an eternal now, is using solutions that were barely effective when she was eighteen months old—although they did enable her to survive. She is still saying to herself, "I can't count on my needs being met. I am good, but the other (my caretaker, or my partner) is bad. I will hurt my partner until he meets my needs." But at an even deeper level of the subconscious is another belief left over from childhood: "I am bad for having these needs. I can't let him meet them." No wonder Will is confused. Of course, given the way things work, Alma has chosen a partner who, like her caretaker, is emotionally detached, an Avoider (and a Minimizer).

THE DETACHED CHILD: FEAR OF REJECTION

Other caretakers are *consistently* emotionally cold and inconsistently available physically. For them it is not that the child's needs are a burden, but the child himself is felt to be one. Such caretakers give rise to the detached child. Unlike the clinging child, the detached child fears the attachment he so desperately needs, because all attempts to attach result in emotional pain. Unlike his clinging counterpart, for whom *not* having contact is frightening, it is contact itself that is painful. Therefore, his defense is to "not approach" his mother, because if she is present at all, she is routinely depressed, disinterested, and emotionally distant. Terrified of the responsibility of a child, somehow caught up in her own problems and personal priorities, she is emotionally rejecting. Because contact results not in the pleasure of acceptance or satisfaction of needs but in emotional pain, the infant makes a fateful decision: avoid contact at all costs. "I am bad, the object (the caretaker) is bad, my needs are bad," he reasons, thus etching on the template of his Imago the impression of the caretaker as bad, and on the other side, where the image of the self is recorded, an impression of the-self-having-needs as bad. This reasoning leads to a primitive but effective defense: "I don't have needs." His caretaker has rejected him, so he rejects the caretaker, and finally he rejects his life force. He doesn't cry; he seems content to be fed whenever food arrives; he doesn't seem to care one way or another whether he is held or talked to. But while the needs are banished from consciousness, the old brain remains in a constant state of alarm, because the denied needs are essential for survival. To muffle the alarm, the detached child numbs his body and voids his feelings, vastly constricting—minimizing—his life energy. To contain it totally, he constructs a false self, which looks independent, but is actually counterdependent. The world admires his independence, but he lives virtually alone in his fortress, determined to avoid the pain of being vulnerable to rejection.[6]

Detached children don't cry very much, and they don't seem to need very much; they take whatever they can get and don't ask for more. Often the mother is proud of her "good" baby, since she finds dependence distasteful and uncomfortable. The detached infant, motivated by fear of contact, is saying, "I don't really need you to get by, I'm perfectly capable of taking care of myself." What's really happening is that he's given up in despair.

THE ADULT: AN AVOIDER

As with the compulsively dependent child, if these patterns are not corrected in later childhood or adolescence (as they are unlikely to be, since the caretakers have usually not evolved), they will show up in adult intimate relationships. He becomes what I call an Avoider. Will, engaged to Clinger Alma, described above, is a good example. As I mentioned, Avoiders tend to hook up with Clingers, for predictable reasons. It is not that Avoiders have no needs; rather, they gave up on getting their needs met long ago and lost contact with their desires. Large chunks of themselves are buried, especially their sensitive, feeling side and their capacity for emotional joy and body pleasure. Their hidden needs for contact influence their selection of partners with excessive contact needs, which provides Avoiders with the contact they consciously deny they want. Consequently, they never have to approach their partners, because the partners' intense needs to be in contact fulfills the Avoiders' denied needs to be in contact. But contact is still painful. As is apparent in Will's case, Alma's needs for closeness both attracted him and made him feel desperate to escape.

In their first session with me, Alma was practically hysterical with rage: "You never approach me. You don't seem to want to touch me. If I did not call or ask you to call, it would be a cold day in hell before I heard from you. If I didn't make plans for us on the weekend, we'd do nothing, and you would sit with your computer and play games or work on business problems. I don't think you have any feelings or needs, and you are never there when I need you."

Will's response was predictable. "I don't know what you are talking about. I am there. You are just too needy (projecting his own denied needs onto her by implying that he doesn't need anything). Nothing I do pleases you. When we are together, you have so many complaints. Who wants to be around that all the time (reflecting the cold and rejecting caretaker of his childhood)?" He said this without emotion and, becoming very rational, continued: "Why do you have all these problems? Why can't we just be together without so much conflict? Besides, we don't have to be together all the time. Everyone needs to be alone sometimes. Why can't you be comfortable off by yourself?" All said in a monotone.

The need for reliable attachment never goes away, but the acuteness of the need depends on the degree to which it was denied in infancy. The family doctor knows that the most effective part of his treatment is the pat on the head and the encouragement to "call me in the morning." I see the implications of reliable availability in my therapy clients. I get very few emergency calls, and I think it's because, knowing that they have my home number and can call me if they need me, my patients feel secure.

For the Avoider, the need for attachment is a secret hunger; for the Clinger, it is an ever-present demand. The ambivalent Clinger and the detached Avoider have found a way to compensate for the untrustworthiness of their caretakers, but a powerful lifelong pattern has been set in motion. If nothing comes along to mitigate their experience, this behavior becomes fixed—the infants become adults frozen in a pattern of clinging or distancing.

Interlude: The Minimizer and the Maximizer

So it seems that nature, with its compulsive passion for survival, has equipped us neurologically to adapt in one of two ways to life-threatening frustrations at each stage of our development. We minimize or maximize our affect. Depending on our genetic makeup and our interaction with the specific ways our caretakers treated us, we choose one of these two responses if our needs are not met. This complementary pattern has a poetic symmetry that cuts across all stages.

Before we go on to the next stage of development, which I call Exploration, I want to pause here to discuss this dual pattern of adaptation that seems to operate on a continuum throughout our development and socialization. It seems that no matter what the frustration, or at what developmental stage it occurs, some of us exaggerate our response to it and the rest of us diminish our response. *Minimizing* or *Maximizing* describes the way we express our energy when danger threatens. Diminishing or exaggerating our affect is an expression of our evolutionary survival instinct to constrict our energy or to explode it in the face of danger—here translated into relational behavior.

The Maximizer is the active one, often expressive and explosive, discharging his high energy, fighting to get what he needs. The

Minimizer is passive, almost immobile, fleeing inward to avoid the danger of being emotionally or physically abandoned.

If we look back at the *Clinger*, we see that in childhood he learned to try and get what he needed by crying, grasping, screaming, clutching—and he never gave up. He actively amplified and exaggerated his affect in the hope of getting a response, however uncertain or inconsistent it was. Alma is an example of the form this can take in adult life. The *Avoider*, on the other hand, gave up in childhood, withdrawing into himself, hardly ever crying, denying his need. He diminished his affect, withheld his emotions, feeling that his efforts were to no avail. Will is an example of an Avoider.

At each stage of development, the child will maximize or minimize his affect, though in each phase the motivation (and degree) differs. Remember the snowball effect: the earlier in life, the more primitive the stage at which the primary wound is suffered, the greater the degree of exaggeration or diminishment. Thus a child wounded at the Attachment stage will be far more volatile—or passive—than a child whose injury takes place at the later stage of Exploration or Concern.

I first noticed the relative intensity of the Minimizer/Maximizer adaptation when I was showing my training class videotapes of couples working on changing their frustrations into Behavior Change Requests. In the exercise, one partner expresses a frustration and asks the other for a change in the bothersome behavior, and they work out a way, and a timetable, for the change to be put into effect. The tape was meant to show the trainees how hard it can be to get some partners to work things out. (You will learn this skill on page 288.)

The first couple was wild and out of control: she screamed and accused, full of venom and vitriol; he got increasingly stubborn, refused to talk, and almost left the room. They could not get the job done. However, the other couple I showed was calm and rational; they were able to cooperate, to accept suggestions, to control their anger and blaming, and to learn and practice the skill.

As I watched the tape, I realized that *both* women were Maximizers, and *both* men were Minimizers. But where the first woman was lashing out mindlessly while the husband became more and more closed and silent, to the extent that they were unable to complete their task, the second couple had a lesser, more functional degree of the same dynamic. She was still talkative and emotional and strayed from the point, and he tended to speak in a quiet and overcontrolled manner. But they accomplished their task; they were courteous to each other, and in the end got results.

The difference is that the first couple's wounding occurred at the Attachment stage (albeit with complementary adaptations), and they were dealing with one-year-old issues. The second couple was wounded at the six-year-old stage of Competence. In most couples, one is as wild as the other is restrained; it's all relative.

I want to point out that all women are not Maximizers, nor are all men Minimizers, though it looks like a gender issue if you measure it statistically. It is rather a function of socialization, having to do with the way men and women are trained to express themselves in our culture. But in my practice I have seen several instances in which the roles were reversed. It is also true that in our culture, which values people who are rational, restrained, and self-contained, the Minimizer, who has buried his feelings and needs, *looks* good, and is more acceptable. The exaggerated, emotional, out-of-control Maximizer looks bad, but he is in fact better off. For while the Maximizer's behavior may be unacceptable, and it may not get him what he wants, at least he is still aware of his feelings and desires. The Minimizer is sometimes more successful in the world, but he is so split off from his emotions, so suppressed, that he has lost his consciousness of his desires. Before he can solve his problems, he must first become aware of his feelings.[7]

Another component of the Minimizer/Maximizer response to stressors in the environment is related to the issue of the rigidity or fluidity of our *boundaries*, of knowing where we leave off and others begin. The Maximizer has minimal internal and external boundaries: he has a hard time separating his own thoughts, desires, and opinions from those of the people around him. Malleable and impressionable, he doesn't know his own mind. He is intrusive, and easily intruded upon. Alma, for instance, constantly interrupted Will when he was talking, and she thought nothing of interrupting him with phone calls at work. She would straighten his tie and tell him what he was feeling in the same movement. The Minimizer has tight, rigid boundaries, and relates everything to himself; he cannot walk in your shoes, or see your point of view. Despite Alma's elaborate expressions of distress, Will never once showed any empathy for her pain or understood her distress. Nor could he show her any affection or say with feeling, "I am concerned about your fears," or "I love you." The most he seemed to be able to say was: "You know I love you. Don't you have everything you need?" He repeatedly diminished the validity of her feelings and told her that she needed help—not that he was willing to give it to her. Establishing proper personal boundaries is a crucial task at every stage of development, but it is particularly critical at the Identity stage, when our task is to establish a clear sense of self.

E X E R C I S E   5 A   ■   ■   ■   ■   ■

Was I Wounded at the Attachment Stage?

It can be difficult to trace our wounds through childhood memories, which are often dim and unreliable. Often we must deduce our childhood wounds from our present circumstances and past liaisons. The chart below summarizes the response to deficit nurturing at the Attachment stage, and its resulting character adaptations, especially with reference to how they translate into partner choice and relationship problems.

ADAPTATIONS TO WOUNDING AT ATTACHMENT

THE AVOIDER: Minimizer, Rigid Boundaries	1	2	3	4	5
Basic Fear (Wound): Contact may lead to emotional and physical rejection, loss of self through contact with parent (partner)					
Internal Message: Don't be					
Core Belief: I have no right to exist					
Relationship Belief: I will be hurt if I initiate contact with you					
Image of Partner: Demanding, all consuming					
Relationship to Partner: Detached; avoidant					
Core Issue: Too much togetherness; too many feelings; too much chaos					
Typical Frustration: You hate me; you feel too much					
Recurrent Feeling: Terror and rage					
Conflict Management: Hyperrational; avoidant; passive/ aggressive withdrawal and coldness					
Growth Challenge: Claim right to be; initiate emotional and physical contact; express feelings; increase body awareness and sensory contact with environment					

THE CLINGER: Maximizer, Diffuse Boundaries	1	2	3	4	5
Basic Fear (Wound): Separation and abandonment; loss of self through loss of contact with parent (partner)					
Internal Message: Don't need me					
Core Belief: I can't get my needs met					
Relationship Belief: I am safe if I hold on to you					
Image of Partner: Unavailable; has no feelings; a rock wall					
Relationship to Partner: Clinging; demanding; attempts to fuse					
Core Issue: Separateness					
Typical Frustration: You are never there					
Recurrent Feeling: Voracious rage and terror					
Conflict Management: Hyperemotional, uncompromising; demanding, then giving in					
Growth Challenge: Let go; do things on your own; negotiate					

While what you have read in this chapter is fresh in your memory, take a few minutes to assess how you fit the descriptions in the chart, rating yourself on a scale of 1 ("that's not me at all") to 5 ("that's exactly the way it is for me"). Remember that most of us were wounded to some degree at *all* stages; but for most of us, one stage will have been the most wounding, the one in which we got stuck, and which we need to heal in our partnership. Also, you may find that your experiences with differing partners may blur the distinctions, for we tend to be different with each partner. But as you check yourself out on all the charts a pattern will emerge. Don't try to tie yourself down to any one stage, but get an overall impression of your wound and the defenses you have chosen to cope with it.

There will be a chart like this for each developmental stage, and a wrap-up exercise at the end. In preparation for doing this exercise, think back over what you have just read about Attachment. Before you look at the exercise, take a few minutes to close your eyes, relax, and take a few deep breaths. Try to recapture the feelings, in your mind and body, of this period of your childhood, and of your past relationships.

Exploration: Love Affair with the World

Now we move into what is probably the most misunderstood stage of a child's development. Once the infant gets his source of supply stabilized, he is anxious to explore the world he is discovering. In the Exploration phase, which lasts from about eighteen to thirty-six months, the infant's task is to be able to securely leave his mother's side and begin to function on his own, with the confidence that he can then return to a secure and loving home base. In other words, the goal of successful attachment is, paradoxically, the ability to be separate.

This stage is usually referred to as Separation and Autonomy, because it has been believed that the child's desire is to break away from his mother, and that his rebellious "no" is a sign that he wants to be on his own, free from her domination. I think that is wrong. The child's drive is not to be autonomous or separate, but to explore the world. He is differentiating from his caretaker, but he is not seeking autonomy. Actually, he is torn between his newfound fascination with the world and his conflicting need for reassurance of his mother's continued availability. He wants to leave, but only if everything will be the same when he returns. Though he is differentiating himself from his nurturing source, he is not separating from it. He still needs to be attached; he will look over his shoulder to make sure his mother is still nearby, or keep coming back to check that she hasn't disappeared in his absence. You can see why inadequate nurturing at the Attachment stage hampers the ability of the child to explore confidently.

At this point, the child is having a love affair with the world; everything is new and interesting. He is the hero setting forth on his journey. He sticks his fingers in the electric socket, eats the toothpaste, plays with his feces, without judgment or inhibition. When the parent curtails his activities, the child's rebellion—the bane of the "terrible twos"—is not so much defiance as his frustration at being boundaried in his explorations. He becomes sneaky and duplicitous. You tell him not to eat Muffie's food, but he gobbles it down the minute you turn your back; he climbs the back fence the minute your back is turned, and figures out how to break into the forbidden cabinet. Like all children, he refuses to go to bed peaceably. He wants more experience, more fun, another story. He doesn't want to miss anything. What seems like defiance is more indicative of the powerful drive to explore and experiment, and the degree of frustration when that drive is thwarted.

Looking at this difficult passage in this light changes our whole picture of the growing child. He is exploring, not rebelling. While he resists the constriction of his boundaries and the expression of his curiosity, he is in no way independent or autonomous; he needs frequent refueling. He needs to be able to go off on his own, but he will never lose his desire for attachment. We are by nature relational, and our attachment needs are lifelong. They do not disappear. It is more accurate to say that a second need appears, namely to go away and return to things as they were when he left. Even the Wall Street executive who goes to work in the morning to move and shake the world wants to come home at night to his safe and sheltering home. As they say in Grenada, "I go out to come back."

At the point when the child is trying to explore his world, when suddenly, and seemingly arbitrarily, he is saying "no" to everything, the astute mother encourages him to explore, as long as she knows he is safe. She sets protective limits, but not arbitrary and unnecessary restrictions. She is not threatened by his newfound self-confidence and his determination to move away from her, nor is she bothered by his seeming contrariness. She understands that this assertiveness is necessary for his growth. Knowing that he is nevertheless a little nervous about wandering off, she makes sure he knows that she will be there and will be glad to see him, and listens to the tales of his adventures when he returns.

I will never forget my son Hunter, when he was about two, leaving my lap in the living room one day to get a toy in his room. Before he left, he looked back to see if I was still sitting there. Since I had moved to get something from my desk, he ran back and sat me down again on the sofa. Then he left again, looking behind him to see if I would stay put. No sooner was he out of sight down the hall when he returned. He stuck his head in the door and smiled: "Stay there," he commanded.

What children want in the Exploration stage can be summed up in two sentences: "Don't worry about me while I'm gone" (i.e., don't restrict my explorations) and "Don't make me worry about you" (i.e., be here when I get back). Children want to leave and come back to find their caretakers exactly where they left them—not off in the yard or the bathroom, and not lost in their own reveries. But even with the best intentions, things can go wrong, as an experience I had recently with Leah and Hunter demonstrates. I had taken them bike riding in Central Park, where there is a long path around a playing field. Instead of sitting by the side of the path as I usually do, I decided to get some exercise by briskly walking around the path behind them. Of course, I couldn't keep up with their bicycles. They circled the track a couple of times, and I was gone, but they didn't worry, and set off again. I was twenty yards behind them at this point, but they didn't see me. A few minutes later I heard the most forlorn screaming and crying, and I rounded the corner and saw them pedaling their bicycles, looking around in near panic and crying, so I ran to catch up with them. "Where were you?" they wailed. "You left us." They had gone exploring, and when they came back I was gone—and I hadn't told them where I was going. I had to reassure them that I would never leave them, that even if they didn't see me I was somewhere nearby, that I was sorry for not having told them that I was going to walk around.

"But where were you? You weren't there and you didn't tell us." They continued to express their fear and anger, to seek reassurance. "Next time you will tell us, right?"

"Of course," I said, "and if I get tired I'll sit down on the path so you can see me, and I'll yell when you go by so you know I'm there."

It all took about three or four minutes and then they were fine, because they know that normally Helen and I are reliable. They rode off again and had a good time.

Now, these kids could have found their way home—they'd been to the park many times, and they know enough to find a policeman and tell him their address—once they stopped crying. Yet for a moment they regressed right back to their two-year-old dependency. But there are no such options for a two-year-old; he has no resources. If he comes back to where he left his Daddy and if Daddy has gone to the bathroom, he cries, and if Daddy doesn't come back very soon, his distress becomes acute. The need to explore and return to things as we left them is the same whether we're two or six or forty-six.

THE DISTANCING CHILD: FEAR OF ABSORPTION

When the Exploration phase is mishandled, children tend either to distance themselves from their parents or to become ambivalent. If the caretaker is overly protective, setting strict limits on the child's wanderings, checking up on him the moment he wanders off; if she holds him on her lap, blocking his access to the world, the child feels stifled, and holds himself aloof. Now, this can happen with parents who are naturally concerned or unsure of themselves, but more often it occurs with the parent who feels abandoned herself and needs the child to stay connected. If the mother grasps at the child as he tries to move away, the distancing child will stay away and not want to return, fearful that he will be absorbed back into the mother's orbit.

Or his response may be to outwardly adapt to the mother's needs, returning to her physically (because in fact he needs her) while cutting off emotionally. Still needing the reassurance of his caretaker's presence and not ready yet to wander too far afield, he plays at the farthest point of the room from the caretaker, or within earshot but at enough of a distance that he isn't within range of her embrace. He will approach the mother, but he is wary of her restrictiveness. She is both a good and bad object in his mind. At this age, he cannot hold these opposing traits together, so he, like the Clinger, views her as "bad" when she restricts him and "good" when she lets him roam, again etching a split image of the caretaker on the Imago template. Sensing her rejection of his defiance, he begins to reject that aspect of himself. Fearing her loss and its consequences, the only strategy the child is able to devise to keep from losing his caretaker and at the same time to keep from being controlled and absorbed is to appear to comply with her wishes while inwardly protesting her restrictions. Here is the passive/aggressive syndrome. This is the child who allows his mother to pick him up, while turning his face away from her kiss. The distancing child is the idiosyncratic form of the Minimizer response to the Exploratory stage. He reduces his affect to deflect his mother's consuming attentions. In a self-protective move to avoid being absorbed, his boundaries become closed and rigid.

On the surface, the distant child looks like the detached child of the Attachment stage, but there is one big difference. The detached child *never* approaches, never asks for anything for himself. He keeps his experience private, for contact is painful and invites rejection. The distancing child made it through the Attachment stage fine; it was when he wanted to *leave* that his troubles started. He's not afraid of contact, but he needs to maintain careful boundaries, for his fear is that if he gets too close, he'll become trapped and unable to escape to explore on his own.

THE ADULT: AN ISOLATOR

In adulthood, the distancing child becomes what I call an Isolator. He is physically and emotionally aloof. He has lots of ways to avoid spending time in the relationship, whether it's a job that involves long hours or a great deal of travel, commitments to clubs and charities outside the home, or always having his head buried in a book or his eyes glued to the television. He spends weekends in the garden, or in the basement workshop, and thinks separate vacations are a great idea. The Isolator needs his "space" and feels threatened if demands are made for his presence, or his emotions. "You want too much," is the complaint, or "You're trying to control me," or "I need some space for myself." Although he has buried needs for closeness, he fears smothering, so he keeps them to himself, and maintains his distance through anger and strict limits on his availability. He feels that if he gets close, he may get stuck like Br'er Rabbit to the tar baby, and never pull free again.

With the freedom to come and go, the adult Isolator is fine, but as soon as he perceives that others have needs, he withdraws, fearing enmeshment, for it was his caretaker's needs that traumatized him in childhood. Only guilt, a desire to please, or his own fear of abandonment keeps him from fleeing. If he feels his partner trying to hang on, he blasts her with anger to get her to leave him alone, or withdraws and stays away until he gathers his armor around him. But when he returns he ignores their fight, and wonders why she is so angry. He tries to jolly her into a good mood, and criticizes her for not wanting to be with him now that he is available. Failing to change the atmosphere, he withdraws again.

Peter, a successful businessman in a pin-striped suit, came with his girlfriend, Julie, "to help her with her depression." It soon became clear that Julie's depression had to do with the fact that she felt excluded from much of Peter's life and thoughts. "Every minute that we're not eating or sleeping, you have something scheduled. You run first thing in the morning, on the weekends you're riding your motorcycle or kayaking. At night you have paperwork, or you need time to 'think.' If I call you at the office, you're just going into a meeting, and you act irritated that I interrupted you. I don't know why you want to be with me."

Peter's calm, weary response was that Julie was simply jealous of any time he spent separate from her. "I like to exercise. I have a lot of interests. I don't see why she's not happy."

"But you always have time to spend with your assistant. If I want to go out to lunch, you're too busy. Who wouldn't be jealous; for all I know you're having an affair."

Now Peter was furious, but he acted calm and cool. "I'm not having an affair. Every time I look at another woman, you think I want to sleep with her. All I get is criticism. I'm not doing anything wrong. I just need some space."

I turned the conversation to what was going well in the relationship. Julie was quick to point out that they had some good times together, that Peter was funny, and interesting to be with when he was around. But, unable to hold on to the good experiences, she continued to complain. "But he often plans things, or says he's going to do something, and then backs off, or something more important seems to come up. You promise a lot, but you come through with very little. It seems the more I ask of you, the less you are willing to do."

By this time Peter had turned and was looking out the window, barely paying attention, containing his fury. "You want too much," he pronounced, unconsciously pushing the bad, smothering mother away by distancing himself from Julie.

Unable to be close to his partner, but afraid of withdrawing to the point where she might leave, Peter's behavior is a case study in passive aggression. Passive aggression is what's going on when we say we're going to do something—spend Saturday with our partner rather than playing poker, clean up the house—but then we don't do it. Afraid to say what we want or feel directly, because it feels too threatening to the fragile bonds of love, we acquiesce or make promises we don't keep. We continue to postpone or make excuses, because we're angry, or we just don't want to do what was asked. It's what's going on when we hug our mates, but our bodies are rigid and our mind is on fixing dinner. We're saying, "I'll do it when I'm good and ready," or "Don't crowd me," or "You can't make me do it."

THE AMBIVALENT CHILD: FEAR OF LOSS

The ambivalent child is the product of a caretaker who is anxious to be free from the dependent child's needs. She encourages him to go off on his exploratory journey before he is ready, or she is not there when he returns, shattering the bonding that maintained his original sense of wholeness through the Attachment stage. Her encouragement for him to separate may take the form of ignoring him or pushing him away, of trivializing his fears, of showing irritation at his attempts to be with her or hold her attention. "Be a big boy," she may say. "Go and play by yourself." She is urging him to grow up beyond his years, before he is ready. He may wander off, and have a good time, but when he returns his mother has disappeared, either physically or emotionally, and he panics. The unemotional "bad" mother is etched on his Imago.

The result is a child who is fearful and dependent. "Where were you? I couldn't find you" is the lament of the ambivalent child. Now he is afraid to leave his mother's side, and needs constant reassurance that she won't go away the minute he takes his eyes off her. He becomes a Maximizer, with diffuse boundaries. Fearing abandonment, he exaggerates his affect with any ploy—tears, threats, stories, questions, anything that will keep his mother's attention and ensure that if he leaves her side, she will still be available if he needs her. When she is there for him when he returns, or reassures him that she will not go away, she becomes a "good" object in his mind, balancing the abandoning mother whom he fears losing.

A client's story illustrates how ambivalent behavior develops: "My mother was always 'setting me up' with games or crayons and snacks and saying, 'Now, be a big boy, Mommy has to rest.' After a couple of minutes, I would always go quietly into her room to see if she was still there. She never seemed glad to see me. 'Can't you see I'm busy?' she'd say. But I kept trying, always thinking of something that seemed like a good reason to disturb her—'I lost my red crayon' or 'Why is the radiator so hot?' "

THE ADULT: A PURSUER

In adulthood, the ambivalent child becomes what I call a Pursuer. He employs all sorts of tactics to keep his partner close by. In a way, he is like the Clinger, with whom he shares a common fear of abandonment. But Pursuers accomplished the task of Attachment well enough; their issue is *remaining attached*. While the Isolator fears being held back, the Pursuer is afraid to stray far from home, if he is able to leave at all. He lives with the childhood memory of terror at finding no one there when he returned from his explorations. To keep this terror from returning, the Pursuer is always being nice and upbeat, trying to keep things comfortable and entertaining, always of service, fearful of anger or conflict that would lead to the partner leaving and re-creating the childhood terrors connected to the ne-glectful or abandoning caretaker. Terrified of being alone, or of being abandoned, there are always plans for things to do together—hobbies, chores, movies, vacations. The Pursuer has needs, but he doesn't give them any attention, because he has to first please his mate. He prolongs every hug, and calls his partner from work. He wants her to stay awake and talk after lovemaking. One client told her partner, "When I wake in the morning and you are in the shower, I get scared. I want you to wake me up and cuddle before you get out of bed."

Julie, the Pursuer partner of Peter the Isolator, was adept at keeping tabs on Peter, and finding ways to keep him close to home. For one thing, she had her ongoing depression, which indirectly demanded his attention and sympathy. If that didn't work, she could always be ill; that had always worked in childhood. When Peter suggested she find friends to hang out with, and a job, she replied, "But then I might be away when you were home and we'd spend even less time together." In one session, she told Peter that she didn't get together with her girlfriend "because that would give you a chance to go out and meet someone new, and you wouldn't be home when I got back." The fear of abandonment often expresses itself as jealousy. Even when Julie had something to do, she would check up on Peter at home, and question what he was doing. If he replied that he was watching TV, she'd be angry that he wasn't thinking about her and wanting her to come home.

You can see from these examples why Isolators and Pursuers tend to pair up; each offers what the other lacks. Of course, every couple has some of this push/pull going on. One wants more and the other less closeness, but they change their minds when they get what they want. It can be almost comical. The Isolator withholds

Exercise 5b ▪ ▪ ▪ ▪ ▪

Was I Wounded at the Exploration Stage?

ADAPTATIONS TO WOUNDING AT EXPLORATION

THE ISOLATOR: Minimizer, Rigid Boundaries	1	2	3	4	5
Basic Fear (Wound): Being smothered, absorbed, humiliated, loss of parent (partner)					
Internal Message: Don't be separate					
Core Belief: I can't say no and be loved					
Relationship Belief: I will be absorbed if I get close					
Image of Partner: Insecure; too dependent; needy					
Relationship to Partner: Sets limits on togetherness; passive/aggressive; acts out absorption fears by distancing					
Core Issue: Personal freedom; autonomy					
Typical Frustration: You need too much					
Recurrent Feeling: Fear and impotent fury					
Conflict Management: Oppositional; distancing					
Growth Challenge: Initiate closeness; share feelings; increase time together; integrate positive and negative traits in partner					

THE PURSUER: Maximizer, Diffuse Boundaries	1	2	3	4	5
Basic Fear (Wound): Unreliability of others, abandonment; loss of parent (partner)					
Internal Message: Don't be dependent					
Core Belief: I can't count on anyone					
Relationship Belief: If I act independent, you will abandon me					
Image of Partner: Distant; has no needs					
Relationship to Partner: Ambivalent pursuit and withdrawal					
Core Issue: Partner reliability; support; standing					
Typical Frustration: You are never there when I need you					
Recurrent Feeling: Panic and anger					
Conflict Management: Blaming, demanding; chasing; complaining; devaluing					
Growth Challenge: Initiate separateness; develop outside interests; internalize partner; integrate positive and negative traits of partner					

feelings, and fears that if he opens up even a little bit, the Pursuer will just march through the door (which is true). The Pursuer feels that if he doesn't keep up the pressure for contact, there won't be any. Not long ago I had a woman in my workshop whose complaint was that her boyfriend did not hold her *after he fell asleep!* The relaxation of his body as he dozed off would wake her up, and she in turn would wake him up and chew him out. She felt abandoned by him. Still dealing with her childhood even when she is sleeping, she gets no rest.

6

Identity and Competence: Becoming a Self

Identity expresses such a mutual relation
in that it connotes both a persistent
sameness within oneself and a persistent
sharing of some kind of essential character
with others.

—ERIK ERIKSON

IDENTITY: "This Is Me"

Now the child experiences a complicated new reality. He wants to know who he is as a separate person in relation to the rest of the world: he embarks on the process of becoming a self. To do that, he must achieve two important tasks that will affect his relationship to himself and to others for the rest of his life: he must develop a stable and consistent inner image of himself and a correspondingly firm and constant inner image of the significant others in his life.

During the early stages of his life, the child feels lost and anxious when his caretakers are not physically present. Now, with his increased mobility and their more frequent absence, he still needs to feel secure. He does that by installing an image of his caretakers in his mind with such clarity that he can evoke that image, and feel secure and connected, even when he is separated from them. This image is like a snapshot you carry around in your wallet, and can take out and recall—emotions and all—the scene depicted. It allows the child to separate physically, while remaining connected psychically.

This stage of Identity (often referred to as Individuation) takes place between the approximate ages of three and four. In the normal course of events, what the child does to create a firm image of himself is to make a series of transient identifications, trying them on for size—with animals, cartoon characters, things, and people (especially his parents)—which are later synthesized into a unique self. There is also an element of testing; he wants to see who he is, and who he is not, how he is the same and how he is different from others. I saw this going on not long ago with Hunter. For a while he was in his "reptile phase," soul mate to lizards and snakes, a character called "Sharptooth," and of course the Teenage Mutant Ninja Turtles. (I have a half-serious theory, by the way, that all kids first identify with reptiles—my daughter Leah went through the same phase, and kids have reptile pets in their kindergarten and first-grade classrooms—because our basal brain is the reptilian brain, so those early connections appear to be with the reptilian phase of the evolutionary cycle. Anyway, to get back to our story . . .) At one point, Hunter was "Mefistofeles," his soul-mate character from the musical *Cats;* he would dress as Mefistofeles and sing every word of the songs. This was one in a whole series of identifications with comic and animal characters, in which he acted out all roles. He also identified with me. He was still mama's little boy, but he wanted to be *like* me. We were walking to church one day wearing similar coats and ties, and he remarked, "We're alike, we have on the same coat."

"Well," I said, "we're father and son."

"No," he corrected me, "we're *fathers*." (Of course, there may be an Oedipal element in this, wanting to compete with me for Helen's attention.)

The important parental task at this point is to notice and to validate the changes of persona, as the child experiments with different identities and behaviors, to mirror back to him the image he is choosing to project. "Oh, hi, Mefistofeles, could you sing me a song?" or "Batman, you sure are strong." If the child is only partially mirrored in the identification he is checking out, he will present other facets to see if he gets a reaction. So the parent has to say, "Well, you *are* a ferocious monster, but you're a furry little kitten, too." If the child is allowed to identify with everything that he chooses, especially if there are enough objects and people in his life to select from, he will integrate all the identifications into a unique, highly individuated self.

The Identity stage is characterized by obsessive self-assertion, with the child continually saying "I," "I want," and "I think," and "This is me," and "I don't like." Again, it's healthy self-assertion, not rebellion. The child wants to be visible; he wants to be sure you notice him. Too, personal opinion is being expressed, as the child tries to explain to you, and to himself, how he is distinct from others. Hunter is determined to be recognized as an individual, which, as any parent knows, can be pretty exasperating. As he establishes a clear sense of himself, he has taken to telling us not only what he is like and what he wants, but how he feels, and what he thinks. He also instructs us as to how we should treat him—what he likes best for dinner, what kind of bedtime story he wants, and who should read it to him.

A final installment in this tale of identity consolidation seems to have taken place recently. A houseguest kept asking him, "Are you a tiger?"

"No," Hunter replied in a dismayed tone.

"Well, are you a turtle?" the guest persisted.

After several more attempts to suggest objects of identification, which even included, "Are you Hunter?" Hunter interrupted and declared: "I am me!"

If the caretakers take all this in stride, and accurately reflect all the varied options of self-image presented by the child, without judgment or criticism, the child will see himself in their mirrored responses, select what feels congruent with his inner feelings, and construct a positive self-image, a firm identity. In addition, he will integrate the good and bad traits of the mirroring caretakers, healing the earlier splits, and etch on the template of the Imago a picture of his significant other as imperfect but constant, thus guaranteeing his emotional security.

THE RIGID CHILD: FEAR OF BEING SHAMED

Again, there are two possible adaptations when things go wrong at the Identity stage. Both are centered around the issue of invisibility, and both have to do with the way the child is mirrored, and how that mirroring affects his sense of personal boundaries.

Many parents, even those who were comfortable at the stage of Attachment or Exploration, do not welcome this "birth of the self." They are threatened by the child's identifications that do not fit their

cultural biases, and suppress the child's emergent identity by rejecting or refusing to mirror those self-assertions that do not fit their
preconceived notions of what they want their child to be. Here is
where the socialization process begins to make its inroads.

The child, fearing shame—or even worse, loss of the parents'
love—if he expresses the core parts of himself that his parents reject,
represses the rejected aspects and resentfully becomes what his
parents approve. Rather than healing the polar experiencing of the
preceding stages, now that his identity is consolidating, he ends up
with a "split self," hiding the disapproved parts from others, and
even from himself.

As we will see in Part III, all too often this kind of selective
mirroring has to do with gender, with boys praised for their assertiveness and stoicism, girls for their cuteness and helpfulness. The
result is that the child, yearning to be whole, develops a false self by
identifying only with parentally or socially approved traits. He
becomes only a partial self, a tightly contained monochromatic
persona, a replication of socially approved stereotypes, typically
overassertive, with dogmatic opinions. His energy is limited to the
mirrored traits, and those unmirrored traits become his recessive
"Lost Self" (see Chapter 10), an aspect of his "shadow." This
compromise salvages his parents' love at the expense of his full
aliveness.

Full and positive mirroring is essential to the child's sense that all
of him—whether he is being tender or assertive, silly or smart, Peter
Pumpkin or Mr. Jones from across the street—is valid and acceptable. If I had said to Hunter, "That's silly, you're not a dinosaur," I
would have interfered with his transient experimentation with a new
trait, and he would no longer feel confident of who he was. The
terrifying feeling would creep in that he was being laughed at, and
he would be ashamed. It would activate a fear that "I am not all
right," or "There is something wrong with me." He would need to
split off the parts of him that were mirrored back to him as good
from the deflected aspects that were deemed unacceptable. He
would also be compelled to split off the affirming caretaker from the
rejecting one. Thus he would end up with a good and a bad parent
in his head—a split object, achieving the goal of object constancy,
but failing in the task of self-integration. Forever after he would see
himself as good and evil, repressing the lost self as bad, extolling the
good part of himself as absolute. You can see why it is vitally
important that parents mirror all of the child's identifications, trust-
ing in the internal process of synthesis to forge them into a unitary
self.

It is at the Identity stage that the child's boundaries are most powerfully drawn. Not surprisingly, the selectively mirrored child strictly defines where he ends and others begin. The boundaries around the disowned core of his natural self are tightly held, to prevent any leakage. On the other hand, the boundary of his inflated self-concept is so global that it includes all others as an extension of himself. He is a rigid child, a Minimizer with a controlling personality.

THE ADULT: A RIGID CONTROLLER

In adulthood, the rigid child becomes what I call a Controller, who is often opinionated to the point of being boorish, and leads a narrowly focused, often self-centered life. He has little access to feelings, and lacks empathy with others. He will choose a partner who carries the traits of his Lost Self, and then find fault with her, as his parents did with him, all the time denying his actions. He can't stand uncertainty, spontaneity, or softness—in himself or others. He engages in a great deal of obsessive thinking and compulsive behavior. Everything in his life is predictable and planned in advance so there's little room for error or spontaneity. Domineering and critical, his complaint is, "You don't seem to know what you want," or "Make up your mind." Others are not seen for themselves, but as objects to be controlled, often for his personal and instant gratification.

Jacob was a pain to be around, even in the therapy session. He constantly complained that his fiancée, Susan, was never on time and was forever changing her mind. His solution was to make a schedule in which every minute of the day was planned, including time for sex, talking, getting dressed. He was convinced that if Susan would follow his plan, she would get her life organized, and get a promotion at her job. Her suggestions that they just go out for a Sunday drive without maps and reservations drove him crazy. He was also quite sure of what the President should do about Iraq, and shocked that Susan had no opinion; yet he denied that he was opinionated or rigid.

"I'm just being rational," he claimed. "There is a logical way of doing things, and I'm just concerned for Susan's welfare." To show softness or indecision, or even empathy, was unthinkable and shameful.

Once I commiserated with him about the pressures of his job, and the burden of decisions he carried, remarking how hard it must have been for him to live up to everyone's expectations, especially in childhood. Suddenly Jacob's sadness broke through, and he quickly left the room as his eyes began to brim with tears. Feeling shamed by the forbidden emotions that broke through his defense, he walked around the block for thirty minutes before he came back in, apologizing for his "weakness" and chiding me for having upset him. Susan was in shock, for she had never seen him shed a tear.

THE INVISIBLE CHILD: FEAR OF BEING A SELF

While some parents inconsistently mirror their children, others, out of their own need to keep the child dependent or because of their intense preoccupation with themselves or other things, are almost completely lacking in the mirroring responses that release the chemistry of individuation and self-integration. The parents are preoccupied with their need to be parented themselves; or they need to be needed, like those parents who feared the child's exploratory impulses would result in abandonment by the child.

With no reflection of his self-expression, the child will lose sight of himself, and remain amorphous and undefined. Failing to integrate and synthesize his transient identifications for lack of consistent mirroring, they float around loose and disorderly in his unconscious, producing a fragmented self. With such diffuse, undefined boundaries, he is unable to distinguish between himself and others. Lacking the necessary self-delineation, he cannot form and store a consistent image of himself. He oscillates between his self parts without consciousness and seems to have more than one personality. He is happy, then suddenly sad, then angry, without a clear connection between his experiences. He becomes emotionally frozen, and suffers the terror of not being seen, overcome with a feeling of invisibility. He experiences himself as "not existing." His complaint is, "You don't even notice me."

If the parents don't say, "Oh, it's nice to see you, Big Bird," or "You certainly are a big boy," then the child has no way of knowing who he is and develops a cloudy, indistinct, unsure identity. He doesn't know where he stops and others begin. His fear is of being *ignored*, so he is always on stage, trying to get noticed, a Maximizer with diffuse boundaries. Failing to see his reflection in the mirror of his parents, without a reflexive response, his energy becomes boundless and directionless, his chatter themeless, his mental associations random and chaotic. He is in a room with no walls, a canyon with no echo. Without the feedback of an "other" he cannot establish self boundaries. And without a sense of where his boundaries are, it is difficult, if not impossible, to become aware of others' boundaries. He is continually invading others' territory, and unable to prevent others invading his.

Nor can he form a consistent image of his caretakers. Having introjected their good and bad traits without synthesizing them, he randomly projects the bad traits onto others, or, when frustrated, identifies transiently with the negative traits of the internalized "bad" parents, and treats others the way he was mistreated by his caretakers.

THE ADULT: A COMPLIANT DIFFUSER

The invisible child becomes in adulthood what I call a Diffuser, whose complaint is: "I don't know who I am" or "I don't know what I want" or "I feel invisible to you." Like a chameleon, he takes on the coloration of whoever or whatever is around, feeling their feelings, swayed by their opinions, unsure of what he feels or thinks, and fearful of being a self. Not knowing himself, he is forever scanning the faces of others for clues as to how he should be, forever dependent on the other for self-definition. When not looking for himself in the reflection of others, his energy is all bound up in ragefully or seductively calling attention to himself, to being noticed. He is a Maximizer.

Many men have had experience with the Diffuser woman, the seductress who looks sexy and is so full of flirtatious energy that you assume she will be fantastic in bed—and it's a big letdown. She is trying to be what she thinks her partner wants her to be, but at the same time she is bitterly resentful that she is not seen for herself, and fearful of the self she wants to be. Her unsuspecting partner ends up in bed with an emotionally labile nonperson, a submissive false self who is trying to become whole by being what others expect of her. Then, shifting from experiencing herself as the invisible child to identification with the internalized "bad" parent, she criticizes her partner's sexuality, devaluing him as she was devalued by her parents. A loose cannon of boundariless rage that she is not valued as a person, she makes her partner invisible. Most of her energy is angrily directed "out there," to the attempt to be visible, at the price of not being anyone, achieving the deflection she fears and deflecting the other in turn. Like her controlling partner who replicates with her his domination by his parents, she renders him invisible as she was rendered invisible by hers.

Susan, fiancée of the Controller Jacob, is a Diffuser. She was only too happy to go along with Jacob's plans, schedules, and opinions. "Jacob is right," she told me, "I'm just too disorganized, and he is so brilliant. But." She glared. "He never sees the things I am good at." Submissive and compromising on the one hand, Susan voiced the classic sentiment of the Compliant Diffuser: "I'll be loved if I please you." Hurt and rageful on the other hand, she says: "I'll be seen if it kills you."

Naturally, the Controller and the Diffuser often end up together, and their power struggle centers around dominance and submission. One is attracted by expansiveness and openness; the other finds decisiveness and clarity appealing. One leads and the other follows. One is excessively dependent and not only allows, but seeks, definition by others, while resentfully rejecting it; the other is rigidly independent, compulsively and angrily refusing any input from others.

A couple I counseled are a good example of this polarity. She is an attractive, nationally known financial consultant in her fifties. Yet she has a very poorly integrated sense of herself, and has all her life felt invaded by the constant demands of her husband, children, and coworkers. Her husband is a brilliant, controlled philosopher type, who is used to thinking of himself as the center of the world. To him, everyone is contained within his orbit; his wife is an extension of him, not a separate person. She was getting fed up with the way he would tell her to do things, with his assumption that she was available to him at all times, that he could just come in and use her phone or interrupt her in the midst of her writing or phone calls. In his presence, she could not maintain her boundaries.

I proposed that she conjure an image of herself living in a cottage with a garden surrounded by a fence, with a lock on the gate. She should insist, I said, that anyone who wanted to come in had to knock, and to ask permission. His immediate response was, "I want you to think of it as *our* cottage"; in other words, "I want you to continue to include your boundaries within mine." Now he was going to have to ask if it was all right to use the phone, if she were willing to have a dinner party. At first he couldn't even understand the concept of a boundary, and heaven knows he didn't want to give up having such a compliant extension of himself. But finally he gave in, saying, "Well, I get it, but I don't like it one bit."

E X E R C I S E   6 A   ▪   ▪   ▪   ▪   ▪

Was I Wounded at the Identity Stage?

ADAPTATIONS TO WOUNDING AT IDENTITY

THE CONTROLLER: Minimizer, Rigid Boundaries	1	2	3	4	5
Basic Fear (Wound): Being shamed; loss of control; losing face; loss of parental (partner) love					
Internal Message: Don't be what you want to be, be what we want you to be					
Core Belief: I can't be me and be accepted and loved					
Relationship Belief: I'll be safe if I stay in control					
Image of Partner: Unorganized; scatterbrained; over-emotional					
Relationship to Partner: Domineering; critical; invasive; withholding					
Core Issue: Partner's emotional lability, chaos, and passivity					
Typical Frustration: You want me to be somebody else; you don't know what you want					
Recurrent Feeling: Shame and anger					
Conflict Management: Rigidly imposes will; super-rational with occasional angry outbursts; takes charge; punishes					
Growth Challenge: Relax control; mirror partner's thoughts and feelings; develop flexibility and sensitivity					

THE DIFFUSER: Maximizer, Diffuse Boundaries	1	2	3	4	5
Basic Fear (Wound): Being invisible, self-assertion, loss of parental (partner) love					
Internal Message: Don't assert yourself					
Core Belief: I'll never be seen, valued, and accepted					
Relationship Belief: I'll be loved if I go along and please others					
Image of Partner: Insensitive; controlling					
Relationship to Partner: Submissive; passive-aggressive; manipulative					
Core Issue: Partner rigidity and dominance					
Typical Frustration: You never see me; you want everything your way					
Recurrent Feeling: Shame and confusion					
Conflict Management: Confused; alternates between compliance and defiance; exaggerates emotions; makes few suggestions; self-effacing					
Growth Challenge: Assert yourself; set boundaries for yourself; respect boundaries of others					

Competence: "I Can Do It"

The first stop on the journey to selfhood is to figure out who you belong to, and to become attached to them. Once that task is achieved, you begin to differentiate from them and look around to see what the world is like. To stay connected with your parents, you install them in your mind so you have them with you at all times. Having achieved that security, you try on different costumes and check out others' reactions until you find one that fits you. When you get most of it in place, at about the age of four, you have succeeded in becoming an integrated self. Then you begin to compete with others, especially your parents and siblings (or your peers if you don't have siblings) to discover your personal power and its limits, as well as to determine what belongs to you and what doesn't. Competence is the last of the major development tasks of early childhood, although the cycle of personal development and growth repeats itself in increasingly complex configurations throughout life. Freud labeled this the Oedipal stage, but I label it "Competence," because much more is going on here than vying with the same-sex parent for the attentions of the opposite-sex parent.[1]

At this stage, the child is trying to become competent in the management of himself in the world of others and things. He experiments with what effect he can produce on his world by impacting it with all his strength in any form he can devise, against all comers. The purpose of all this aggressive initiative is to experience the extent and limits of his power in the social world. The degree to which he succeeds will determine the way he values himself.

Hunter is caught up now in building with blocks, with endlessly drawing, changing his picture until he gets it right. He's trying to complete tasks, to play games, to win. His sister Leah is wiping him out these days at tic-tac-toe and he's frustrated. If he comes to a word he can't read, he gets upset and has to know it right away, and then is proud that he got it. When he plays the piano, he fusses at himself if he gets the notes wrong. He ties his shoes and brings them for our inspection with a proud smile on his face. He also has the really annoying habit of bopping people, testing his strength. But he looks to see if he has gone too far, and if Leah cries while they are tussling, he says he is sorry. As parents, we teach him boundaries by setting limits, and teach him appropriate ways to use his power. He can disagree with us, but he cannot disobey us, and he can't hit us.

At this point the parental task is basically a continuation of the mirroring—of affirmation, validation, and praise for effective doing and accomplishing—and teaching proper limits of behavior. The child wants to learn and to succeed. The parent must never tire of saying, "What a great tower you built," or "Your letter 'A' is really clear," or "Wow, you read that whole page," or "I like the way you solved your problem with Janie," or "That didn't work; why don't you try it this way?"

Hunter's Oedipal stuff is showing up in his wanting to sit between Helen and me or plopping between us on the bed, refusing to let me read to him, or take him to school, and smirking victoriously whenever he gets his way. The message is, "I want to be more special to her than you are." Tacitly, he's asking, "She belongs to me . . . doesn't she?" Helen's task is to be available in appropriate ways, to let Hunter know he is valuable to her, but that our relationship is primary, and to set appropriate limits. If I take my place with Helen without punishing him, he will eventually identify with me, which will cement his gender identity and clear the way for him to shift his interest and affection to another female. He's clearly competitive, but the competition is not just for Helen, but for competence and a sense of personal impact.

If all this is done well, the child experiences himself as able to manage his environment, and, as a by-product of feeling competent, he will have a high level of self-esteem. In addition, he will internalize his parents' values as he did their traits and develop an autonomous conscience to guide him in his behavior with others in the larger world. In Freud's classic aphorism, he will be able to "love and work."

THE COMPETITIVE CHILD: FEAR OF FAILURE/DISAPPROVAL

Some parents are threatened by the child's initiative and competitiveness. Like the parents of the detached, distant, and rigid children in the preceding stages, they *selectively* reward and punish their child's expression of competence.

"I remember how my parents bragged about my attempts to play the piano, and how my mother was endlessly patient with my attempts to make pancakes or help with the dishes," reported a young woman. "But when I started to like to play the 'boys'' games, she would yell at me, and make fun of my friends, and complain about my dirty clothes. And when I asked for Lego blocks for my birthday, she absolutely refused."

The child who does not get sufficient, consistent, reliable mirroring is caught in a bind. Since his efforts sometimes meet with approval, he keeps trying, never knowing when his efforts will produce results. Driven by feelings that nothing he does is good enough, that if he just tries a little harder, he will make it, he gets "stuck" performing and competing, trying to win, to get noticed, to produce an effect. Overburdened by guilt and fear of failure, he deadens his conscience in order to relieve his pain. He gives up on intimacy and settles for success as an indirect bid for approval. When things go well, if he wins or gets approval, he is euphoric, but when he loses or fears he has disappointed others, he falls into depression. Alternating between rage and despair, desperate to avoid failure or disapproval, he knuckles under even harder. But no matter how successful he becomes, he is unable to enjoy his life, because he never feels successful. The competitive child becomes a Minimizer with rigid boundaries who is compulsive in his own efforts while deprecating the efforts of others.

THE ADULT: A COMPULSIVE COMPETITOR

The competitive child, who becomes what I call a Compulsive Competitor in adult life, is, not surprisingly, often outwardly successful as an adult, but without empathy for others; he occasionally skirts moral values. Competitive and combative, he ends up managing a big company, or becomes one of the big shots on Wall Street. He's preoccupied with winning and enjoys beating the daylights out of others to do it. "You're not even trying," he complains, or "Can't you do anything right?" What happens is that he often ends up overreaching, unable to employ subtler tactics when called for; or he reaches his goal, and then can't figure out why he still feels empty.

Paul is a good example of a Competitor. Paul's ambition had been to make a million dollars, but as soon as he succeeded, he felt compelled to go for his second. His earlier plan to retire when he got rich faded in the emptiness of success. He resigned from his job, formed his own company, and built a fifty-million-dollar empire in five years—a process that involved compromising his values, and impersonally exploiting others in the interest of achieving his grand scheme.

When he came to therapy with his girlfriend Amy, he was depressed. In therapy, he came to understand that his father was alive in his head, telling him that nothing would ever be enough. Paul had thus spent his life trying to silence that voice and finally win his father's approval—though his father had died twenty years earlier. Amy had taken over his father's role with her desire for a larger house, new cars, exotic vacations, fine jewelry—the same things she had gotten as a child in lieu of love and affection. Both were starved, one for praise, the other for emotional warmth.

THE HELPLESS/MANIPULATIVE CHILD: FEAR OF
AGGRESSIVENESS/SUCCESS

Unlike the preceding parents, who alternately praise and criticize
their child's initiatives, some parents are consistent in their lack of
support of the child's attempts to achieve a sense of personal power.
Their constant criticism confuses the child about how to express
himself; he alternates between feelings of helplessness and resentment. The child's way of winning is a kind of manipulative passive/
aggressive stance. He never competes openly; he wins by appearing
not to compete, or by getting others to fail. Like his counterpart, the
Controller, at this stage, he also lacks empathy and experiences
lapses of conscience.

If a child is habitually criticized or not affirmed—"You didn't do
that right," or "That doesn't look like a tree to me," or "Why can't
you read as fast as Sally?"—he gives up, feeling he can't do it right
anyway. He is like the clinging, ambivalent, and invisible child. He
shuns self-assertion because of the pain of repeated deflection,
disapproval, and fear of failure. He feels *helpless* to find a way to
make an impact on the world, and to please his parents. He withdraws from the competition, complaining that he is not appreciated,
or never given a fair chance to win. Full of resentment, he feels at
the mercy of his environment. To combat the emotional pain of
consistent deflection, he identifies with the deflecting parents and
treats others as incompetent. A Minimizer with constricted boundaries, he is manipulative, sometimes a saboteur.

THE ADULT: A MANIPULATIVE COMPROMISER

The grown-up Compromiser never wants to play games, or do
anything where he is compared to others. When placed in a competitive situation, he behaves in a way that will make the other person
look bad, and he seldom feels remorse over the other's discomfort.
At work, he keeps a low profile, staying in jobs below his capabilities,
and he may subtly undermine the efforts of colleagues. He never
openly pursues the partner who seems "too good" for him, but
arranges to be pursued while denying any interest in being courted.
His complaint is "You don't value anything I do" or "Can't we just
play for fun?" Behind these complaints is a hidden resentment: "I'll
get even."

During their therapy, I learned something about Paul and Amy's
courtship. She had flirted with him, but rebuffed his attempts to
date her until she finally "gave in" and accepted his invitation to
dinner. After several dates, Paul, in his highly competitive manner,

sought to complete his conquest by seducing her. But he made the mistake of bragging about his sexual stamina. Amy "gave in" again, but during their lovemaking she became very aggressive and caused him to ejaculate prematurely, and in the process of their jousting complained that he hurt her. In one act of exquisite manipulation, she shamed his view of his sexual self and pricked his Achilles heel of guilt. Amy, with her passive/aggressive Compromiser behavior, is a perfect match for Paul the Competitor.

The Competitor/Compromiser couple on the tennis court is a case study in adaptive behavior. She agrees to the game even though she doesn't really want to play. He plays every ball as if his life depended on it, counting every point, sweating and cursing, "Why did you let that ball go? You could have gotten that." She cowers with her head down, swatting listlessly at the ball as it whizzes by, feeling put upon. "Can't you just play for fun?" she wails as she walks off the

EXERCISE 6B ▪ ▪ ▪ ▪ ▪

Was I Wounded at the Stage of Competence?

ADAPTATIONS TO WOUNDING AT COMPETENCE

THE COMPETITOR: Minimizer, Rigid Boundaries	1	2	3	4	5
Basic Fear (Wound): Being a failure, guilt and disapproval; fear of parental (partner) disapproval					
Internal Message: Don't make mistakes					
Core Belief: I have to be perfect					
Relationship Belief: I'll be loved if I am the best					
Image of Partner: Manipulative; incompetent					
Relationship to Partner: Competitive; aggressive; puts partner down					
Core Issue: Control; battle for who's boss					
Typical Frustration: You are never satisfied					
Recurrent Feeling: Anger and guilt					
Conflict Management: Competes for control					
Growth Challenge: Accept competence; become cooperative; mirror and value partner's efforts					

court. He gets upset and feels guilty; she sulks, saying, "I'm doing the best I can," and he apologizes. A variation of this scene repeats itself around every issue. They go to a cocktail party; his goal is to meet everyone, while she sits in a corner and talks to one person all night. He's upset that she's being a wallflower, she's upset that he pays no attention to her. They alternately push each other's buttons of helplessness and guilt.

Keep in mind that the repercussions in adulthood of a malfunction at the Competence stage are not as devastating as if it happened earlier. The Maximizer (Compromiser) is not as volatile and intrusive, the Minimizer (Competitor) not as closed off and rigid as they might be if their wounding occurred earlier in childhood. The Minimizer wounded at this stage can look and act downright hysterical next to someone even more withheld. The Maximizer may seem docile, almost passive, relative to a Maximizer wounded at the stage of Attachment. In some situations, the Competitor is able to relax and enjoy himself without having to win; the Compromiser can assert himself in a comfortable situation. Fluidity and rigidity are relative and situational, affected by the interrelationship with others.

THE COMPROMISER: Maximizer, Diffuse Boundaries	1	2	3	4	5
Basic Fear (Wound): Being aggressive, successful, competent, and powerful, losing parental (partner) approval					
Internal Message: Don't be powerful					
Core Belief: I don't know what to do; I can't be aggressive or express anger					
Relationship Belief: I'll be loved if I am good and cooperative					
Image of Partner: Never satisfied; has to win					
Relationship to Partner: Manipulative; compromising; sabotaging					
Core Issue: Feeling controlled; efforts not valued					
Typical Frustration: You always have to win					
Recurrent Feeling: Helpless and resentful					
Conflict Management: Compromises; manipulates					
Growth Challenge: Be direct; express power; develop competence; praise partner's success					

7

Concern and Intimacy: Moving Out into the World

True engagement with others is the result
and test of firm self-delineation.

—ERIK ERIKSON

At about the age of seven, an important change takes place. The egocentricity that characterized the child's drive to establish a secure, competent self abates somewhat, in part due to his "loss" in the Oedipal struggle. That loss, one in a series of life experiences that confront us with our insignificance, demonstrates that we are not center stage in life's pageant. This realization reactivates the survival drive, and initiates a new phase. Needing to become significant in a new arena, the child shifts the agenda of his search for healing and wholeness beyond the family to a larger world, to nonfamilial adults, and to his peers.

I want to talk briefly about the emergence of two other impulses and their development stages: the caring impulse, which is expressed as concern for peers (spanning the ages between seven and thirteen), and the striving for intimacy (which appears in adolescence between ages thirteen and nineteen). It can happen that a child who successfully negotiated the tasks of ego development will suffer his greatest wound during this period, which is the precedent-setting foundation for his relationships with equals. And even though his healthy self-development up to that point will mitigate the severity of this later-life injury, it may nevertheless be the core around which later relationship problems congeal.

The healthy outcome of the early years is a secure, competent child with a conscience. His emotional base has been solidified by the ingenious process of internalizing his caretakers, in essence installing them in memory so that they are with him whenever he needs them—an achievement referred to as object constancy. He has integrated his identifications with a variety of models to achieve a sense of personal identity with some continuity, which will evolve and change throughout his life. He has achieved a sense of personal competence and has internalized the social directives of his caretakers. And he has been tested in the Oedipal battle, and lost.

Now his behavior shifts from external to internal control, from a morality of constraint to a morality of cooperation. Having passed the initiation of childhood, he is ready for the larger social world. He seeks to belong to, and become intimate with, his peer group. In both the Concern and Intimacy stages, the task cycle of early childhood development will now repeat itself (as it will in each subsequent stage throughout life). He will have to become *attached* to his peers, and in particular to a special "chum"; *differentiate* himself from them; establish his own *identity* among them; and develop *competence* in his dealings with them, so that he emerges secure and confident in his dealings with others. Further, he will at each stage tend to get "stuck" at the same phase of the cycle in which he was stuck in childhood. At the stage of Concern, for example, he may have no trouble getting attached to his peers, but may have trouble finding his own identity within the gang. During the Intimacy stage, he may find it easy to get attached to a girlfriend or boyfriend, but have problems holding on to his identity in the couple.

It is important to note that these stages offer an opportunity to correct the unresolved issues of his earlier experiences within the family, since he now has some freedom and emotional distance from it. In lucky circumstances the parents will cope in constructive ways; the teenager will resolve the old conflicts or reduce their intensity to the extent that he makes healthier adult choices; and the internal alarm will subside. Unfortunately, the old problems are usually exacerbated, for they present themselves to the same caretakers (who have in little likelihood changed their own attitudes or behavior) and in the same community in which the damaging social standards hold sway.

I'm sure that the *sturm und drang* of adolescence is not natural. If you had a childhood in which your needs were met, you would be using the intense energy of puberty, and your growing sense of self, to do adolescent-appropriate things. In adolescence healthy kids consolidate their selfhood, solidify peer relationships, fall in love for the first time, integrate their sexuality, and go on to establish their arena of competence. But because there is usually unfinished childhood business, they hit the same impasse, and have to deal with the same problems. Only now they have power and independence (and raging hormones). They can run away from home, take drugs, steal cars, get pregnant, and do all kinds of things to distract themselves from (and call attention to) their pain, in an effort to get their parents to provide the love and security they didn't get in childhood.

Concern: "I Belong"

At about the age of seven, the child's attention turns for the first time to the world outside himself and his home. His focus shifts to others who are equal rather than superior. He learned from his lost Oedipal battle that he cannot have a relationship by conquest, by capturing another who belongs to someone else, so he moves on to establish friendship with his peers. Then his task is to form a special bond with a same-sex person within this new group, his "chum."[1]

The relationship with this best friend is intense, serious, and exclusive, based not on competition but on cooperation. The child learns that the bond with his chum can't be taken for granted; it has to be nurtured and developed. As the chum becomes an object of care and concern, the child learns that interest in his friend's welfare is the best strategy for success: it is an adaptive response, necessary for survival. Since the chum is also a mirror of himself, he becomes more self-aware, self-compassionate, and empathic. Here are the rudiments of altruism, the foundation on which he may later learn real love.

During this period, part of the parental task is to teach the child social skills. Healthy parents encourage the child's forays into the world, remaining available while keeping their distance as needed. They are supportive of his peer relationships, and in particular show approval of his friends and his "chum." "I like your friend Aaron," they say. "He seems to be a live wire, and he's a good pal. Maybe he'd like to come with us on our picnic next weekend. That would be fun for us."

Supportive parents recognize that the child's friends are a mirror in which he sees himself, and also objects for his new identifications. Their approval enhances his self-esteem; any rejection is a personal rejection. If the parents compliment him on his friends, invite them to share family meals, include them in family outings, encourage overnight visits, the child sees that who he is in the world is of value.

THE LONELY CHILD: FEAR OF OTHERS/OSTRACISM

Some children fail to make friends and are thwarted in their attempts to be included in the group. Such setbacks produce an adaptation that I call the "lonely child." There are usually three possible explanations for this. Often his parents, overprotective and overrestrictive, fear the loss of the child. They are quick to voice disapproval of his friends, criticizing them and the child's social behavior. Failure may also be due to the lack of social skills in his home; his parents are unable to guide him in his new task of developing friendships and resolving conflicts. Now that the child is out in the world, and subject to its judgments, he may also be ostracized because he is different—too smart or not smart enough, too tomboyish or too effeminate. His religion, nationality, race, or economic background may isolate him. Although he may have one close chum, probably a loner like himself, he has few other friends. Rejected, socially inept, he turns his energy back on himself, becoming self-preoccupied and immersed in a self-constructed fantasy world of relationships that are closed off to him in real life. Though he looks independent, and denies that he needs or wants friends, he is acutely lonely.

Amy, a painfully shy woman, told me that she spent her after-school hours writing poems and plays with her best friend, who was as heavy as Amy was tall. "We wrote about people who were 'different' and who would someday be famous. We dreamed that someone would find our plays (though we never let anyone see them) and that we would be discovered and we'd move to New York." When I asked Amy if she ever asked her parents for help, she said that her parents had few friends themselves and that her mother was forever trying to buy her clothes that would make her look "smaller."

THE ADULT: A LONER

The lonely child becomes a Loner in adulthood, a rigid Minimizer, a private person who has a hard time sharing his feelings. At the core of his being is a void, for he has failed to satisfy his needs for healthy dependency and interdependency. He is filled with intense, often painful feelings, including the powerful belief that he is unlovable. This may have positive value as the source of creative output, but he is also vulnerable to addiction—to drugs, alcohol, work. To make up for what he lacks, he is attracted to someone gregarious, intrusive, and self-sacrificing, someone who will spearhead the making and keeping of friends and draw him, kicking and screaming, out of his privacy, while at the same time he does his best to exclude the partner from his inner life.

Martin had avoided the world pretty well by devoting his life to microbiological research, spending his time in the lab unless a specific "place" were carved out for him to present his findings at meetings or conventions. He was overwhelmed with love, and relief, when Monica, a science writer assigned to interview him, took him under her wing and drew him out into her world of movies and museums and potluck get-togethers. But now, six months later, he was resenting her intrusions: "She never leaves me alone. She's always including friends in our evenings together. I don't know what to say to them, and they don't know or care much about me. She thinks I should be telling her everything I think about. Doesn't she understand I'm not like her?"

THE GREGARIOUS CHILD: FEAR OF NEEDINESS/BEING ALONE

The gregarious child is excessively interested in the welfare and caretaking of others. He asks little for himself, seeming prematurely to take on his parents' role. Outgoing and accommodating, he has many casual friends, but only his chum is close to him. His caretaking may focus on his chum, his classmates, his family or pet. The problem is that his self is defined by the approval of others, and is sacrificed to their views and needs. Defined by others' views of him, he cannot see himself. Thus he is terrified of being alone, for he feels invisible to himself, not sure that he exists except in others' eyes. He is trapped trying to please others to validate his life. Subservient, self-sacrificing, needy to be needed, swayed by the opinions of others, his boundaries are diffuse, and he is easily dominated, often the scapegoat. This pattern is the basis in later life of codependency.

Parents of the gregarious child convey their belief that self-care and self-worth are bad, and that personal feelings and concerns are unimportant. The child is trained to give, to feel bad when he doesn't give, and to overly appreciate whatever he receives. The parents praise the child's social responsibility and leadership skills, selectively mirroring and supporting only approved caretaking behaviors, while diminishing his desire for autonomy and self-care.

A case in point is a recent visit from friends I hadn't seen since my seminary studies. They bragged to me about their daughter Emily, who lost no time helping my kids with their homework and clearing the table after meals. At one point during the visit, Emily came in all excited because Helen had offered to take her for a carriage ride in Central Park. "Oh, no, honey, you can't do that," they said in obvious disapproval. "It's not right to take up Helen's valuable time."

Once the child becomes involved with his peers, the parents of the gregarious child often withdraw their support, relieved that they don't have so much responsibility, and turn their attention elsewhere. Pushing the child away, they make the child feel he has to make himself valuable in order to get their approval. He forgets his own needs, or chastises himself for having them.

THE ADULT: A SACRIFICING CARETAKER

The Sacrificing Caretaker adult gets his recognition—at work, in his community, in his relationships—by making himself indispensable. He finds out what others need and provides it. Often he is a community leader, a scout-troop master, an indefatigable worker for local charities. He's respected and admired; others see him as self-sufficient, and turn to him for advice and help. He commiserates with his secretary about her life, he gives up his afternoon golf to register voters, he helps his girlfriend with her sick cat. He is a magnet for needy people, and sometimes supports them when they should be supporting themselves. If he doesn't feel needed, if he can't *do* something, he doesn't know how he fits in. But often, under his cheery "I can do it" exterior, he is depressed, and feels that something is missing. And sometimes, weary and exhausted, he is angry that no one cares about him, or appreciates all that he is doing.

The lonely, awkward Martin was a likely target for Monica's caretaking. He seemed so welcoming of her efforts to make his life better, so approving of all she did. But it was getting to her that he still seemed so wrapped up in himself, and so unwilling to let her in on his life, after all she had done for him. "Martin is a good, kind man," she told me, patting him fondly on the thigh. "And I try to understand how hard it is for him to open up. But he doesn't seem to appreciate how much I care for him and how much I've done to try and help him. Why won't he let me get close? Why can't he tell me he loves me? After all, I don't ask much."

Exercise 7A   ■   ■   ■   ■   ■

Was I Wounded at the Stage of Concern?

ADAPTATIONS TO WOUNDING AT THE STAGE OF CONCERN

THE LONER: Minimizer, Rigid Boundaries	1	2	3	4	5
Basic Fear (Wound): Ostracism by peers; parental (partner) rejection					
Internal Message: Don't be close					
Core Belief: I am not lovable					
Relationship Belief: I'll be hurt if I try to be close					
Image of Partner: Gregarious and intrusive					
Relationship to Partner: Exclude partner from inner world; make unilateral plans; counterdependent					
Core Issue: Partner intrusiveness					
Typical Frustration: You don't like me; you won't leave me alone					
Recurrent Feeling: Resentment and depression					
Conflict Management: Avoids conflict; sulks					
Growth Challenge: Develop same-sex friends; join partner in socializing; share feelings and thoughts with partner; become inclusive					

Intimacy: "I Can Be Close and Loving"

The adolescent's task is to separate more definitively from the family, to solidify his place in the social order of his peers, and to establish a satisfying sexual and emotional intimacy with someone of the opposite sex. At this point the parents are charged with accepting the budding sexuality of the emerging adult while providing a model of appropriate behavior as to the boundaries of intimacy. The message they want to convey is, "We are close and loving with each other, and we want the same for you. We are going to support you. We hope you find a nice girlfriend. We look forward to meeting her and getting to know her."

THE CARETAKER: Maximizer, Diffuse Boundaries	1	2	3	4	5
Basic Fear (Wound): Having or expressing needs; being excluded; parental (partner) rejection					
Internal Message: Don't have any needs of your own					
Core Belief: Others need me					
Relationship Belief: I'll be loved if I meet your needs					
Image of Partner: Unappreciative					
Relationship to Partner: Self-sacrificing; intrusive					
Core Issue: Partner's exclusion					
Typical Frustration: You don't appreciate me or my efforts					
Recurrent Feeling: Resentment; depression					
Conflict Management: Tries to be understanding and nice					
Growth Challenge: Express needs to partner and others; self-care; respect partner's privacy; take time alone					

The teenager may have avoided serious wounds in his earlier caretaking, but if his parents have a troubled dynamic, if he remains enmeshed in the Oedipal tangle or has been appropriated by either of his parents for their own gratification, he is bound to carry that baggage into his first attempts at intimacy. In addition to their example, he needs their support. If he can bring his new love home to his caretakers with their approval, if they are not threatened, jealous, or embarrassed by his emerging sexuality, and if he can integrate his new relationship into the rest of his life—at home, at school—then the impulse toward intimacy becomes right and natural.

THE REBELLIOUS CHILD: FEAR OF BEING CONTROLLED

Some parents, fearful and envious of the child's power, freedom, and sexuality, pull in the reins at this point. "Don't grow up," they are saying. "You're not ready for the world, and we're not ready to let you go." The child is angry at any restriction of freedom as he tries his wings, angry that his parents don't trust him to make the right choices. His only defense is to break the rules that he finds too limiting, for he fears that to acquiesce would trap him, that he would lose his fragile sense of self.

Most teenagers test their limits, challenging authority in an attempt to see how far they can go before they're reined in, and to test how much of the larger world is open to them. They also want to see if their parents are there to support and protect them, i.e., do they still have a safety net to fall back on if they go too far? But the rebel is more extreme; he has a hair-trigger sensitivity to anyone—his parents, his teachers, his girlfriend—telling him what to do. His dress and language are not just indicators of his individuality; they're meant to provoke. Any negative response gives him an excuse to rebel further, and confirms his belief that all authority figures are rigid and reactionary, so he must be vigilant against others' encroaching on his rights.

THE ADULT: A REBEL

In adulthood, the rebellious child becomes a crusading Rebel, railing against social rules and behavior, compulsively going against the grain, despite the fact that no one is telling him what to do anymore. He's full of contrary opinions, and goes out of his way to set himself apart. He's suspicious of others' motives, wary that they are trying to control him or to impose the status quo. In a way, he doesn't grow up. He relives the rebellion of the "terrible twos," defying all limits, still acting as though people are trying to boss him around. His relationships tend to be adversarial, and he fears that his partner will dominate him if he isn't on guard. He needs his freedom and his "space," but he can easily be made to feel guilty.

On the other hand, the rebel, if he has not been too wounded in childhood, may become a social reformer. He will fight for the whales, march on Washington, refuse to eat meat, and champion any cause that guarantees freedom or extends the limits of social behavior. If his wounds are deep, he will become an outcast or criminal.

Not surprisingly, he is usually attracted to a conformist, a model citizen who is compulsively committed to the rules of the social game. He desperately needs the structure and order he defies, and projects this need upon his model partner. At the same time, he criticizes her for being so proper, for belonging to the in crowd to which he secretly yearns to belong.

Tony was so afraid that his girlfriend, Gail, was going to get the upper hand with him that he perpetually tested her, to be sure she wasn't going to try and keep him "on a leash" after their wedding. She seemed "too nice" to him; he thought she was just putting on an act that would change drastically once they married. Somehow she reminded him of his mother, who always seemed to want the best for him but cared more about what the neighbors thought than what he wanted to do. He challenged Gail with experimental sex and tried to take her to wild parties and let it all hang out. Tony's mother liked Gail, and that also made him suspicious. "When we visited my folks last week," he reported, his voice laden with hidden meaning, "Gail seemed to agree with all my father's fascist views, even when I was disagreeing with him. She says she was just trying to be nice and to avoid an argument, but sometimes I feel like she's not on my side."

THE MODEL CHILD: FEAR OF BEING DIFFERENT

Conservative, rigid caretakers who are afraid of being different often raise a model child. The parents never stop pointing out what's odd, or weird, or unusual about the child's friends or clothes, interests, or taste, sending the unmistakable message: "Don't be different." Their range of acceptability falls into a very narrow band. "If you try to be different," they warn, "you'll never have any friends. You won't be accepted unless you get along with others. If you stand out, you will become a target." In addition, they warn, "You'll get into trouble." The child buys the party line that the only way you'll be loved is to be like everyone else and "do what is right." Though the child might still have secret longings, opinions, or interests, he is afraid he will lose the love and acceptance of his peers, his parents, and other adults if he dares to be different. Thus is born the model child, the well-behaved, well-groomed paragon of TV commercials and family sitcoms. He is the one who volunteers to be homeroom monitor, puts up the decorations for the school dance; often he is the confidant to whom his peers tell their troubles.

THE ADULT: A CONFORMIST

The model child becomes a Conformist in adulthood, and lives in a world of model citizens, fighting for the status quo. He is full of self-righteousness about what's wrong with the world, full of certitude about how things *should* be, convinced of the decadence of the new generation, pining for the "good old days." Conformists don't make waves, and they are offended by the waves others make. They see themselves as preservers of the common good, traditional values, and moral standards.

Critical of "individualists" and rule breakers, they are nevertheless attracted to rebellious, childlike partners who carry their hidden rebelliousness, their resentment of their failed adolescence, missed

EXERCISE 7B • • • • •

Was I Wounded at the Intimacy Stage?

ADAPTATIONS TO WOUNDING AT THE STAGE OF INTIMACY

THE REBEL: Minimizer, Rigid Boundaries	1	2	3	4	5
Basic Fear (Wound): Being controlled by others (parent/ partner)					
Internal Message: Don't grow up					
Core Belief: I am not trusted					
Relationship Belief: I'll be controlled if I give up dissent					
Image of Partner: Too nice; counter-controlling; guilting; parental					
Relationship to Partner: Rebellious; controlling; devalues partner					
Core Issue: Freedom to break the rules					
Typical Frustration: You are never on my side					
Recurrent Feeling: Anger and disappointment					
Conflict Management: Rebellious; suspicious of motives					
Growth Challenge: Maintain self-identity; be responsible to others; learn to trust others					

opportunities, and lost freedom. They often have rich fantasies of aberrant sexuality, dreams of murder or flying. Secretly they yearn to be free of constrictive rules, which they often break in private. Often, behind the facade of propriety lives a depressed child or a criminal in disguise. Yet Conformists are condescending to rebellious partners and try to control them and make them behave, feeling like they have to be good and hold things together for their immature, uncooperative mates.

Tony's suspicions about Gail were not far from the mark. Though she was patently fascinated with Tony's "bad boy" persona, she was also embarrassed that he was so different from her friends and coworkers, embarrassed that he made his money demonstrating

THE CONFORMIST: Maximizer, Diffuse Boundaries	1	2	3	4	5
Basic Fear (Wound): Being different from others; disapproval of parent (partner)					
Internal Message: Don't make waves					
Core Belief: I have to be good					
Relationship Belief: I have to hold things together					
Image of Partner: Rebellious child					
Relationship to Partner: Condescending; critical; controlling					
Core Issue: Stability and cooperation					
Typical Frustration: You won't grow up; you always want to be different					
Recurrent Feeling: Angry self-righteousness					
Conflict Management: Tries to impose rules					
Growth Challenge: Experiment with being different; take risks, develop identity					

appliances in department stores, volunteered at a soup kitchen, and was a vegetarian. She also had subtle ways of making him behave, whether by taking charge of the logistics of their life, which he was too "irresponsible" to handle, or by agreeing with the pedantic rantings of Tony's father. But when Tony didn't do what she felt he should, she was full of indignation that he had offended her, at the same time condescending toward him as though he were a recalcitrant teenager. "If I don't hold things together," she claimed, "nothing gets taken care of. It's like living with a child."

It is interesting to note that the push/pull dynamic of couples whose wounding occurred at these later stages of Concern or Intimacy is more fluid. Their character structure is looser, and the partners tend to alternate roles more easily than those injured at earlier stages when the character structure is more rigid. Character structure is always relative to the person we are relating to: when the Distancer comes closer or starts to pursue, the Pursuer suddenly becomes distant. But it is even more malleable here. Thus, in about 30% of cases, I have seen couples in which the Rebel is the *Maximizer* and the Conformist is the *Minimizer*.

E X E R C I S E   7 C   ■   ■   ■   ■   ■

Am I a Minimizer or a Maximizer?

If you are at all unclear about whether you are a Minimizer or a Maximizer, take a look at the chart below. On the left is a list of traits that describe the Minimizer; the traits on the right describe the Maximizer. Circle the phrases that describe you.

MINIMIZER	MAXIMIZER
Implodes feelings inward	Explodes feelings outward
Diminishes affect	Exaggerates affect
Denies dependency (counter-dependent)	Tends to depend on others
Generally denies needs	Generally exaggerates needs
Shares little of his inner world	Is compulsively open; subjective
Tends to exclude others from his psychic space	Tends to be overly inclusive of others in psychic space
Withholds feelings, thoughts, behaviors	Tends toward clinging and excessive generosity

MINIMIZER	MAXIMIZER
Has rigid self-boundaries	Has diffuse self-boundaries
Inner-directed; takes direction mainly from himself	Outer-directed; generally asks for direction from others, distrusts own directions
Mainly thinks about himself	Focuses on others
Acts and thinks compulsively	Acts impulsively
Tries to dominate others	Usually submissive, manipulative
Tends to be passive-aggressive	Alternates between aggressiveness and passivity

E X E R C I S E   7 D   ■   ■   ■   ■   ■

Identifying the Wounded Child in the Adult

Now take a few minutes to complete the following summary. Look back over your responses to the questionnaires in the three preceding chapters to determine at which stage most of your responses fell in the 4 to 5 range, and note if there were any other stages where your responses were consistently at the high end of the scale.

I am a _____ (Minimizer or

Maximizer) with _____ (rigid or diffuse) boundaries who

was most deeply wounded at the stage of _____.

(Example: Identity.) Therefore I am a _____ (Coping

response. Example: Controller.) My Basic Fear (wound) is _____

_____ (line 2 of chart for pertinent stage). I also seem to

have problems in the area of _____

_____ (any additional stage or stages where your

responses consistently fall in the 3 to 5 range). My Basic Fear

(wound) there is _____. Thus my

Growth Challenge is _____

_____

_____

Well, that's pretty depressing, isn't it? It's a wonder we can get out of bed in the morning, and dress and feed ourselves, with all the baggage we're carting around, all the indirection and defensiveness. I agree that this is the hard part; but it is also the hopeful part. Fortunately, we can repair the damage if we work at it. In fact, in doing so we are aligning with our fervent unconscious wish to be whole.

8

Traumatized Relationships: Legacy of the Dysfunctional Family

All happy families resemble each other;
each unhappy family is unhappy in its
own way.

—LEO TOLSTOY, *Anna Karenina*

We have just looked at how the particulars of early childhood nurturing result in specific wounds that affect our partnerships. But many people have wounds that go much deeper than what we have explored, and they must face the repercussions of a possible history of abuse. They are the victims of parenting additionally impaired by alcohol and drug abuse, physical and emotional battering, incest, violence, and trauma that affect more than half of American families. You may belong to this large population, which has become highly visible in this last decade of the twentieth century. If so, you will have to contend with more severe difficulties and complications in your attempts to establish a lasting relationship.

It is not my intention here to go into detail on specific dysfunctions. These serious and, unfortunately, commonplace problems are dealt with in hundreds of widely available books, workshops, and programs offering counsel, comfort, and recovery strategies. But because children from toxic environments are fated to repeat the problems of their childhood as adults, I want to make some general observations about dysfunctional family dynamics, with particular regard to their devastating impact on relationships, and to add my voice to the ongoing dialogue about how to repair the damage.

A Matter of Degree

It sometimes seems as though families torn by violence or abuse are a very far cry from "normal" families. If yours was such a family, you may have felt that the seemingly happy household next door lived on a different planet. In a way, you were right, for serious dysfunction has a far-reaching impact on children.

But however extraordinary they may seem, the dynamics of toxic families differ *only in degree* from those of a "normal," functional family. The process of wounding is the same. Everyone's troubles are the result of the deprivation of pleasure, the infliction of pain, and the lack of emotional safety; this is the core of the human condition. But in the traumatized family the damage is extreme. All children are wounded through the failure of their caretakers to meet their needs for reliable attachment, to be allowed to explore the world and return to a safe environment, to be mirrored in their search for identity, to be praised in their efforts to become competent, to be supported as they venture into the world of peers, and, in adolescence, to be assisted in integrating their sexuality and entering into adulthood. But the caretakers in the disturbed family are mortally wounded themselves, and thus are incapable of providing even marginally adequate sustenance and gratification to others.

Parents carry the burden of their own history of deprivation and neglect, and children suffer the consequences. Such parents have nothing to give, no resources to draw on. In many cases they themselves are so needy, and their resources so slim, that they turn to the child for their own sustenance. This powerful, largely unrecognized pattern, which psychologist Pat Love calls emotional incest, is what happens when parents rely on their children for the fulfillment of needs that should be met by another adult.[1] It's easy to vent anger at a helpless child; no challenge to win an infant's love; unthreatening to ask a child for help.

Because the damaging environment is in place at birth, the child from the dysfunctional family is deeply wounded—deprived, abused, neglected—during the crucial early stages of Attachment and Exploration, in ways that the old brain will not forget. Ineffective response patterns—the feeble, unsophisticated, inchoate defenses of a desperate infant—are laid down, imprinted, and carried through life in a desperate attempt to deflect further pain. The fact that these defenses are destructive, unproductive, and unnecessary in a more functional world, and that those same defenses serve to distance the child (and later the adult) from others, doesn't even register. It's all he knows.

All too often the amplification of dysfunctional dynamics is provided by a substance, such as alcohol or drugs. The substance is the medium through which the dysfunctional behavior is filtered. It exaggerates the mother's detachment, depression, and unavailability. It enhances the father's anger and lowers his psychological barriers to molesting his daughter.

The point I want to make here is that all family dynamics, from those of the healthy, functional family to the family riven by strife and abuse, should be viewed as a continuum, not a polarity. The major difference is the *degree of amplification* of the same problems, as a consequence of the functional level of the parents—their degree of self-absorption, their addictions, their abusiveness, their neediness, their competence level. In a healthy family, the exhausted, over-stressed mother finds some way to be with her child, even if it's just having the child sleep in her bed; the exhausted mother in the dysfunctional family ignores the child, becomes angry at his cries, or attends to him erratically when she emerges from her drunken stupor. An angry, frustrated father in a healthy family may lose his temper and yell at his daughter; the troubled father hits her.

The Minimizer/Maximizer adaptation operates here too, but on a grander scale. The Maximizer parent feels too much; he drinks to deaden pain, anger, and hopelessness. The Minimizer uses drugs to jump start deadened feelings, to overcome a sense of detachment and isolation, to make him feel alive. I once asked a friend who had been sober for five years what he understood about his reasons for drinking. He responded immediately: "It made me feel alive. Between drunks my body felt like cement, and I lived in a mental stupor."

At the Attachment stage, for example, the avoidant Minimizer parent withdraws into alcohol or severe depression, in near total abandonment of the child. Rejected in every attempt to get nurturing, the child withdraws into a shell, never to emerge even in adulthood. At the Exploration stage, the clinging Maximizer parent, often fueled by her own neediness and depression, may smother and control the child, with escalating demands for affection, friendship, favors, or time, cutting off the child's opportunities for exploring the world and gaining independence. And so it goes at each stage, the problems magnified by the unremitting severity of the parental deficit.

Let me use a couple of instances from my practice to illustrate the severity of extreme parental deficit.

Ann was drawn to highly sexual men, yet felt little pleasure in intercourse. She could not remember feeling sexual desire. All her relationships ended the same way, with her partners leaving her in anger and frustration at what they felt was a double message: "I like your sexuality, but don't try and have sex with me." During the course of her therapy, she dreamed of having sex with a stranger whose face she couldn't see. This broke her amnesia about having been molested by her father in late childhood and his subsequent rejection of her in her early teens. She had come to look upon her body as evil, wore bulky clothes to hide her breasts, and shut down all sexual feeling. Unconsciously identifying with her repressed sexual self, she stated to all contenders, "I want you, but I am not a sexual person." In the depths of her sexual denial, Ann would get hysterical at the mention of sex in books or on TV. If a man looked at her, she would think that he wanted to rape her. She would come to our sessions with stories of men who tried to touch her, and "lascivious" looks that the man at McDonald's was sending her way, and the "filthy" couple she saw kissing and petting on the street.

Victor suffered a different fate. Having played the role of surrogate husband for his alcoholic mother, he had an eroticized body, but no access to his feelings. Diverting all his core energy into his mind and body, he became a lawyer, and a stud. He was compulsive in his search for partners, needing an inexhaustible supply. He'd have sex twice a day—he claimed he *needed* sex twice a day—but could not express tenderness to or empathy for his partners, nor could he understand why women didn't like the kind of instrumental, unencumbered sex that he did. Using his highly developed mind with legal precision, he would skewer every woman who tried to defeat his rationality or failed to match his sexual athleticism, or who became emotional during a discussion. His mother was still the only woman in his life.

It's All Trauma

The second point I want to make is that while the particulars of the abuse or dysfunction differ from family to family, and from child to child, there is nevertheless a great similarity in the wounding itself. And therefore there is a commonality in the impact on adult relationships and the path of healing and recovery. The similarity of the many twelve-step and other rehabilitation programs that have sprung up in answer to the need for healing of these widespread wounds corroborates this point. Because the wounds are similarly affecting, with similar consequences, the path to wholeness (whether from alcohol, drugs, incest, battering, overeating, over-spending, gambling, or emotional abuse) is the same. And it is the same for the alcoholic and the codependent, the abuser and the abusee. The similarities in the course of healing and treatment of diverse wounds can be compared to the special diets that are peri-odically publicized for the treatment of heart disease, cancer, stroke, or arthritis. While each has its specific refinements, all are addressing the physiological needs of the body and so are basically the same: human bodies need a diet low in fat, moderate in protein, high in fiber and complex carbohydrates—and free of alcohol, tobacco, and caffeine. In other words, while the foreground in every case is different—and I don't mean to minimize the particulars of your pain and suffering—the background of fear, neglect, abandonment, and abuse is similar in all troubled families.

SHELL-SHOCKED CHILDREN

The seemingly inescapable, tenacious hold that childhood abuse continues to exert on the adult—even the aware adult who has tried to escape the past—is illuminated by recent research on Post-Trau-matic Stress Disorder.[2] PTSD is usually associated with soldiers who suffer lasting effects of the terrors of combat. New findings demon-strate that even a single traumatic or terrifying incident, and certainly repeated incidents, can actually alter the chemistry of the brain, so that victims respond to normal events as though they were repeti-tions of the original trauma—with nightmares, sweats, rage, insom-nia, irritability, and flashbacks to the original terror—though years or decades may have passed. And this response is the same whether the original trauma was the result of combat, torture, an earth-quake—or abuse as a child. All PTSD sufferers are responding to a life-threatening experience over which they had no control. A child with no skills, resources, or means of escape is certainly without control over his circumstances. And what he is responding to—whether it's the original trauma or the harmless everyday event that brings the original memory flooding back—is the threat of death.

WHY ARE ONLY SOME CHILDREN AFFECTED?

Even though scientists have been able to identify the malfunction-ing brain circuitry of PTSD and are developing drugs that they hope will help the brain to correctly rewire itself, they are still puzzled as to why some people sustain lasting damage in response to combat, for example, while others do not; and why some people recover from a traumatic experience in a short time, while others are troubled for years and probably lifetimes.

But there are some clues, and these clues also suggest parallels to the legacy of family dysfunction. Animal studies have shown that animals who are repeatedly subjected to mild stresses in early life are more likely to undergo brain-chemistry changes as a result of a major stress later in life than those animals who were not stressed as infants. So it seems that if we receive adequate love and guidance early in life, we are able to better tolerate later stress and setbacks. This would explain why one person recovers quickly from an airplane flight in which an emergency landing was made after the engine caught fire, for example, while another is haunted by it long after. This phenomenon is known as the "kindling effect," where sensitivity to a stimulus builds up over time to an incendiary level, so that the person becomes like a tinderbox, ready to burst into flame at the slightest breeze. It can be compared to lightly rubbing an area of the skin with sandpaper. After a while the area is so raw that a minor touch produces a maximal response. It is not surprising that a little girl whose mother left her home alone to go out drinking becomes an adult who goes into a hysterical panic when her boyfriend does not call for her exactly when he said he would. A boy who was beaten for every slight infringement of the rules will go through life reacting to every sideways glance or mild criticism as though he'd been hit.

Sam was two when his father died and six when he was orphaned by his depressed mother. Discussing his relationships with women, he reported that he goes into a panic at the slightest hint of rejection or negativity. He compulsively looks at the faces of his dates, expectantly hoping for a smile, fearing a frown or the barest hint of disinterest. He cannot bear to be around anyone who is sad. After his mother's death, he was placed in an orphanage where he was beaten and yelled at. Now the slightest anger from someone he cares about will send him into a tailspin of fear and self-recrimination. At the orphanage he ran and hid in a closet. Now he flees the room, and will even flee the relationship, if his partner shows any annoyance or the slightest frustration. Eventually his partners leave, convinced that nothing they can do will convince Sam of their love, since all he can see is evidence of betrayal.

Evelyn, whose parents drank and had blatant affairs, tends to become sexually involved with whomever she dates right away. She's indiscriminating in her choices, and seems to feel that she should go to bed with any man who's civil to her. Her sexuality is all she feels she has to offer. But once she has slept with someone she somehow feels she's kept her end of the bargain, and her emotional needs are overwhelming. The minute her lovers go home or go off to work, she is on the phone asking them if they are available for lunch or when they can get together next. If they betray a hint of reluctance or distance—as they are bound to do, since they are like her parents—she cries and becomes hysterical and punitive, even threatens suicide. Then she refuses to see them again or to answer the phone.

UNEXPERIENCED EXPERIENCE

Why is it that childhood trauma continues to hold such power over our lives, and why is the exaggerated, irrational response pattern so hard to break? I believe it is because, as children, having no wherewithal to understand the trauma or to do anything to stop it, we repress it. Because we cannot connect our emotional pain with the devastation that caused it, we literally don't know it's there. We deny the depths of our pain, the hopelessness of our situation. After all, we have little choice; we have no other home, no other parents to turn to for love and comfort, so we have to pretend that everything is really OK. The truth is inadmissible, so we hide it from ourselves. Yet our old brain and our body carry the truth inside us, split off from our awareness. Instinctually we respond to all life situations as though the original threat to our survival still exists. To a shell-shocked soldier, a slammed door or a strange noise in the night brings back in full force the terror of battle. To the adult traumatized in childhood, the girlfriend who comes home an hour late brings on full blown the fear of abandonment. A sarcastic remark or an angry look from her boyfriend triggers a woman's vehement rage, or anxiety; she lashes out in anger, or compulsively leaves the restaurant or the relationship.

For some, the early trauma is so devastating, or so prolonged, that they can never allow any of the feelings associated with the trauma to surface. They live in an ever-threatening world, with their memories suspended outside of time. This *unexperienced experience*, as psychiatrist Ivor Browne terms it, is literally "unthinkable."[3] Seemingly innocuous everyday events trigger the leakage of emotions locked into the sensitized unconscious about memories too painful to confront, setting off the symptoms of panic, anxiety, rage, flashbacks. The more this happens, the more the early events are replayed, even in their current, seemingly harmless form, the more hard-wired becomes the pattern of response in the limbic system.

Once, when I was about nineteen years old, a group of us "preacher boys" were headed back to college one Sunday night when the driver of our car swerved to avoid an oncoming truck. We careened into a ditch, rolled over, and came up on the other side of the road. After our initial shock and relief, we continued on home and didn't say much. But about three hours later I began trembling and shaking, and crying uncontrollably. I was experiencing the trauma of facing death—but hours later. For a while my old brain had been too paralyzed to experience the emotional content of the event. This is what happens with soldiers—and with traumatized children—except that their trauma is buried for years instead of hours. Unable to confront their inner demons, they can't even begin to let the experience out, and so carry it coursing through their bodies and nervous systems, where it wields a powerful control over their lives.

Seen from this vantage point, *all abuse is trauma*, and the reaction will be that associated with trauma: continuous, instinctive, repetitive, exaggerated—and inappropriate—responses. Wounds suffered while in the womb—from a depressed or addictive mother, or from a man beating his pregnant wife—even from the trauma during or before birth, must also be considered as having long-term consequences if they remain outside our awareness, and if life experience doesn't correct them.

ALL LOSS IS ABUSIVE

Other trauma stems not from the parents' failure but is the fallout of some unforeseen disaster—the death of a parent, the loss of a house in a fire, serious financial reverses, a crippling parental illness when the child is very young. In a way, the result is the same, for the child suffers from the parents' unavailability or distraction. However, whether this loss translates into lasting trauma depends on the context in which it occurs. Factors surrounding the tragedy— the age and ego strength of the child, the love and availability of other caretakers (in the event of a parent's death or illness), the foresight to protect the affected child—make the difference. Recent studies have shown that divorce is far more devastating for children than had been originally thought. But what made one child more resilient than another was his age, the concern of the parents for his welfare, and the volatility of the home ambience *during early childhood*.[4]

All loss, whether the result of dysfunctional emotional dynamics at home or an act of God, is abusive. Fortunately, many children hit by unforeseen tragedy, unlike those from chaotic homes, are guided through the loss and compensated emotionally. When the traumatic event is mitigated by a caring environment, its effects are not as deep or long-lasting.

I now know from my own years in therapy that the loss I felt during my early years as a consequence of my mother's depression was far more devastating than my pain over her death when I was six. The first was a constant, gnawing pain that I could neither understand nor do anything about. She was there, but she seemed to have no energy for me, no interest. Was there something wrong with me? But when she died I was cared for by my older siblings, fussed over and given tremendous attention and sympathy. Outwardly it was a greater trauma. But I had love and support, which softened its impact.

Emotional Abuse

Emotional abuse is not usually mentioned in the same category with battering or incest. Less obvious or dramatic, it is harder to recognize. But it deserves special mention for two reasons. One, it is probably the most widespread form of childhood trauma. Two, because it often masquerades as caring and appears benign, it can be particularly devastating. A parent who wouldn't dream of hitting his child will cut him to pieces with words; this is criticism raised to the level of violence. Then there is "Daddy's little girl," the product of a father who tells his daughter that she is special and beautiful, who showers her with presents and takes her out to lunch at his club while Mommy stays at home. This is emotional rape. There is the single mother who relies on her son for the companionship she doesn't have from a mate, telling him what a big, grown-up boy he is, thus robbing him of his chance to be a child. Or the daughter who cares for her alcoholic father, making sure he eats enough and gets to work on time, looking for him in the neighborhood bars when he doesn't come home. This accesses latent nurturing in the child which is age inappropriate and deprives the daughter of the nurturing *she* needs to become a self.

Charlotte vividly recalls protecting her alcoholic father from the rage of her codependent mother. Lacking any sense of self, and dependent on her unavailable husband for support, Charlotte's mother only knew how to use criticism and complaint to be in contact with her husband. In later life Charlotte found herself drawn to a series of men who had no resources to spare for her. She became their caretaker—and the thorn in their flesh. Alternating between the needy child inside and her identification with her rage-filled mother, she both took care of the men in her life and punished them for their dependency. "Every man I date at some point accuses me of de-balling them," she said derisively. "They're such wimps." At a deeper level, she was unable to commit to any of her suitors because of an unconscious loyalty to her father.

Walker was caught up in a failure cycle at work and with women. Recalling his unrelentingly critical father, with his daily "inspections" of his mother's housekeeping and cooking and of Walker's room and homework, and the compliant pill-addicted mother who never protected him from his father's abuse, he found himself unable to get close to women "because they are too weak." Inevitably drawn to weak women nevertheless, he would initially take care of them in a highly romantic way. Inevitably, though, they would "reveal" their helplessness and their inability to make decisions, and he would criticize them brutally. At first he would keep his judgments to himself, carrying on an ongoing inner dialogue about how they looked and dressed, their grating voices, their lack of intelligence and social graces, their lowbrow tastes. Slowly his criticisms would ooze out, and he would abuse them verbally.

One day, for example, he took a car trip with a woman who he discovered couldn't read a road map. He became so furious and scathing at her "feeble efforts" to navigate that she became completely confused and collapsed in tears. Feeling guilty, he turned to comfort her, only to find himself being "clawed by a tiger."

Emotional abuse is particularly confusing because it often feels good. The child revels in the parent's attentions and trust, and feels somehow grown-up and special to have been singled out over Mom or Dad or siblings. Put into the mate's slot by the parent, the child feels both flattered and guilty. It is the only way he knows to feel loved and valued—and not to be abandoned. But his emotional development will be arrested in childhood, and later he will not be able to have an equal relationship with an adult without feeling that he is violating his loyalty to the parent.

Horrible as it may seem, I sometimes feel it is preferable for the child's recovery if he has been beaten or kicked around. Many emotionally abused adults cannot, will not, admit that what happened to them was abusive, even though the repetition of the pattern in their adult relationships is making them miserable. This is abuse that looks like indulgence, with the parent so wrapped up in his or her own needs that the child is sacrificed to fulfill them.

Who's to Blame?

In my practice I see couples from dysfunctional families, acting out their unexperienced traumas, subject day in and day out to the same pains—and reacting in the same way—to the wounds of their childhood. I see the addict and the codependent couple, the abuser and the abusee.

In many abusive families, there appears to be a victim and a tormenter. Perhaps this takes the form of the alcoholic and her all-suffering husband. Or it is the man who beats his wife and then children, while she cowers in the corner and silently comforts her children when it is over. It seems easy to fix the blame in these situations, but this is dangerously misguided. It takes two to create this warped ballet. What is rarely acknowledged is that the battered wife knows only one way—the way she learned from her own mother—to get attention, and that is to provoke her distant, silent husband with relentless, though perhaps subtle, criticism, complaints, and rejection—until he explodes. It's her only strategy for getting his attention, for making him available to her. His violence is the only behavior she recognizes as love and caring. What is going on is a replay of the unavailable parent and the needy child, the Clinger/Avoider dynamic carried to its dysfunctional limit, the ultimate in Maximizer/Minimizer behavior. It's an intact system in which both parties have something to gain from their exchange. What we treat as social problems are often actually psychological dynamics being acted out on the world stage.

It is crucial, if problems are to be solved, to take a *blameless* look at partner dynamics. The emergence of an understanding of codependency is an important step in acknowledging shared responsibility rather than meting out the lion's share of blame to the wife beater or substance abuser. Addressing the complicity of the passive/aggressive woman who provokes the batterer's wrath, the suffering wife who neither leaves her partner nor defends her children—however unsympathetic it seems—has gone a long way toward reevaluating the unproductive "poor victim"/"awful tormentor" scenario.

A couple I was seeing demonstrated this victim/tormentor impasse. She was furious, full of hurt and blame and vituperation, because her husband had had an affair. What she couldn't see was that for two years he had been telling her—she admitted this was true—that he was hurting and lonely, that he felt unloved, that she didn't seem to want his sexual advances. As she continued to withhold her affections, he became more and more demanding. But no matter how he pleaded and cajoled and threatened, he couldn't seem to get her attention; as he became more aggressive, she was more repulsed and withdrew further.

One day she found him in their bed with her best friend. Now, that's an act of desperation, and certainly he was wrong to act out his frustrations, but he got his message across. If he had just wanted sex or companionship, he could have had a discreet affair with no problem. But his unconscious drove him to a rash act, and she provoked it. He was later profusely apologetic and remorseful, but he was a desperate man, having exhausted his entreaties. She's right to be furious, but she's playing the victim and still can't see what her part was in this drama. She can't comprehend that her emotional unavailability to her husband was in any way connected to him having the affair.

For a true understanding of dysfunctional behavior, we have to look more deeply into what is happening when a man beats his wife—or when she conspires to provoke him. I want to sound my old refrain again: what we want is to feel fully alive. We want to recover our lost selves, to regain joy and pleasure, to be whole. We want ourselves back. The couple above are trying, albeit in a crippled and counterproductive way, to get what they need to be themselves again, to jump start their deadened batteries.

Violence, substance abuse, provocation, depressive withdrawal: are all frustrated, angry, inappropriate reactions to powerlessness. People who feel that they have an impact—that they are listened to, that they have the wherewithal to get what they want—do not need to resort to violence, nor are they depressed. Studies show that hyperaggressiveness is connected not to power but to the lack of it, and that the attainment of real power makes one *less* warlike. Delinquent teenagers and violent criminals almost without exception come from troubled homes.

Love deprivation is equally devastating. Deprivation of physical pleasure—the lack of love and affection, the inhibition of sexuality— also leads to violence. Cultures that are sexually repressive often revere military glory. Child abusers typically lead notoriously pleasure-deprived lives. A University of Colorado study showed that only a few of one hundred mothers who abused their children had ever experienced orgasm, and that the parents in general reported impoverished sex lives.[5]

IS THE CHILD AT FAULT?

Only the child is innocent of blame. He has no need for sexual contact with his father, no need to be beaten in order to experience pleasure or to confront his self-image. He is only complying with a system which he feels protects him from death, which keeps him connected to the parent, and to which he sees no alternative. But this is an unwitting act of self-betrayal, which he will pay for later. His behavior becomes part of a habituated survival response, frozen into character adaptation and rigid belief that is not easily altered by contradictory life experience. Any new environment is perceived as being the same as the one he came from. Robotically, he will respond to the new situation with whatever behavior he felt enabled him to survive at home. Perhaps that means submitting to abuse, because he saw that it was the best way to survive. Or he becomes the abuser for the same reason. The child will usually identify with one or the other parent's behavior as having greater survival value. He may come to the conclusion that "if you fight back, you get killed"; just as easily he may reason that "if you *don't* fight back, you get killed." Neither behavior effectively changes his situation, but there isn't much choice.

Additionally, there is often a gender component involved. The daughter sees that her mother's submissive compliance seemed to lessen the severity of the father's abuse. She unconsciously comes to feel that this is a woman's role; she figures out that her mother survives because she is clever in protecting herself from further harm. The son may see that his father is mean and awful for beating his mother, but he sure does get his way, and he doesn't get hurt.

But the roles can also switch in an altered context. A woman who was abused may go out of her way to choose a placid, passive mate. But then she will behave aggressively and abusively toward him— because his passivity is as frustrating to her as hers was to her father. In family dynamics, there is often a triangle—the tormentor, the victim, and the rescuer. But the players can switch roles, moving around the triangle in relation to the behavior of the others.

However blameless the child, though, the adult who takes on the responsibility of a partner or children must own his behavior, no matter how rooted in childhood trauma over which he had no control. And the first step is to recognize the family dysfunction and its present-day impact in his relationships.

Are You from a Dysfunctional Family?

Many children from troubled families grow up with some awareness that something was grievously wrong at home. Some spend years trying to understand what happened to them, and to undo the damage. Others can't face the pain of confronting their pasts, and choose to avoid any intimacy which might put them in danger again. Yet others go through life on the giving or receiving end of pain, their aliveness subverted in constricted behavior and habits that they hope will forestall crisis, unaware that their pasts have poisoned the present.

But ignorance is not bliss. Alcohol and drugs, or compulsive behavior such as obsessive work or play, only mask the pain, and can do so but temporarily, until the house of cards collapses and one's life and relationships lie in shambles. The only way out, as they say, is *through*. No healing is possible until the truth is out in the open. Let's look at some of the characteristics that dysfunctional families share.

1. There was secrecy and denial.

It is not only the pain of a dysfunctional childhood that makes it hard to face up to. Unless the problem was such that it became public—a murder, a falling-down-drunk parent, a beating that brought the police—secretiveness, denial, and deflection are hallmarks of a toxic home environment. This has several implications. It means that what was wrong—the incest, the violence, the alcohol—was not talked about, and the child was unsure of the validity of his own experience. A prisoner of the family cover-up, he colluded in the lie. If he tried to get at the truth, to articulate what was happening, he was an outcast.

Adults from dysfunctional families often face an amnesiac barrier about their childhoods; they are split off from an inner awareness of their trauma. If you cannot remember your childhood, you probably had a childhood that you cannot bear to remember. Conversely, you may idealize your childhood, though your memories conflict with evidence that your present life and relationships don't work: your childhood was so bad that you can remember *only* the good. If you remember your childhood as all bad, that too is a defense. Children from wholly toxic homes are in institutions or jails or bars, or they are already dead. If you are intact enough to be buying this book, there was some level of functionality.

In my family, overfunctionality was part of our dysfunction. My father was dead, and when my mother died when I was six, leaving nine children behind, we didn't talk about it. It wasn't that it was a secret, but nobody mentioned it, or cried about it. We just worked from sunup to sundown, and prayed, and filled up our time. We didn't allow ourselves to mourn, or to acknowledge the pain of our loss. I paid for this denial with a series of relationships with depressed women who "covered" my own unacknowledged depression for me while I criticized them for their unhappiness.

2. You have a distorted sense of yourself.

Deprived of their childhood, not seen for who they are, children from dysfunctional families experience extremes of either abandonment or overprotection. Never mirrored, their needs subordinated to that of the family, and thus denied the ability to develop a distinct identity, they instead forge characters or roles that help them cope.

Moderation and appropriateness are foreign to the traumatized child: the Minimizer/Maximizer effect operates at full tilt. The adult either feels worthless, or has an overblown sense of his importance. His boundaries are far too loose, or constricted to the point of suffocation. Either he is overadaptive, going along with everything and everyone, or he rebels against every single demand. The traumatized child lacks problem-solving modalities, because he reacts rather than acts. Impulse and instinct override thought and planning. Unable to experience himself accurately, without exaggeration or diminishment, he neither knows what he wants nor has the tools to get it.

A gender component is at work here too, compounding things. The pressure on a male to be strong is coupled with denial, intensifying his withdrawal. The culture also reinforces his tendency to be the abuser. A woman's training to have her feelings exacerbates her oversensitivity to her surroundings. And the culture encourages her tendency toward codependency.

Life patterns are restricted and inhibited, governed by unacknowledged rules and fears, rigid beliefs, magical thinking, and cut-off feelings. The inner child was abandoned in the cause of survival, but that child is screaming for attention.

I once asked a client why she continued to explode at her partner. At first she blamed his behavior and claimed he deserved her abuse. Pressing her further, I asked how the episodes of conflict served her, but she was still at a loss. I then pointed out to her that all behavior is purposeful: it prevents your facing up to a reality that is more terrifying than the terrible situation you create. "If you go to the grocery store, no matter how much you dislike going, it prevents you from starving," I said by way of illustration. She then understood what was going on. "It's the only way I can hold his attention. If I'm nice, or don't bother him, he ignores me. When I am upset and full of blame, he fights with me, and I feel he's involved. The pain of fighting is more bearable than being ignored. Then I feel like I'm going to die. I don't know any other way to get close to him."

3. Your relationships have been haunted by the specter of the problems of your childhood home.

The pull to repeat the patterns of childhood in our relationships is especially irresistible for the traumatized child, whose rigidity and fixed belief systems cause tunnel vision about what to expect in a relationship. However flawed our models of relationship, they are all we know. Experience must be corrected by experience, and it is inevitable that we will gravitate to the ambience of childhood in an attempt to heal. But since, whether overdependent or overdetached, we lack the tools for intimacy, and since our internal wiring has us rooted in the past, we are in no condition to face present realities, or to find solutions.

4. You rarely experience joy or pleasure.

No matter how difficult, stressed, or complicated life gets, most people can still laugh at a joke, enjoy a bath or a friend's story, take pleasure in watching the sun set or in making love. However, anhedonia—the inability to feel pleasure—is not uncommon in those from dysfunctional families.

Timothy's father was an alcoholic and workaholic, and his mother, though always attired in her "persona" clothes and makeup to keep up their "good name" in the community, was chronically depressed. Timothy became a workaholic himself, and turned to drugs in his mid-twenties, after his stint in Vietnam. He came to therapy in response to his girlfriend's complaint that he never asked for sex. His report was that he never felt any pleasurable sensation during intercourse, so he wasn't much interested. Since he'd gotten off drugs, he claimed, he enjoyed nothing—food, drink, sex, play. His only passion was work, and he'd come to the conclusion that this compulsion had replaced drugs as his anesthesia.

Timothy and others like him have lost contact with their own life energy, which provides the most exquisite pleasure of all. To the traumatized adult, there are no "simple" pleasures. Hampered in the ability to feel pleasure as well as pain, only intense, compulsive exercise, drinking, shopping, eating, sex, or danger—often with the aid of drink or drugs—wakens the deadened pleasure receptors.

5. You are an addict.

If you drink or take drugs, gamble, work sixteen hours a day, exercise or eat compulsively, you are filling up a gaping black hole that threatens to engulf you, in the only way you know how. Chances are you came from a dysfunctional home.

How Can I Break the Pattern?

The way to a loving, conscious relationship is no different for someone from a dysfunctional family than for someone less seriously wounded. You must examine your childhood courageously, using the questionnaires in Chapters 5 through 7. The exercises in Part V, which are geared toward changing behavior patterns, will work for you, too.

But the process will be longer, harder, and more painful. There is more to heal, and the lost child is more deeply buried. Denial of the past is stronger, the fear of facing it greater. Beliefs and behavior are more rigid. The anger, and the tendency to blame, are greater. The shame may feel paralyzing. But you, especially, must acknowledge the wrong done to you, express your anger, and be able to *let go of blame*—of yourself and your caretakers. Surrendering to the process is essential.

There is no way around this. You cannot avoid choosing partners with the devastating problems you had at home. Many times I have had people approach me after my lectures distraught because I've said that they are fated to repeat the devastating problems of their childhood. "Isn't there any way I can avoid marrying an alcoholic (or someone who is physically abusive, or emotionally frigid)? Isn't it enough that I have been in therapy, that I faithfully attend AA (or ACOA)?" It is heartbreaking for me to tell them that the work they are doing is of tremendous benefit, but they cannot avoid the problems, that in fact they need to confront those very problems as adults in order to heal. "All you can hope for," I have to tell them, "is to find someone who is aware of his or her problems and willing to do, with you, the hard work necessary to heal."

I have had clients tell me that they were encouraged at their AlAnon meetings to leave their drinking spouses. This is appallingly ignorant. The idea of the disposability of the troubled spouse is dangerous and destructive. Relationship problems are a dynamic between two people: until you are perfect, there is no perfect partner. Until you correct your codependent behavior, you will choose an abuser partner. While you are an addict, the only partner you find will be codependent.

Wanting to escape a troubled relationship is an understandable human impulse. There are plenty of times when I've wanted to go away myself, just to be alone for a while, to have a break from dealing with the conflict, ill will, and day-to-day hassles that arise in any relationship. But the relationship itself is always a vital part of the cure. It is the ambience in which the early trauma can be experienced, dealt with, and *integrated*, so that it loses its power to cause pain. Running away solves nothing; eventually the same problems show up further down the road. The criteria for leaving a partner, to my way of thinking, are few, regardless of the severity of the problem. When it is clear that a partner is unaware of his problems or unwilling to do anything about them, there is probably no way to salvage the relationship. Often, I know, this is the case where there is chronic abuse and addiction. However, when the addict or abuser is willing to acknowledge and work on the problems, I feel the attempt to save the relationship should be made.

Your awareness and your intention will make the difference. You must surrender to the process, and have faith that your efforts will move you toward wholeness. I urge you to do as much as you can now to become aware of your past, to find a supportive environment in which you can open up your wounds, however horrid, and begin to feel the experience that has so long been shut out. Make the changes you can make on your own—through therapy, a twelve-step program, and some of the exercises in Part V.

Because trauma is so often locked in the body, people from dysfunctional families often benefit from therapeutic bodywork, such as deep tissue massage or other body therapies. It is also possible that you would benefit from short-term medication under the supervision of a doctor, judging from my experience with troubled couples. I've seen couples so entrenched in their behavior that it has been impossible to make any headway in therapy until one or sometimes both of the partners takes medication to de-escalate their exaggeration and temper their hair-trigger responses, so that they are emotionally *available* to work on the relationship. The work still has to be done; the medication doesn't make the problems go away. The paranoia is still there, the delusions and the abandonment fears, but the paralyzing, life-threatening, "combat level" intensity is reduced. The partners are able to feel normal, and have breathing space to look inside, without feeling that they are suffocating.

Though it may require great effort and courage, whatever you can accomplish now will put you in a position to attract a healthier partner, one who also has serious problems to deal with, but who is available to work on those issues.

PART

III

THE IMAGO PUZZLE II: CHILDHOOD SOCIALIZATION

9

"For Your Own Good": The Messages of Socialization

This above all: to thine own self be true.
— POLONIUS, in *Hamlet*

We have just talked about the unmet childhood needs that arise from inadequate nurturing in our early years and how they influence the type of person we are attracted to. Knowing this is important preparation for the journey of love, but there is another important aspect of your childhood that you must understand in order to make your self-knowledge more complete and to deepen your preparations.

How we were nurtured is but one ingredient in the complex recipe of our Imago, that inner picture of the opposite sex that guides us like a homing device to our intended. For while we were being fed and cuddled and protected from danger, our caretakers were involved in an additional activity, which would have equal weight in our partner choice. Our parents were educating us in the ways of the world we live in, so that we would be safe outside the walls of our home. We were being *socialized*.

As is by now apparent, the distinctions between nurturing and socialization are often blurred, for they are parallel but overlapping

137

processes. While nurturing is internal, a private and personal process, concerned with the warmth and availability of our caretakers, socialization is external, concerned with our interaction with the outside world. As we began to respond to our environment, to walk and talk and explore, we were bombarded with messages—through instruction and example, praise and punishment, rules and role models. These messages conveyed to us exactly what to do and say, how far and fast to walk, what was (and what was not) permissible to feel, to think, and to do. We were even told how to relate to our own bodies. The lines of acceptability were drawn.

In the next three chapters we will look at how the messages of socialization mold our personalities so that we repress certain essential aspects of ourselves and develop a false veneer that we hope will be accepted and loved. We will see how, just as we choose partners who have similar nurturing wounds and complementary defenses, we also choose partners who are able to express the traits that we repress.

SOCIETY'S CHILD

This process of being shaped into social beings is carried out under the survival directive. But while biological survival skills seem to be instinctive—a genetic legacy of our evolutionary history—social survival is learned. Mothers and fathers are representatives of society, charged with the responsibility of seeing that their children will be accepting of, and acceptable to, their surroundings. Their objectives and intentions are honorable: to protect you from outside forces that might harm you. The premise of socialization is twofold: that society is dangerous to you and that *you*, without proper shaping, are a danger to society. Only through the institutionalization of measured constraint can society protect itself from your natural wildness, the free expression of your life energy. Wild creature of nature, you must be tamed to live in the zoo. "The animals out there are trained," we are told, "and you are not. If you don't learn to fit in with them, they will kill you; at the very least they will cast you out."

All social systems view the individual as dangerous and constraint as therefore necessary. However, the method of constraint differs according to the cultural philosophy, be it belief in a theology of inherent evil, a theory of the individual as self-centered, or a political ideology that designates some people unequal by virtue of race, sex, or class. Whatever the rationale, all such views concur that we must be tailored to fit into society, and not the other way around.

Since that tailoring requires a modification of our original selves, we are inevitably wounded in the process.

But the shaping of the individual is not necessarily evil. Our life force is morally neutral and dedicated to its own survival; we do not inherently know how to live with others and let them live with us. All creatures, from bluejays to chimpanzees, live in a collective; socialization is the parental responsibility at all levels. Because of our plasticity and complexity, we humans must be directed and molded to become constructive social beings, to care for others and the collective of which we are a part. It is necessary for our survival.

The damage comes as the result of the method, and the ideology that informs it. Unfortunately, no society has yet devised a way to preserve the wholeness of each person and integrate him into the collective without repressing essential aspects of the self and dimming his full aliveness. Until we reach that level of enlightened evolution, the potential for injury remains great.

Ironically enough, much of the damage is done at the hands of those who want most to protect us. Our parents are the conduits of whatever social norms are in vogue. But they themselves carry the wounds of their own socialization, by-products of a lifetime of assorted fears, beliefs, and disappointments, often the remnants of a rigid or difficult upbringing. Since, consciously and unconsciously, they inevitably pass their wounds on to us, we suffer the fate of their limitations. Acting on his or her own inculcated belief that conformity is in the child's best interest, it is the rare parent who sees the potential dangers and actively guards against his or her child's loss of self; rarer still that the child's uniqueness is encouraged. Too, our society, which pays lip service to the autonomy and dignity of the individual, is no hotbed of tolerance, flexibility, and forbearance for idiosyncracy. Society is by nature biased toward the protection of the collective good and values acceptability and conformity to majority values.[1]

THE PRICE OF SOCIALIZATION

"For your own good" is the battle cry of socialization. But conformity exacts a high price. The nature—and the tragedy—of socialization is that it thwarts our individuality in the service of survival, censoring and editing our thoughts, actions, and feelings. In their zeal to homogenize us so that we will fit in, our caretakers fail to sustain us in our wholeness. We were made for ecstasy, but our sense of full aliveness must be tempered; our freewheeling energy must be controlled; our spontaneity must be dampened.

"You cannot have all of yourself and live in this world," they tell us. It is an insidious process of invalidation, in which we give up pieces of ourselves in order to survive.

However, since we have an innate drive for wholeness, a compulsion to recover our true selves pursues us relentlessly throughout our lives. *Just as the degree and type of wound we carry from the way we were nurtured varies according to our circumstances, so it is with how we are socialized. And to a lesser but nonetheless significant degree, how we were socialized affects our Imago picture.* By understanding how our wholeness was violated, how we were pruned and abridged—and how that wound affects our relationships—we can begin to repair the damage.

SHUTTING DOWN THE ENERGETIC CORE

To understand how the socialization process works, look at Figure B. The circle represents the energetic "core" self, and the "outside" world—nature, society, the collective unconscious. For the sake of simplicity, I like to divide the core self into four functions. These are our avenues of connection to the outside world: thinking, feeling, sensing, and acting. As long as our thoughts are free, our feelings flowing, our bodily senses intact, and our muscles flexible, we have full access to the outside world and to our inner experiencing. Our borders are open, and energy can flow freely in and out: we are whole. But all these functions are the targets of socialization, and in the indoctrination process of life, our wholeness is challenged at every turn.

By the time we are adults, we have done as we were told and erected fences at strategic places to control the flow of energy. Depending on what was encouraged and what prohibited, we selectively closed off our boundaries, so that energy was hampered in its flow to some areas of our psyche. Our connection to the outside was broken, distorted, and devitalized, and our interactions with the world became limited and rigid. To the degree that we are cut off from aspects of ourselves, to that degree we feel cut off from others, and from the cosmos. The consequence is a sense of separateness, or, at the extreme, alienation and loneliness.

In my practice, I see countless examples of the selective censorship of socialization. Alice is a highly expressive singer who feels deeply about everything, but she goes into a tizzy over trying to balance her checkbook. When her accountant tries to explain her taxes to her, she gets agitated and confused. Alice can't *think*. Susan, the daughter of a college professor, is a successful investment

FIGURE B
The Four Functions of Socialization

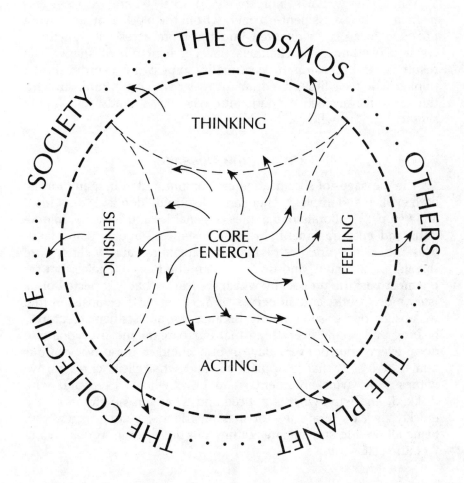

banker, but she feels no pleasure during intercourse and has never had an orgasm. To her, a massage is the height of self-indulgence. Her body anesthesia is so extensive that she hardly feels pain when she hurts herself. Susan's *sensing* functions are shut down. George is a computer whiz, but he can never relax and has difficulty showing affection. He's cool as a cucumber; he never cries, and he prides himself that nothing upsets him. No wonder the women in his life see him as cold, and criticize his sexuality as mechanical. George's *feelings* are cut off. Harry is a couch potato. He says he hates exercise; it's hard to get him to walk a few blocks. He's awkward and plodding on the dance floor, carrying his body as if it will break. Harry is cut off from spontaneous *action*.

While energy flows more freely in areas where we were less restricted, the excess pent-up energy from the blocked areas, having nowhere to go, gets diverted into the more accessible functions, creating overburdened channels. We get bent out of shape. The result is certain common personality types: the overdeveloped thinker who feels little, the dramatic feeler who can't think straight, the compulsively active sports nut who never reads, the highly sensate intuitive who can't make plans.

Getting the Message

The messages of socialization are communicated in many forms, both explicit and implied. There are "dos" and "don'ts," "shoulds," and "stops," elaborate hierarchies of penalties and rewards, injunctions and encouragement. In some instances—and in some families—the tactics are pretty blatant: screaming and yelling, dire threats, punishment, and rigid rules are the tools of choice. But for the most part the process by which we learn what is expected of us is far more subtle, and all-pervasive. It is similar to osmosis, in that we absorb our lessons simply because we are sentient creatures, hearing and seeing everything that our parents and everyone else does, every hour of every day, in public and in the privacy of our homes. We see what is applauded, and what elicits criticism; we witness who wins arguments, and how; who is liked and who disliked, and why; what is noticed and what gets no attention. We quickly develop strategies for making friends, getting a new toy, being allowed to stay up late, getting our big sister in trouble, being Grandma's favorite.

THE MODEL MARRIAGE

Our parents' marriage is a powerful, ever-present teaching tool, especially when it comes to learning how to conduct ourselves in a relationship. Do they talk to each other, spend time together, have fun? Are they affectionate with each other? In front of the children? Who makes breakfast, sees that you get to school, goes to the meeting with your teacher, takes you to the dentist? Who brings in the money, and how are decisions made? When there are arguments, is there calm discussion, give and take, or yelling and name-calling, tears, hostile silence, dirty looks, accusations? Is the arguing done in front of the children; does one parent bad-mouth the other to the children? It is a never-ending lesson in how to live in the world. In one way or another, we absorb and evaluate our parents' way of being together, whether we approve or disapprove, adopt or reject it. "Do as I say, not as I do" is a pointless admonition, for children model their parents' behavior, despite any contradictory verbal messages. (At the end of this chapter, you'll find an exercise which will help you remember what you "learned" from your parents' marriage.)

As we move away from our families, we find more models of what works in the world: the examples of our teachers, the church, the police, books and music, movie stars and television. We expand our repertoire of possible behaviors, refine our body language and turn of phrase, increase our feedback from the outside world, and adjust our ideas of what's OK and what's not, modifying the parental messages.

The copycat nature of modeling is humorously illustrated in one of my favorite movies, *The Last Starfighter,* in which an extraterrestrial android is sent back to earth to replace a young man whose exceptional video-game skills are needed to fight an intergalactic war. The android finds himself at a picnic with "his" girlfriend, and though he is an exact clone of the earthling he's replaced, he completely lacks the social skills and graces that he needs to pass himself off. When his girlfriend playfully sticks her tongue in his ear, he doesn't know how to react and replies by clumsily sticking his tongue in her ear. When she gets upset, he sees a guy nearby whose girlfriend has turned away from him, too, and he hears him say, "Oh, darling, I'm sorry." So he says this to his girlfriend, in exactly the same tone of voice. And it seems to work, so he keeps listening with his supersensitive hearing to the other guy, imprinting every gesture on his supersensitive brain. This strategy works perfectly until he tries another one of his "model's" phrases: "Honey, all the other girls didn't mean anything to me, only you do."

We model our behavior in a similar process of trial and error, choosing what seems to get results in the context of our particular environment. If yelling and screaming kept you in line as a child, you will likely adopt the same tactic as an adult, however much you hated and feared it. If your mother cowed you with stony, hurt silence, you will come to believe that that's the most effective way to get what you want. You may abhor the way your parents dealt with each other, but find to your dismay that when you are irritated with your partner, you give him a withering look that implies he is a thoughtless brute—the very same look your mother gave your father whenever he dared to stand up to her.

Ironically, sometimes the smarter and more sensitive we are, the more quick and complete our capitulation to society's plan for us. Clever at figuring out how to thrive in the world, we succeed all too well at getting rid of anything that doesn't advance our cause. Soon we have so successfully digested the incoming messages that they become part of us. We not only model the behavior that seems to work for us, we internalize and believe the attitudes behind the behavior. We have *introjected* society's lessons. No longer do we need our mother to tell us that we shouldn't cry, or that men are good-for-nothings, or that we're not going to get the job we want. There's a voice inside us, doing the job. My daughter Leah said to me one day: "When I am angry at Hunter, I hear your voice in my head telling me not to hit him." After age four or five, we no longer need those messages to come from the outside; they have been carved on the neurons of our brains. We have met the enemy, and he is us.

Bullied by Our Beliefs

Which brings us to the subject of belief systems. Your self-knowledge is incomplete, and your preparation for marriage limited, without insight into how you were affected by what you saw and imitated. Without such insight, your ideas about relationships can become so fixated that you cannot function in a partnership that deviates from your ideas about how things are supposed to be.

I recently counseled Maria and Ted, an engaged couple who had begun their relationship by playing distinct, traditional roles. But Maria became unhappy with her subservient role and entered psychotherapy. Now she was insisting on changes before the wedding, while Ted kept talking about what a woman was "supposed" to do. I tried to explain to Ted that *in his experience* that's what women did, but his idea of a wifely role model was antithetical to the relationship that he seemed to want. Maria may have fit his image when he met her, I pointed out, but she had changed, and become aware that she is a person first, not someone acting a part, and that she would never be able to go back to her role-playing again except under the strongest duress, unless her survival felt threatened by it. But Ted felt threatened and was unable to rise above his own role: "It's either the way I want it or we call it off," he insisted. To which his fiancée replied, "Well, it's no marriage then."

It is sad, but not surprising, that Ted was unable to make the changes that would enable him to stay, and grow, in this relationship. His ideas about the roles that he and his fiancée should play were part of his belief system, a gospel about how the world is and how people should act, a catechism that had been drummed into him all his life.

In some ways, our belief systems perform a valuable service, for they temper our instinctual nature. Animals live pretty much in a stimulus/response environment, with fixed reactions and adaptations to life, doing the bidding of the old brain. Our clever cerebral cortex enables us to be more discriminating in our responses. And the way we temper the mindless reactions of the old brain is to develop a set of beliefs. Beliefs offer order and stability in a chaotic world. By conceptualizing our repeated experiences into a codified canon that is fixed and stable and logical, we can say, "This is the way my mother behaves when . . . ," "If I do this, then *that* will happen . . . ," "This is how a family acts when someone is sick . . . ," "Men don't like it when. . . . " Our pattern-forming brain enables us to digest blizzards of stimuli and to formulate what we feel are proper and effective responses, so that we are not at the mercy of our primitive instinct to fight or flee, and don't have to start from square one to figure out how to react to every little byte of input.

But we get tripped up by our belief systems. They begin to function in us as instincts do in animals, becoming fixed and un-yielding. We develop models about how to act, what to do, how people are—and the *models*, rather than each discrete experience, become the reality. Unfortunately, studies show that the more troubled and dysfunctional our family, the more we need belief systems to protect us from chaos, to assuage our fear, to *cope*. The daily stress and unpredictability of living with an absent or abusive father, an alcoholic or withdrawn mother, can be tolerated only by creating a system of beliefs within which to make some sense of their unloving behavior. The bottom line about the brain, says Robert Ornstein in *The Healing Brain*,[2] is that it yearns for stability, especially if we are in a volatile, fragile environment. The brain needs to be able to make predictions, and fears the unknown—which is what unpredictable behavior is—so it codifies and ritualizes its experience in order to make sense.

But however useful beliefs are in a stressful environment, their rigidity has to be tempered if we are to be able to find, and function in, relationships. If, from your experience and what society tells you, it becomes part of your canon of belief that all a man cares about is sex, that all family members shout at one another, that the best response to criticism is to keep quiet, that women care most about how much money you make, or that you have bad luck with men, you will find it hard to distinguish on a case-by-case basis and will react according to what you believe rather than the actuality.

Richard Pryor tells a story about his wife coming home and finding him in bed with another woman. "Who are you going to believe?" he challenges her. "Me, or your lyin' eyes?" This is what belief systems do.

Every second of our lives, we create our reality with our thoughts and behaviors, but we cannot change our beliefs at will. We cannot think our way out of pain, cannot override our instinctive reactions. We must become aware of the price we pay for our rigid thinking, and we must experience the pain of holding on to our old beliefs. As a single, part of your preparation for the journey of relationship is to uncover the world you carry around in your head; if it is not the world you want, you have to take the responsibility for changing it. But to fully change your beliefs, you need new experience that contradicts the old, and changes those beliefs naturally over time. This experience is what a conscious relationship provides. (An exercise that will enable you to identify the belief system you developed while living in your parents' marriage appears on page 152.)

The Crybaby and the Bitch

Now I want to go back to the four avenues of socialization shown in Figure B (page 141) and give you some examples of how cultural values determine what is repressed and what is permitted. The norm which we contort ourselves to conform with represents the collective values of our society, but in our society things are hardly in perfect balance. (As Gandhi replied when asked what he thought of Western civilization: "I think it's a good idea.") "Normalcy" is itself highly valued, though what is considered normal produces an unbalanced personality, and also conflicts with any attempt to be oneself. Normalcy in our society means that we can think but not feel, act but not sense—with allowances for gender and environment. If we look at how we are socialized in each area of expression, we can see what a cruel distortion of our own integrity results.

THINKING

What's going on when we flash "learning cards" at infants through the slats in their cribs, and pray that they will be toilet trained in time to start preschool—at age two? *Thinking* is what's going on—analysis, rationalization, deduction, intellectualizing, the exercising of the mighty cerebral cortex. Thinking is what we are trained, encouraged, and rewarded for, the fuel for our economy and our technological progress. "I remember," said one client, "that my father often helped me with homework, and when I got a new toy, he would make me read the instructions and figure out how it worked. But he was a research chemist, and thought sports were rough and bullyish and a waste of time. So we never played games, and I never learned to skate or even ride a bike. I grew up feeling very self-conscious about my body, and any demand for 'action' paralyzed me. I've had to overcome tremendous feelings of clumsiness and frivolousness just to be able to dance or play volleyball."

The expectation of intellectual accomplishment is not the same for everyone, though. "When we would bring our report cards home from school," a female client tells me, "my brothers were given fifty cents for each 'A' on their card, and a quarter for each 'B.' I was not, because it didn't matter if I was smart. On the other hand, the first time I remember my parents making a fuss over me was when I came home with a very cute boyfriend and started going out to the movies and dances. I think they were afraid I was becoming an egghead and wouldn't be popular." Not surprisingly, this woman ended up spending most of her life trying to be popular and pretty, hiding her intelligence, struggling with daunting "blocks" in her creative endeavors.

FEELING

Thinking's polar opposite is feeling. Emotions are not held in high esteem: we are expected to control them through calm and rational thinking. Thinking becomes the *outlet* for repressed feelings; we think our way out of sadness and anger, hurt and grief. "What did you feel," I asked one client, "when they foreclosed on your plant?" "Nothing," was his response. "It was a problem to be solved; I just began to work harder. What was I supposed to do, cry about it? What good would that do?"

Women are cut a little slack in this area. They are allowed to cry, to be fearful or sentimental. In fact, such behavior is preferable to a show of bravery or stoicism. Talking about her childhood, one woman related this tale: "I remember being terrified about performing in a ballet. My mother took me in her arms and encouraged me to cry, saying, 'It's all right, just let those tears out.' " Although this is good parenting, her complaint was that her mother held her and supported her *only* when she was tearful or needy. For her, crying became almost the only way she got attention, a tactic she was still using in her relationships.

Big boys, of course, don't cry; they "act like a man." During a therapy session, I asked Charles to put his dead father in the chair opposite him and tell him about his lifelong sadness. (This tactic is known in Gestalt therapy as a two-chair dialogue.) As he visited his father in memory, he described the scene—his father's funeral, viewing him in his casket. He felt some heaviness, but no tears came. When I asked him to "let the tears out," he stiffened and choked his emotions back. "I see my father saying to me, 'Stop crying, that's for sissies.' The only time I cry," he admitted, "is when I see movies about fathers and sons, and I cry alone."

The rules are different for anger. In most families, anger isn't "nice." Your laughter and smiles were probably noted and encouraged, but it's not likely that you were allowed to show your anger. Your show of angry feelings may have been ignored; you may have been spanked or sent to your room; you may have been cajoled into smiling ("Oh, c'mon now, what's the matter? It's nothing to be upset about. Let's go play in the yard"). The chances that you were allowed your feelings of upset and frustration—"I understand that you're angry that you can't watch the movie, but it's way past your bedtime"—are slim indeed. Is it any wonder that the TV, movies, video games, comics, and foreign policy of our "nice" society seethe with violence? We clean it up, compartmentalize it, intellectualize and ritualize it—as we do to a lesser extent other emotions like love and grief—so that we can cope with it in a safe, acceptable way.

Anger is also genderized. While under some circumstances anger is considered an appropriate and manly response, an angry woman has crossed the line of acceptability. She is a bitch, or a shrew. It's a powerful prohibition, as any smiling, compliant woman eventually learns. "When I was little," explained Felicia, "I was sent to my room if I showed any angry feelings. I had to stay there until I could control myself and was told not to come out until I could smile and apologize. That was so humiliating that I still dash to my room when I am angry and close the door so no one can see me. I'll throw myself on the bed and beat on pillows until I'm exhausted. I'm not sure my mother wasn't right. Just recently my boyfriend left me, saying that he likes me when I'm generous and fun, but he can't stand the negative part of me."

ACTING

For a society that prizes action, accomplishment, and a "can do" attitude, there are nevertheless substantial restrictions on what we can do and when—just how we can flex our muscles. "Walk, don't run," "We don't do that around here," "Sit still," "Look before you leap": by the time childhood is behind us, we no longer question these injunctions. I remember being told not to sing at the table, and my church labeled dancing a sin. But what is wrong, after all, with running, with singing at the table, with spinning around until you're dizzy and fall down? So great is society's need for us to behave ourselves, to be quiet and nondisruptive, to plan ahead, to wait our turn, to subordinate our wishes to those of the group, that we lose touch with our spontaneity and our confidence in our ability to act.

Not surprisingly, what we can *do* is often influenced by gender considerations. A couple of years ago, at an annual church picnic, I witnessed a classic example of this kind of gender bias. A colleague of mine, a competitive squash player, couldn't hide his irritation at his young teenage son, who had been helping some of the younger children blow up balloons and was now reading a book he had brought along. "Why aren't you playing volleyball? I thought you liked volleyball. There's a basketball game going on over by the barn . . . " He was getting more and more exasperated, and each time his remarks would become a little more pointed—"Is there something the matter with you?"—and the boy would shrink into himself a little more, making less and less of a response. As he reached the breaking point, his ten-year-old daughter showed up, panting, smiling, and dirty, to announce that she'd hit a scoring run in her softball game. The father blew up. "Look at you, is that any way for a young lady to behave? Why aren't you with the other girls? Your mother didn't bring any clean clothes for you." Though this kind of scene has become more of a rarity in this age of feminism, in more subtle forms such messages are still influential determinants of our behavior and self-image.

SENSING

It is in the realm of the senses, with regard to our bodies and our sexuality, that we are most proscribed. Ever since the fifth-century theologian St. Augustine decreed that the body was evil and sex sinful, the body has taken a beating in the Western world. You'd think, from the combination of silence and admonition that most of us receive, that it would be better if we didn't have bodies, or if we covered them completely and only used them when necessary—when walking and eating, for example, but never for sex and other bodily pleasures.

A client related a poignant story about a much-anticipated visit to her grandmother's house when she was about six. "I had finished my bath, and I ran down the hall naked to her room and jumped into her bed. She was horrified. 'Cover your shame, young lady,' she screamed. 'Don't ever let anyone see your naked body.' To this day I can't make love with the light on or sleep in the nude. I still hear my Granny's voice and see the consternation on her face." This woman's story is not unusual. One of my clients who cannot enjoy sex told me his parents made him wear gloves to bed to prevent him from masturbating!

As with violence, repressed sensuality oozes out in distorted forms, from sadism to celibacy, from pornography to impotence and frigidity. In no area is the polarization of the way men and women are socialized as strong as in this one. Because this issue is so central to relationship, all of Chapter 11 is devoted to gender and sexuality.

LOCAL CUSTOM

Even within our society, the way we are socialized differs mark-edly from one part of the country to another, and from one commu-nity to the next. A child growing up on a farm may receive few prohibitions around the area of the body or sex, while it will be a furtive and forbidden subject to a child raised in a strict religious home. Anger will be quickly quelled and punished in one home, while next door the nightly squabbles are audible the length of the block. A child from a working class family will be chided for his intellectual "pretensions," while the son of Ivy League graduates who grows up on New York's Upper East Side will not win many friends with the announcement that he wants to be a carpenter.

"I've always felt that I was 'saved' when we moved from the lower-class neighborhood where I grew up to the upper-middle-class community where I went to high school," a friend once told me. "There was no value placed on reading or studying where I grew up, you were expected to be tough and pretty. I was a voracious reader, and I liked to draw, but I mostly kept it to myself and spent my time in the streets with my friends, looking 'cool,' chewing gum, smoking behind the police station after school, and feeling like an impostor and like I didn't have what it takes. Then we moved to another town, where on the very first day of school I realized that my classmates enjoyed their studies and were working hard to do well. I'll never forget my immense sense of relief, of joy, really, that here was another whole world in which I could feel a part, and be more myself, where the things I valued and excelled at counted."

Can we hold on to ourselves in a society that devalues huge chunks of who we are and insists that we strain our feelings and sensuality through a puritanical social sieve? A society that shapes boys and girls very differently, and then expects them to live together intimately and lovingly, to understand and value each other's feelings and opinions? Is there any hope for a relationship in which a man's tears make him a crybaby, and a woman's anger labels her a bitch?

The Whole Self: Missing in Action

Now if we redraw our diagram (Figure C) to reflect the messages we've had drummed into us, we see that the cumulative effect of our indoctrination is that the energy that sustained certain aspects of

FIGURE C
Core Energy Blocked by Socialization

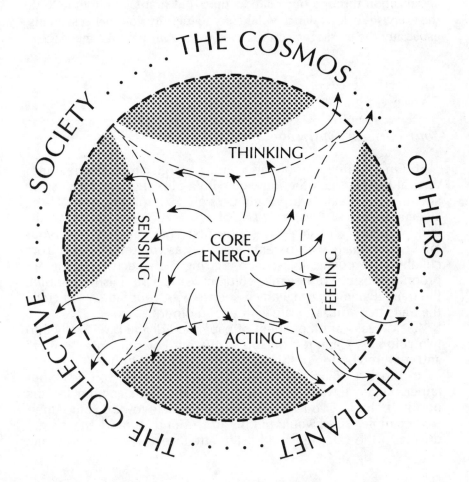

ourselves was blocked from flowing freely in and out. Parts of ourselves became deadened and devitalized, closed off to the outside world. Our energy was deflected into areas that were left relatively undamaged, channels that still allowed energy to move freely. When Woody Allen says, "I am at two with nature," he is talking about the urbanized, intellectual filter through which his feelings and senses cannot penetrate. While all of us have in some way been restrained in all areas, there are likely one or two areas that are most repressed. And while some of us have been left relatively free to be ourselves, others' socialization has been heavy-handed, and they are substantially blocked off in all areas, powder kegs of unexpressed thoughts and feelings, inhibited actions and senses—alienated from themselves, from nature, and from others.

In Chapter 10 we'll look at what happens to the suppressed and fragmented self, and how we attempt to repair the damage of socialization through our relationships. But first take the time to do the exercises below, which will help you identify your belief systems, especially the messages you received from your parents' marriage.

E x e r c i s e   9 a   ■   ■   ■   ■   ■

Your Parents' Marriage

1. On a blank sheet of paper, draw a large circle. Divide it into vertical halves. Mark the left side with a plus sign (+) for positive and the right side with a minus sign (−) for negative. Using adjectives such as "warm," "sexual," "affectionate," "cold," "distant," "tense," "hostile," describe first your mother, then your father, and finally your parents' *marriage* as you remember it from childhood through adolescence, placing the adjectives in the appropriate positive or negative column. When you finish, underline the traits that you particularly associate with your father and circle the traits that you associate with your mother.

2. Now take another sheet of paper and divide it vertically into two columns. Centered on top of the left column write "Father" and centered on top of the right column write "Mother."

In the left column, list the *positive behaviors* you saw your father initiate toward your mother. In the right column list the positive behaviors you saw your mother initiate toward your father. (For example: "Dad would put his arm around Mom when we were driving in the car. He would listen attentively when she told him about her day. He made breakfast for everyone on Sunday mornings. He called if he was coming home late.") When you have finished, draw a horizontal line under the lists across the page.

Below the positive behaviors in the "Father" column, list the *negative behaviors* you saw your father initiate toward your mother. (For example: "Dad would complain if dinner wasn't ready on time. I rarely saw him kiss Mom or say anything affectionate. Dad would blow up if Mom talked for long on the phone. He never helped with housework, even if Mom was sick. He would often interrupt Mom.") When you finish, draw a line under both columns. Repeat the above process for your mother in the right-hand column.

3. Take another sheet of paper and divide it in half horizontally. Put the word "Father" at the top of the page and the word "Mother" centered at mid-page. Now divide the top and bottom of the page into four columns vertically. Label the columns as follows: Column 1, "Frustrations"; Column 2, "Feelings"; Column 3, "Reactions"; and Column 4, "My thoughts." In the first column list all the *frustrations* you saw or heard or believe your father had with your mother; in the next column, write the *feeling* you saw or heard or believe your father had when he experienced that frustration; in the next column write the *reaction* you saw or heard or believe your father had with the frustration in the first column. In the last column write the *thought* you had then or now as you recall your father's frustration and his feeling and behavioral reaction to his frustrations with your mother. Repeat the same process on the bottom half of the page labeled "Mother." (For example: "My mother was frustrated because Dad would come home and watch television all evening. I think she felt hurt that he ignored her and angry that he took her for granted. She reacted by giving him the silent treatment and complaining to us kids about his behavior. I thought Dad was lazy and a bully, but I hated that Mom complained to me and didn't stand up to him, although I was afraid of him, too." Or: "My father was frustrated because Mom usually rebuffed his affection, saying that she was too busy, or the kids shouldn't see it. And he complained that she never dressed up for him. I think he felt that she thought sex and affection were taboo, and that she was repelled by him. Dad's reaction was to have a brief outburst—"For crying out loud, Esther . . . "—and then storm off to the basement or to his office. As a child I also thought that he was bad and should leave Mom alone; now I see that she was angry and prudish.")

4. SUMMARY. Complete the following sentences, using the information from above.

1. I grew up in a marriage that was (somewhat/mostly) [positive adjectives from the left half of the circle in step 1]

_____

_____

2. and also (somewhat/mostly) [negative adjectives from the right half of the circle in step 1] _____

_____.

3. In their marriage, my father (sometimes/often) [positive behaviors from step 2] _____

_____

4. and my mother (sometimes/often) [positive behaviors from step 2] _____

_____.

5. Sometimes/often my father felt [negative feelings from step 3, Column 3] _____

_____

6. because my mother frustrated him by [father's frustrations from step 3, Column 1] _____

_____

7. and then he would [father's reactions from step 3, Column 3]

_____

8. and would [father's negative behaviors from step 2] _____

_____.

9. Sometimes/often my mother felt [mother's feelings from step 3, Column 2] _____

_____

10. because my father (often/sometimes) [mother's frustrations from step 3, Column 1] _____

_____:

11. Then she would [mother's reactions from step 3, Column 3]

_____

12. and would [mother's negative behaviors from step 2] _____

_____.

13. Because of these interactions, I decided that my parents were [my thoughts from step 3, Column 4] _____

_____

14. and that marriage is (usually/sometimes) _____

_____.

15. I also decided that a husband is _____

_____

16. but he *should* be _____

_____

17. and a wife is _____

_____

18. but *should* be _____

_____.

19. I now feel that if I ever marry (or marry again) I will _____

_____.

20. It is also my belief that an ideal marriage is _____

_____.

E X E R C I S E 9 B　　　■　　　■　　　■　　　■　　　■

What Do I Believe?

Earlier in this chapter, I talked about how our belief systems can become so powerful that they screen out our actual experience. We need to know our beliefs, so that we can be aware of how they influence our behavior. The Self-Knowledge Inventory (Exercise 2A, page 24) and the exercise above reveal important information about what you believe, especially with regard to love, marriage, and sex.

I'm going to list the responses that elicited your beliefs by category, so you will be conscious of those beliefs in your relationships. Read over what you wrote; I think you may be surprised at how many entrenched "beliefs" you harbor. You may even want to write down your responses and refer to them when you get "stuck" with your dates or partners.

What I believe about marriage:
Exercise 2A (page 24): Responses 11, 12, 72, 78, 80, 84, 86, 107
Exercise 9A (above): 20

What I believe about love:
Exercise 2A: 57, 83, 105, 106, 108

What I believe about sex:
Exercise 2A: 4, 5, 24, 55, 56, 67, 73, 75

What I believe about women:
Exercise 2A: 28, 44, 63, 90, 92, 94
Exercise 9A: 17, 18

What I believe about men:
Exercise 2A: 23, 37, 39, 59, 90, 94, 106
Exercise 9A: 15, 16

What I believe about families:
Exercise 2A: 42, 43, 62, 70, 87
Exercise 9A: 13

10

Recovering the Missing Self: Love's Agenda

She likes herself, yet others hate,
For that in herself she prizes;
And while she laughs at them, forgets
She is the thing that she despises.
—WILLIAM CONGREVE

What happens to the parts of us that are buried or distorted by the socialization process? Where does the blocked energy go, the parts of us that are unacceptable, suppressed, ridiculed, or unacknowledged? The fugitive self goes underground, as we will see, only to resurface in our Imago partners and in the conflicts we have with them.

THE HIDDEN SELF

All of us have a "secret life"—things that we do, or believe—that we keep to ourselves. As children we learned to talk with our imaginary playmate only when we were alone, because Mom and Dad thought it was babyish. We'd be in trouble if we got caught playing doctor, so we did it when Mom wasn't paying attention.

157

Dancing was for sissies, so we only danced alone in our room. Unless we were too guilt-ridden, threats and propaganda didn't keep us from masturbating—and hopefully enjoying it. In these instances, we overruled society's demands (perhaps in spite of guilt or shame). If we were lucky, we learned that our own standards could deviate from those of the collective. We had enough perspective to see what we wanted, and needed, to preserve our wholeness. We just went underground with these unacceptable parts of ourselves, consciously privatizing them.

The high-school basketball star writes his poems in secret, fearing that his teammates would tease him without mercy. But he allows a part of himself to emerge that he needs to survive. A young woman counts the days until she can leave her stifling home environment, knowing that there is another world in which her "weirdness" will be accepted.

As adults, on our own, we still carefully protect our private lives, keeping secret even from friends our quirky eating habits, our twice-weekly showers, our meditation practice, our attraction to the mailman. This is the *Hidden Self*, consciously suppressed in the service of living acceptably in the world: we know about it, but others don't, and we're not telling. But we yearn to have someone in our lives who will accept these hidden parts of ourselves.

THE LOST SELF

Other parts of us are hidden not only from others, but from ourselves. So strong is their prohibition, so completely have we taken to heart the messages that have been drummed into us, so uncomfortable or painful has it been to be ourselves, that we lose awareness of certain aspects of who we are, forgetting they ever existed. If you look back at the "Four Functions" diagram (Figure B, page 141), you can probably figure out where your energies, talents, and interests were restrained and criticized.

Our imaginary playmate is lost to memory. We were discouraged from learning carpentry, or writing stories, or wearing the odd costumes we came up with. We forget we loved to dance to songs we made up, because we were ignored or laughed at. In my own case, I recall that in the ninth grade I wanted to sing and play the trumpet. But the school music teacher assured me that I couldn't sing, and should stick to talking, "which you are good at." I never tried to sing again except in church. One day when I was bellowing out next to a friend who is a musician, she said, to my astonishment: "You have a beautiful voice. Have you ever taken lessons?"

We forget how good it felt to touch our genitals as we went off to sleep, or that we dreamed of climbing mountains in faraway lands. We buried our belly laugh, lowered our eyes, and became convinced that girls didn't like boys who looked like us. What our parents used to tell us, we now tell ourselves, and believe it wholeheartedly: dancers *are* sissies; I *won't* have friends if I show my anger; I *am* too fat; people *don't* like me because I'm an egghead. We don't remember the time when what we now reject was part of ourselves, and it was OK. These repressed and prohibited parts of ourselves are the *Lost Self*. While on some level we remain aware of our suppressed and inhibited Hidden Self, our Lost Self is out of sight *and* out of mind.

There is another component of the Lost Self that I want to mention. Chapter 9 discussed the gender biases of our socialization. Given the prohibitions men and women are given about how they are supposed to look and talk and act, it is inevitable that part of the fugitive self is our culturally unacceptable gender energies and interests. Thus for men part of the Lost Self may be such feelings as tenderness, or an interest in baking or decorating; a woman's fierce competitiveness and her love of adventure may have been sacrificed to propriety, and are now lost to memory. This part of the Lost Self, which I call the *Contrasexual Self*, will be discussed at length in Chapter 11.

THE DENIED SELF

There is another split-off part of ourselves that we are unaware of but *others* know all about. These are the traits that we possess but deny having. Sometimes they are traits that many people would consider acceptable, or even laudable—if you were a member of the opposite sex. A girl, for example, may sincerely deny that she's a "brain" and may affect the persona of an "airhead," when in fact her analytical mind is apparent to those who know her. Gender-defined traits that we disown as unacceptable, but others see in us, are also part of the *Contrasexual Self* discussed in Chapter 11.

But it's usually negative traits too painful to acknowledge that we deny having. Some of our denied traits are introjected aspects of our parents that we particularly despise—their anger or pettiness or petulance. To admit to them is to recognize that we are like our parents.

Often our denied negative traits are compensatory. They are adaptations we made to our childhood environment that have survival value in that they replace traits that our parents and society considered unacceptable. A little girl who has been taught that sex is dirty later decides that celibacy is the answer or becomes frigid. A tough, combative exterior covers the tender spots of a boy whose crying was jeered at or punished.

But these adaptations get us into trouble. Our youthful sexuality may have been too threatening to live with, but the frigidity that replaced it causes tremendous conflict in our relationships. The tough-guy exterior that seemed so protective keeps us from forming close friendships. The stinginess that enabled us to hoard the meager scraps of love that were thrown our way is criticized by our coworkers.

This confounds us, because we need our compensatory adaptations to cover our wounds, yet we want to hold on to our good self-image. Our only defense is to deny the accusations. "How can you say I'm frigid? What are you, some kind of sex fiend?" "I'm just frugal; if I left it up to you, we wouldn't save a penny." This is our *Denied Self*, the parts of ourselves that those around us are all too aware of, but that we refuse to acknowledge.

THE FALSE SELF: FILLING IN THE GAPS

All of the disowned pieces—the Hidden Self and the Lost Self and Denied Self with their Contrasexual Self aspects—together form what I call the *Missing Self*, which is often referred to as the Shadow.

But now major pieces of our original selves are missing in action, and there is a void that must be filled to replace our Missing Self. How do we compensate for being so fragmented and incomplete? Of necessity, we construct a new, substitute self that is more in alignment with the wishes of society, a public persona that will get us the love and work and approval that we need in order to survive and that rechannels our energy in approved directions. We compensate for our inability to think by exaggerating our feelings, and everyone seems to love our enthusiasm and our giddiness. We cover our stinginess by loaning money to friends and bragging about our generosity. A chronic smile and rigid body replace the natural body aliveness of the child who was told not to show her anger or run in the house. The child whose spiritual longings were thwarted becomes a theologian, so he can think and write about and analyze what he is unable to feel and experience directly. This is our *False Self*, the part that papers over, or compensates for, that which we gave up. The False Self preserves the illusion of wholeness.

IS ANYBODY HOME?

So what's left of us? We have whatever parts of our original, unique nature were nurtured and accepted. But most of what we're left with is a facade, made up of our False Self and, like it or not, the Denied Self, which we would rather not acknowledge. Together they comprise our *Social Self*, the grab bag of traits that we present to the world. But much of our true self is lost, fragmented, and split off, swept under the lumpy rug of conformity to the social order.

MUTILATED, BUT ALIVE

Socialization, then, is essentially a process of mutilation, of chipping away at our wholeness, masking or getting rid of what's undesirable and what doesn't fit, then adding on whatever is needed to patch over the gaps left by the jettisoned parts. In the process, we lose contact with the exquisite pleasure of our own pulsating life energy, which our old brain interprets as dangerous. Restricted, warned, admonished, rejected, punished for being ourselves—our essential unity is shattered, our generic spirituality evaporated. Our life energy itself, what the Greeks called *eros*, is menacing and fearsome. Fearing our essential aliveness, we become stick figures, unrecognizable shadows of our unique and joyful selves. What's left is a cobbled-up hodgepodge of defenses and adaptations, interspersed with what remains of our true selves. We may no longer remember who we are and may have to keep forbidden aspects of ourselves under wraps, but we have found a way to be allowed to live in the garden. Depressed, lonely, mute, anxious, blunted, angry, alienated, antisocial, rebellious, sociopathic, psychopathic—but alive.

Which brings us back to our innate human yearning. Our search for wholeness is compulsive and nonnegotiable. We are hooked on life and will do whatever is necessary to feel fully alive. As I've noted, in our culture we generally purchase our aliveness in the form of goods that represent love or sex or success, from toothpaste and fine wine to Porsches and prostitutes. Our repressions are assuaged with orgies of sex and eating, jogging and laser tag, violent sports and films, wheeling and dealing, and trying to get the best of Byzantine video games. Our deadness is temporarily overcome with drugs and other transient stimulants. We become addicted to anything that stirs our inner life force: work, religion, people, exercise, even love itself—whatever numbs our pain or stimulates our senses, at whatever cost. It is our peculiar way of searching for the holy grail, the modern but misguided equivalent of crusades and jousting, fierce monsters and life-threatening deeds. The grail is never found on the journey, and the art of the deal never assuages our longing. Eventually we must come home again, to ourselves. All of our yearning is connected to our Missing Self, and it is not "out there." If we are lucky, though, we meet someone who brings us alive, someone who makes us feel that the journey is over. We fall in love—with our Missing Self.

Falling in Love: What's Lost Is Found

When we fall in love we feel whole again, for in our beloved we annex the qualities dormant and missing in ourselves. In love, our inner drive for wholeness breaks down the wall of the social prison in which we live. Rescued from our torpor, we vibrate with aliveness. Basking in the glow of our all-accepting lover, we become witty where once we were dull; our benumbed body opens to sexual pleasure; our monochromatic world shimmers in full-spectrum color.

We feel lucky to have been rescued from our apathy and sadness, from our anger and alienation. But it's not luck; there is method to this madness. What we have here is another piece of the Imago puzzle: *Just as partners are attracted to each other on the basis of their symmetrical wounding on the developmental scale, they are also attracted on the basis of their complementary adaptations to the socialization process.* Nature is up to her old tricks again, easing us into a relationship that has the potential to heal our wounds. With sly wisdom, it pairs you with an incompatible partner to create the chemistry for growth.

Think of the couples you know, and you'll uncover ample evidence of this unacknowledged collusion. Your cool-headed mathematician friend Nate has dated a series of emotional basket cases. A couple you know is in constant conflict about sex. She enjoys massages and everything that appeals to the senses, while he is embarrassed about showing affection and seems to recoil from being touched. A man I've worked with loves to kayak and climb mountains; he loves action and physical challenge of any kind. But his new fiancée is a couch potato who loves to knit and listen to music, and seems allergic to the outdoors.

Chances are that the people you are drawn to and admire possess qualities that you long for or that were dismissed and disdained in your home. If you get close to such people, you feel good about yourself, more complete, through the association. You never cry at the movies, perhaps, but you love to go with your friend who sobs through the sentimental scenes. You may love to laugh and dance, but find yourself drawn to dating partners with logical, buttoned-down minds.

To demonstrate how the subterranean self surfaces in the partner, I'm going to use the example of Earl and Christine, each of whom seems tailor-made to make up for what the other lacks. In my office, Earl sits straight up in his chair in his three-piece suit and regimental tie, hair clipped, nails buffed, looking the perfect picture of the business executive. Christine slouches a bit, knees crossed, in a casual, sleeveless summer dress, running her fingers through a loose tangle of dark curls. They met at the Christmas party of friends. Earl recalls falling in love at first sight with Christine's bohemian look, her long, wild hair, and her rambunctious laugh. He asked her to dance, and felt lifted into a world of sensual delight. Christine recalls being enthralled with Earl's intellect, his knowledge of philosophy and history, his sense of command. She "could have listened to him talk for hours."

What did Earl want from Christine? Her ease with her body, her open sexuality, her crazy laugh, her *feelings*. And he got all of that. But what did Christine see in Earl? Disorganized and indecisive, she was attracted to Earl's "take charge" attitude, to the efficient way he takes care of business, his sure opinions—his *thinking*. And she wasn't disappointed. If we look again at our diagram (Figure D), we find that Earl and Christine, in finding in each other what is lacking in themselves, have created a unit with open boundaries that allows them to express aliveness in all areas.

So why are they here in my office, even before they get married? It seems that they got more than they bargained for. Earl is complaining that Christine thinks about nothing but sex, and her "outbursts" of enthusiasm over every little thing are driving him up the wall. Christine says that the slow, plodding way that Earl approaches every task makes her want to scream, and she's tired of hearing his opinions spouted as gospel truth. "Every man I meet," complained Christine, "turns out to be a bore, a computer with no feelings." To which Earl countered, "And you seem to have many sisters who do nothing but wallow in their feelings and make demands, all of which I seem to have met."

What they once adored about each other is now the source of their complaints. And what they want from each other they are least capable of giving, until they grow and change. Unless they come to grips with what is really going on, they may not make it to the altar.

FIGURE D

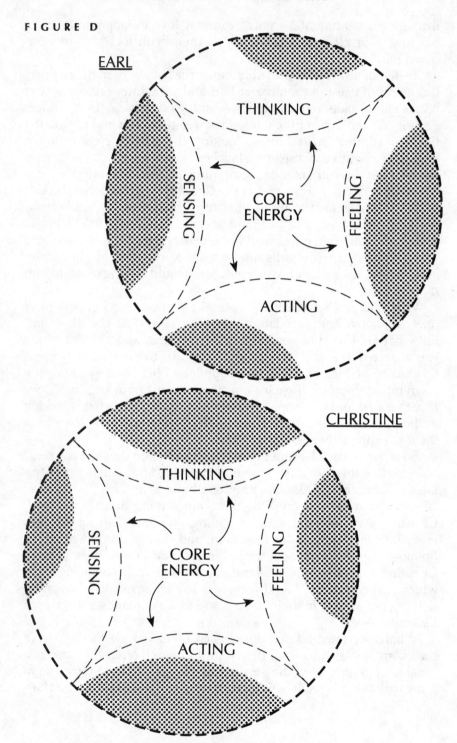

AWAKENING THE SLEEPING BEAST

What is going on here? Well, merely falling in love with someone who makes up for what is missing in us is no miracle cure. For in recapturing our lost traits, we are awakening a sleeping beast: the part of ourselves that we were told—and unconsciously believe—is dangerous to have. What you love in your partner is what you buried in yourself in order to survive. What first attracted you, and momentarily liberated you, will eventually stir up what has been forbidden, causing you to squirm in discomfort. Christine's sexuality awakens Earl's repressed sexuality; Earl's probing mind awakens Christina's dormant intellect. Remember, that blockage was not arbitrary; it was done with a purpose, and with a specific cautionary message from society via your parents, which you have taken to heart. Your old brain reacts with alarm, telling you that it is dangerous to have these forbidden needs met, and your partner is pushing you beyond the brink of safety. You lash out at your partner, in order not to have to wrestle with your own sleeping beast.

Such is the nature of relationships that our discomfort grows as the stakes get higher. A commitment of any kind, be it a decision to see each other exclusively, moving in together, an engagement, or a marriage—sends the old brain into panic. For commitment makes demands on the parts of the self that have been blocked. Fear of facing the Lost Self, that remnant of our original core, explains why many couples break up when problems start to surface. As long as the relationship remains casual, things may go along fine.

But intensity intensifies anxiety. The usual explanations for a couple's breakup—fear of commitment, sexual incompatibility—are often masks for the deeper underlying tensions: the terror of giving up the safety of the acceptable, if limited, False Self. This awakened terror explains why many couples have their first serious fight within forty-eight hours of their engagement. It is also the source of honeymoon blues—when suddenly the buried frigidity, the rigidity, the hysteria, the dogmatism, and the passivity that have served us so well up to now show up among the palm trees and in the honeymoon suite.

Ellen and Jack concurred that something pivotal happened in the store where they were buying the engagement ring. Ellen had pushed for commitment, but suddenly felt panic, covering it with anger when Jack made a facetious comment about the cost of the ring. Suddenly she saw Jack as stingy, rigid, and emotionally insensitive, traits similar to aspects of her father which she had blinded herself to in Jack. Jack, who had been enamored of Ellen's easy ways, suddenly saw her as demanding and picky, reminiscent of his mother. They completed their purchase and left the store in stony silence to mask the trauma of their new awareness. What had happened? The scales had fallen from their eyes; their collusion in serving as each other's Missing Self had ended, and they were in shock. They are getting a peek at the work they must do for their mutual wholeness.

OWNING THE MISSING SELF

Understanding the nature of your Missing Self can not only predict the kind of partner you will attract; it foreshadows as well some of the problems you will face. For while we choose partners who possess the positive traits that we have buried, we also pick partners with our disowned negative traits. Remember that the Denied Self is not really a part of our original core nature, but an internalization of our identification with traits in our caretakers that are in such conflict with our self-image that we cannot admit to them. The Denied Self represents the discrepancy between how we need to think of ourselves and how we actually are—a reality gap that psychologists refer to as *ego-dystonic*. Since we can't live with a bad image of ourselves, we project our inadmissible negative traits onto our partner.

The awful truth is that what is most intolerable to you about your mate is at least partially your recognition in your partner of what you cannot bear to recognize in yourself. The degree of emotional reaction to a trait in someone else is the degree to which that trait exists in you, whether the trait is viewed as negative or positive. Ellen, in the instance cited above, had met her denied stinginess in Jack, and he was confronted with his hidden anger in Ellen. When the blinders came off, it was almost too much to bear. It is safe to say that if you can't stand your partner's laziness, your appearance of great activity is a cover for sloth. Your anger at your partner's vindictiveness masks your own, however much of a nice guy you seem to be.

Your Denied Self may rear its head in the course of daily life, or it may show up in dreams. A clergyman client dreamed of a political figure who he perceived as cold, ruthless, and manipulative. When confronted with the projective interpretation of dreams, he vigorously rejected the thought that he could be that way. "After all, I am a man of God," he protested, "I think I have a good heart." The next week he brought a dream of another political personality who he disrespected even more. When I heard the dream, I humorously told him he should have listened to his first dream. Since he hadn't, his unconscious was sending him an even stronger message about the part of him he was denying.

Clearly shaken by the dream and the interpretation, he began an earnest self-exploration. In a therapy group, he asked the members to give him honest feedback about whether they had seen such traits in him. Since the group was charged with telling the truth, they pointed out several instances when they had seen him try to manipulate the group in a cold and insensitive way.

Whether we admit it or not, our intimate others—partners, colleagues, and children—know about the traits that we deny to ourselves. They are the "mirrors" in which we can see hidden aspects of ourselves. In Chapter 13 we will see how the projection of our disowned traits onto our partner becomes the core of the power struggle in our relationships, setting the stage for the reenactment of our childhood behavior with our caretakers.

FACING THE TRUTH

Intimate commitments force us to own what we deny in ourselves; we cannot indefinitely mask the undesirable traits we are able to camouflage in public. Like it or not, these qualities are part of the Missing Self, and in order to be whole, we *must* own them, and integrate them. Our wholeness—our total self—includes the shadow. In my own case, I once had no patience with anyone who was depressed and sad. Yet I kept putting sad, melancholy people in my life. In one of my own therapy sessions, as I was talking about my life in general, my therapist shocked me by asking how long I had been depressed. After several weeks of denying my depression, and even considering leaving the therapist because of his off-the-wall diagnosis, I decided to explore his theory so that I could prove him wrong.

In talking about my childhood, it became clear that I had not grieved the loss of my mother when I was young. Other people's depression and sadness stirred those feelings in me, feelings too painful to let into my awareness. But I had consistently brought into my life people whose depression functioned as a mirror to my own, so that *I* didn't have to admit it in myself; then I would get rid of those people to destroy the reflection.

In the course of exploring my childhood memories, the depression surfaced as enormous sadness. Allowing myself to grieve my mother's death after twenty-seven years, the hidden depression lifted, and I felt more alive than ever. The feeling side of me was restored.

Putting Ourselves Back Together

The conflicts you will have with your partner are externalizations of the conflicts going on inside you. Whatever you either idealize or despise in your partner is likely to be true, to some degree, about you. To one degree or another, your partner embodies the denied negative traits you can't live with in yourself, and the positive traits of the Lost Self you can't live without. In other words, there's actually a self-betrayal going on—in projecting your own buried qualities onto another, and then treating them accordingly, you are denying yourself. This is what is going on when we worship movie stars: we idealize them for qualities that we have repressed, essentially disowning ourselves in the process and remaining partial selves who live vicariously through others. When we admire Mother Teresa, or are attached to the fortunes of a sports hero, what often attracts is the part of ourselves that is missing, that we were not allowed to express.

How do we break this impasse? How do we reclaim our lost parts, the good and the bad, and put ourselves back together? We come back to the same answer: through the long, demanding work of a conscious relationship with an Imago partner. What appears to be nature's dirty trick is actually benevolent: there is a beautiful symmetry to the healing process, as there is to our wounding.

They say that breaking up is hard to do, but that is wrong. It's easy to walk away before the going gets tough, to find another dreamboat—until the ship starts to sink again. It's *waking up* that's hard to do.

THE BIG PICTURE

We have just spent a great deal of time looking at the complex issues of our nurturing and socialization. Understanding how the process of unhealthy parenting works can be confusing. Before we go on to a series of exercises that will help you identify your socialized self, take a look at Figure E, which pulls together the interacting cycle of nurturing and socialization deficits from birth to about the age of nineteen. It graphically illustrates the progression of losses and repressions that lead to the fears and adaptations that arise at each stage.

FIGURE E
Effects of Nurturing Deficits and Social Repression

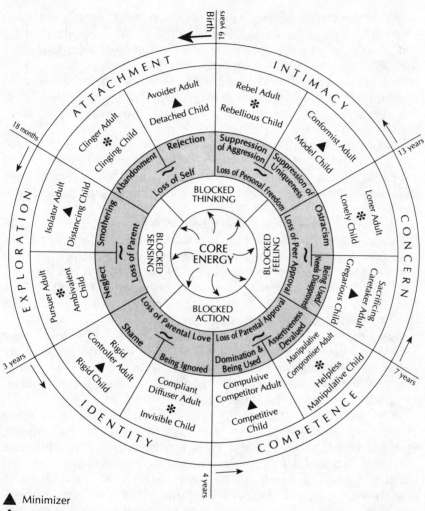

▲ Minimizer

✳ Maximizer

Shaded area indicates "THE WOUND"

~ FEARS

E X E R C I S E   1 0 A   ■   ■   ■   ■   ■

Your Hidden Self

Allow yourself a relaxed, uninterrupted hour for this exercise. Close your eyes, take a few deep breaths. Think about those traits and aspects of yourself that you keep hidden from others, images that don't fit your public persona or that would embarrass you if others knew about them. Some of these traits may be acceptable to you, but you feel they would be criticized or rejected by others. Ask yourself: "What would people think if they knew . . . " Here are some examples: " . . . that I cry in movies." "I have a cache of hard-core pornography magazines." "I write love poems." "I have a crush on the teller at the bank." "I cheated on my boyfriend." "I masturbate a lot." "I'm cheap about buying gifts." "I return clothes that I've worn to the store." "I often eat dinner straight out of a can."

Now ask yourself the same question with particular regard to the opposite sex. What would they think, or do, if they knew, for example, that "I have mystical experiences," "I believe in UFO phenomena," "I sleep in the nude," "I steal from the supermarket," "I dream about being famous," "sometimes I don't change my sheets for weeks?" As the images come, write them down quickly in whatever order they appear.

On a blank sheet of paper, draw a diagram like the one on page 171. Write each of your Hidden Self traits into the appropriate sector of the circle, and add anything else that comes to mind as you do this. Any items that do not fit into one of the categories should be entered in the inner circle.

Now you have a picture of your Hidden Self. To keep these aspects under wraps requires energy and vigilance that deplete your life force. Some of these traits are aspects of your authentic core self that need to be integrated into your self-concept and perhaps into your interpersonal relationships. You may have to actively overcome your fear of letting others know you write poetry or cry in movies, or you may have to seek out an environment in which such things are acceptable. Other parts may be compensations for aspects of yourself that you had to repress. For instance, pornography may be a substitute for loneliness or sexual deprivation. When such is the case, real needs must be identified and met, again in the service of your wholeness. You may find in your future relationships that you can share these hidden traits with a partner, and that s/he can assist you in dealing with them appropriately.

FIGURE F

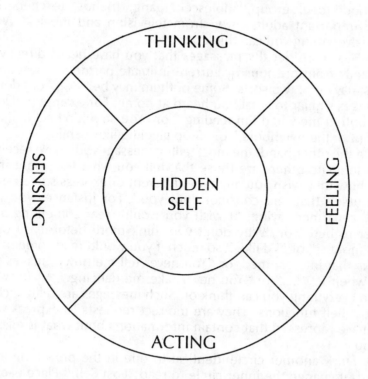

EXERCISE 10B   ■   ■   ■   ■   ■   ■

Your Lost Self

To retrieve the data for this exercise, we must use an indirect method, because the information is not in your conscious mind. Again, you need an hour of privacy and relaxation. You may have to repeat this exercise to retrieve all the relevant data.

1. While in the relaxed state, allow yourself to recall childhood memories in which your parents gave you "don't" or "shouldn't" or "stop" messages about your body, thoughts, feelings, and behaviors, and about your "self." For instance, your caretakers may have said, "Don't touch yourself 'there,' " or "Stop running," or "Don't sing at the table," or "Big boys don't cry," or "You shouldn't think that," or "We don't do that in our family," or "You are bad." In addition, you have picked up unspoken messages such as "You are a bother," or "You don't belong here," or "You're too smart for your own good," or "Nobody likes you when you're sad," or "You

should not exist." Other messages may have come from your childhood peer group, adolescent gang, friends, teachers and other important adults, even from television and movies. Write down everything you can think of.

2. Next consider the messages that you have heard directly or indirectly from previous or current intimate partners. These messages may be of two sorts. Some of them may be "stop" or "don't" messages similar to what you heard at home. For example: "Don't ever bother me when I'm reading," or "You shouldn't act like that in front of the neighbors," or "Stop giggling like a child."

On the other hand, the most telling messages you have received from intimate others are those that tell you what they want from you, how they wish you might be different or express some aspect of yourself that you consider "not you." For instance, you may recall a partner saying, "I wish you would wear something a bit sexier to bed," or "Why don't you think more before you open your mouth?" or "I'd like it so much if you would read some of the books that interest me," or "You never tell me how it makes you feel when I . . . ," or "You never take me dancing." Again, write down everything you can think of. Such messages are telltale clues to Lost Self functions. They are indirect requests to express what you have repressed that contain information about what is missing in you.

3. Draw another circle identical to one in the preceding exercise, but change the inner circle to read "Lost Self." Place each of the messages in one of the four categories. Put the ones that apply to your core energy, such as the "don't exist" messages, in the center circle. As you record them, others may come to mind about specific functions as you focus on that part of you. Be sure to include them.

Now you have an impression of your Lost Self. The categories that contain few messages suggest that you did not have to repress that function. The categories to which most of the messages apply identify parts of your authentic self that are missing. In your drive to wholeness, you will gravitate toward partners who did not have to repress the same functions you were asked to repress. Later in the relationship, however, you will tend to criticize those "alive" parts in your partner that are "dead" in you. You will need to develop the repressed functions to become a whole, separate person, so as not to require your partner to "carry" your missing pieces. Your partner will, no doubt, prod you to develop those missing parts by criticizing you for not having them. I am certain you have already heard some of the complaints.

EXERCISE 10C   ▪   ▪   ▪   ▪   ▪

Your Denied Self

Now you are going to look at that part of yourself that you have a hard time accepting, your Denied Self.

1. On a blank sheet of paper, draw a large circle and divide it in half horizontally. Mark the top of the circle with a plus sign and the bottom with a minus sign. Using adjectives to describe yourself, list your positive traits in the top of the circle, and the negative traits you see in yourself on the bottom. Do this thoughtfully and thoroughly.

2. Draw the circle diagram as above on five or more additional sheets of blank paper. Ask at least five people you know, including at least two with whom you've had an intimate relationship (i.e., an ex-lover or -partner) to describe you, using the same method as above.

3. When you collect all the responses, *underline* each description, whether positive or negative, that is identical or similar to an adjective you used to describe yourself. *Circle* the positive and negative ones that were *not* on your list.

4. Draw another circle identical to the ones above, but divide this circle vertically as well, so that it is quartered. Transfer the positive *underlined* adjectives *that were mentioned more than once* to the top left quarter of the circle and write next to each one the number of times it was mentioned. Transfer the underlined negatives that were mentioned more than once to the bottom left quarter of the circle. Transfer the positive *circled* adjectives that were mentioned more than once to the top right quadrant of the circle in the same manner, and the negative circled adjectives that were repeated to the lower right quadrant.

5. Write "Traits Known by Me and Others" on the left side of the circle. Label the right side "Traits Unknown by Me But Known by Others." The adjectives in the right half of the circle describe your Denied Self. Although people who know you well see the positive qualities, you may be embarrassed or fearful of owning them. For instance, you may downplay your sharp mind if your parents thought that "women should be seen and not heard" or if you unconsciously believe that "men seldom make passes at girls who wear glasses." Or you may still downplay the artistic nature that your teenage friends thought was wimpy. The most troublesome part of your Denied Self, however, is the negative qualities that you disown but that you are likely to project onto others. You

may have experienced these aspects of yourself in times of stress or crisis and thought, "That's not like me." You may have suddenly exploded with anger and then thought, "I don't know what came over me."

Now you have a rather complete picture of your Missing Self. In Chapter 11 you will examine your Contrasexual Self more closely, and in Chapter 15 you will find exercises to assist you in integrating all these disowned aspects. All your fugitive traits must be owned and integrated, and some must be changed, for you to become whole. In a relationship with an intimate other, any unintegrated self parts will tend to be projected upon your partner and may result in destructive conflict. You will have a more constructive relationship with this knowledge available to your conscious mind, and it will not be the source of conflict between you and your partner. Too, your future partner can assist you in changes you want to make in the service of becoming whole.

11

Gender and Sexuality: Making Love, Not War

Why can't a woman be more like a man?
—PROFESSOR HIGGINS, in *Pygmalion*

One of the most troublesome ingredients of relationship conflicts is so glaringly obvious that it is often overlooked: *your partner is a member of the opposite sex.* No kidding, you're saying, I didn't need to buy this book to figure that out. But the biological and culturally maintained differences between men and women are a core source of conflict for most couples, particularly because those differences—some of which are changeable and some not—are often ignored as they search for the root of their predicament. Part of your mission as a single is to understand those differences and, beyond that, to *transcend* them. (NOTE: I want to mention that while this chapter is addressed quite specifically to heterosexual couples, the same push/pull of gender roles and energies—and thus similar conflict—operates in homosexual couples as well.)

When we socialize children to be "men" and "women," what we end up with is the "battle of the sexes." Relations between men and women in our society have indeed become so polarized, so dominated by anger and mistrust, that they often resemble war. As in

175

most wars, no one truly wins. All men and women locked in this no-win conflict lose the individual wholeness that is attainable only when we integrate our innate male and female energies. As a single, in particular, you forfeit the freedom to be yourself in the mating game: you are pressured to conform to societal ideas about how to present yourself as "a man" or "a woman" if you hope to attract dating partners. Which means that right from the start, your relationships get off on the wrong foot.

Is there a way out of the gender wars, given the long-standing history of misunderstanding between the sexes? Men and women are at odds because they literally don't understand each other. Misconstrued interpretations and miscommunication are often behind the confusion, judgment, and hurt that characterize so many male/female relationships today. Resolution, therefore, requires first becoming aware of how men and women differ biologically and psychologically, and then seeing how these differences are culturally magnified and distorted. Only through awareness of our gender heritage can we understand how conflicts arise and learn how to resolve them with acceptance and empathy rather than blame. Only when we understand and value the energies and sensibilities of the opposite sex can we open up to our own contrasexual energies, aspects of our Lost and Denied Selves that we have sacrificed in the cause of socialization. Only then can we be balanced and whole.

Let me clarify my terms. I want to make it clear that "masculinity" and "femininity" do not refer to gender but describe particular traits and energies. Biologically, all embryos start out as females, and remain so until about the sixth week of development, when the existence of a Y chromosome in the genetic coding initiates the development of "maleness" characteristics in those embryos destined to become males. Thus, men have a transsexual change early in life! (Biological reality also contradicts the biblical dictum that woman was created from the rib of man, which has been a rationale for the subordination of women.) The essence of the human being is a polarity of male and female: the original unity of the self is biophysiological. When we begin to dissolve the barriers between our male and female energies, we are getting back to where we began, to our wholeness, and the relaxed joyfulness we started out with.

After the sixth week male and female embryonic development diverge in the ways we have previously noted. But it is in the socialization process that the repression of contrasexual energy— what Carl Jung calls the "animus" in females and the "anima" in males—takes place. And it is this culturally unacceptable energy that splits off to become part of the Lost and Denied Selves. Thus, our conflict with the opposite sex is also a conflict with our own denied masculine and feminine side.

Ironically, we are attracted to the contrasexual energies of our partners *because* we have not developed them in ourselves, yet their very "foreignness" breeds anxiety, suspicion, and conflict. As long as we continue to deny and repress our contrasexual energy, we will continue to seek wholeness through the other who embodies what we disparage. Jung calls this "projecting the opposite"; women project *animus*, their denied masculine energies, onto the men in their lives; men project their denied feminine sensibilities, or *anima*. We expect our opposite-sex partners to heal the emptiness created by the repression of our contrasexual energy, counting on them to fill in for the split-off part of ourselves and to carry the load for the energies that are missing in ourselves.

Unfortunately, we expect too much. Our partners are bound to disappoint us, as we are them. If we want to regain our original wholeness we must awaken and integrate our rusty gender-opposite energy. We must look to our partners not to make up for our Missing Selves, but to help us to jog our memories, to refamiliarize us with our buried aspects, to reclaim what we gave up. When men recognize and develop the split-off female energies in themselves, and women allow their masculine side to emerge, they no longer need to get what is missing in themselves from their partners, and they no longer see each other as the enemy. Conflicts with the opposite sex dissolve to the degree that partners can integrate in themselves their dormant polar aspects.

"ALL YOU DO IS COMPLAIN"

The list of complaints that women have about men, and men about women, are seemingly endless, the fodder for countless books and articles, TV sitcoms, sociological studies, and therapy sessions. "What's wrong" with the opposite sex is the lingua franca of the locker room and the beauty parlor.

Women accuse men of a number of perceived failings: they don't listen, they don't communicate, they won't express their feelings, they don't do their fair share, they are condescending, domineering, and all they care about is looks. What's more, they are sexually demanding, sloppy, unreliable, and insensitive.

It is not surprising that many of the most common gripes that men have about women are the flip side of women's complaints about men: women are too emotional, they talk too much, they're sexually unresponsive, too demanding, too sensitive, and overly concerned with their appearance.[1]

Most of you have probably heard these same or similar criticisms. As a therapist, I hear them repeated in one form or another, countless times, with escalating anger and blame as time goes on and "nothing changes." The bottom line seems to be: Why can't a man be more like a woman? Why can't a woman be more like a man? And implicit in these questions is the value judgment: women are "better" than men, or men are "superior" to women. The battle lines are drawn.

The perceived inequity in value attributed to masculinity or femininity in our culture exacerbates the polarization. In a patriarchal society such as ours has been for most of recent history, male energy is dominant and prized, while there is a coincident devaluation of the feminine. The subordination of women has led to a limited and distorted view of *all* humanity. Our culture prizes reason over intuition, competition over cooperation, the workplace over the home front, etc. Because it has been mostly men who have studied and defined human development and behavior, male biology and male psychology were until recently considered the "norm" by which human development and behavior was measured. Females were often found lacking by default—their development "abnormal," their behavior "deviant"—when judged by these standards. Thus stoicism is "good," while showing emotion is "bad." Autonomy is "strong," dependency "weak." Pragmatism is superior to intuition. Recent feminist scholarship has rightly debunked these truisms, not by emphasizing the *sameness* of the sexes, but by identifying those *differences* between males and females that make the male "norm" inapplicable to females, and by challenging the mind-set by which women are judged.

RUMBLING IN THE PSYCHE: THE EMERGING FEMININE

What *is* true is that the human psyche, male or female, is not static: it *evolves*. And what we are currently witnessing is the emergence of the feminine. This emergence parallels—and is a continuation of—the evolution of our society from monarchy to democracy, and the parallel emergence of the individual from the collective, which I spoke of in Chapter 2. Individual freedom, a relatively recent concept in our psychohistorical evolution, has in reality amounted to a freeing of the masculine only. The creation story of woman being fabricated from the rib of man reflects the patriarchal society from which it emerged; it is a social rather than biological reality. But the feminine has remained "embedded" in the masculine and is only now emerging in its own, separate but equal, right.

This emergence of the feminine has stirred up considerable alarm and discomfort, particularly on the part of role-embedded males. Women's dissatisfaction with the status quo has found an articulate and powerful voice in the women's movement, which has raised the level of anger and distrust (as well as the decibel level of the name-calling), and challenges the already shaky foundation on which male/female relationships have traditionally rested. Men are disoriented; they feel blamed for women's troubles, and they feel their power base threatened. No wonder they fight back. As the power struggle settles into an impasse, as the gap between men and women yawns into a seemingly unbreachable chasm, men and women retreat to their own corners.

While both sexes have a history of seeking support within single-sex groups—for example, women gathering in their kitchens and men gathering at the local pub after work—now the groups are more polarized and more politicized, more exclusionary. It's not surprising that the currently emerging men's movement, exemplified by the poet and workshop leader Robert Bly, focuses on helping men get in touch with the "warrior" or "wildman" in them, with their "deep masculinity."[2]

Meanwhile, women gather in groups to worship "the goddess," performing rituals that elevate feminine principles and sensibilities. Now we have *female* superiority, in which once-vaunted male traits—power, aggression, linear thinking—are denigrated, and women's nurturing, inclusive thinking and pacificity are revered. "If women ruled the world," the new thinking goes, "there would be no more war." I recently heard a woman politician say that women are *by nature* "cooperative" and "inclusive," while men are *by nature* "competitive" and "excluding." This is antagonistic, specious logic, and we've had enough of it. No rapprochement is possible when one faction is "good" and the other "bad." The genders are trading places these days, maintaining the polarity, when what is needed is synthesis. Although men and women are socialized to reflect a dominance of one over the other, all aspects are present in both sexes. Both sexes have the ability to be both cooperative and competitive if culture is not an intervening variable.

While "sisterhoods" and "brotherhoods" can provide positive and healthy nurturing and support, and while I sympathize with the need to seek succor from the gender wars, my concern is that same-sex settings not become forums for increased gender polarization. It seems to me we've got it backward. Perhaps it's time for women to celebrate the masculine in them, and men to take pride in their femininity!

Both the men's and women's movements need to imagine different roles for the future. The emergence of separate men's and women's movements is analogous to partners who go into individual therapy, rather than couple counseling. Both may evolve, but their growth occurs separately and often leads to further estrangement. If men and women continue on this course, I feel the polarization will increase. What is needed is dialogue, so that men and women can come to "know" each other as well as the recessive parts of themselves.

It is urgent that we *cooperate with the evolution of the psyche*, which in our time involves the emergence of the feminine, not only for social and political reasons, but because the process ultimately contributes to the wholeness of all human beings, male and female. When we resist what is after all an inevitable progression, we contribute to our own repression, our own stagnation.

Gender is an *ethical* issue as well. Inequality is unethical, and we human beings have an innate drive for equality that parallels the drive for individual freedom on which our country was founded. Our democratic government is no accident; it is a manifestation of the current status of our evolution toward equality. Since inequities are inconsistent with individual freedom, the drive for the equality of the feminine is a natural phenomenon. It is the human spirit expressing itself, the next step in the process by which the human psyche is evolving to a higher level of development—ultimately to a partnership of equals. We are all participants in this psychohistorical process, in which we are moving toward the integration of the masculine and feminine, societally and individually. Though we are in a difficult transitional phase these days, it is a process from which we, and our relationships, stand to gain tremendously.

Vive La Différence

So, why can't a woman be more like a man? Because men and women *are* in some significant and fundamental ways different from one another. Gender differences, be they a function of biology or culture or some combination of the two, are real and for all intents and purposes immutable. Whether they can change over time and in response to changes in environment or culture, or through direct efforts, will be discussed later. Suffice it to say at this point that most true gender differences, as opposed to roles and stereotypes, will persist without significant change for the life of a relationship. Therefore, they cannot be ignored. By identifying gender differences and accepting their equal validity, we can work with them rather than against them, and we can develop what is missing in ourselves, regardless of its gender "assignment."

Pointing out gender differences is not a popular thing to do in these times of struggle for equality. I feel somewhat like the fool rushing in where wise men fear to tread by adding my voice to those debating the differences between men and women and the causes and consequences of those differences. However, it is increasingly clear—to biologists, to social scientists studying the sexes, to therapists counseling them, and to men and women struggling to maintain loving relationships with each other—that men and women *are* inherently different in more than just their reproductive organs. The debate centers on the degree of difference, and the source of the difference—the old "nature or nurture" debate.

PHYSICAL DIFFERENCES

I want to enumerate some of the quantifiable differences between male and female, with the understanding that this oversimplification is meant merely as a basis for discussion. Some differences seem to be a matter of simple physiology: Males are on average 10 percent taller than females, have a significantly higher percentage of muscle, and more and coarser body hair. Females have more flexible joints, a significantly higher percentage (and differing distribution) of body fat, and a longer life span (although 60 percent of this life-span gap is the result of increased social risks for men).[3] Many of these purely physical differences—men's physical strength and women's childbearing capacity in particular—had a much more significant impact on sex roles and the division of labor before industrialization and birth control than they do, or should, have now. But other differences appear to significantly affect how males and females perceive, interact with, and function in the world.

DEVELOPMENTAL DIFFERENCES

Developmental differences in male and female children appear at early infancy and in every stage thereafter. Girl babies sit, crawl, walk, and talk, on the average, earlier than boys. There is some evidence that they are already more "sensitive"—to touch, to smell, to sounds. Girls show an early advantage in verbal skills that continues to blossom in adolescence, while boys exhibit early superiority in visual/spatial ability and by puberty outperform girls in math skills. Although our culture participates in emphasizing or de-emphasizing these differences—by what it expects, encourages, or teaches—they have been identified by too many studies to be ignored. "Remedial reading," for example, seems to be a response to the fact that boys learn to read more slowly; yet there is no "remedial math," probably because education is not considered as vital for girls.[4]

HORMONES AND THE BRAIN

Another crucial difference between males and females is hormonal: the presence of estrogen in women and the significantly higher level of testosterone in men. These hormones have an impact on health—estrogen protects the arteries, for example; testosterone strengthens muscles—and on brain development as well. Male and female brains develop differently and those differences are increasingly being linked with differences in perception and behavior. Brain function in men is more localized in the left hemisphere, which explains their lead in logic, reasoning, and rational thinking. Women's brains have a much thicker corpus callosum, the nerve cable connecting the left and right halves of the brain, so their skills are more evenly divided and they are better able to integrate left- and right-brain thinking.[5] Since right-brain functions include abstract thinking and communication skills, the open channel between the left and right sides of women's brains probably explains their enhanced ability to communicate; they are better at expressing their own feelings and intuiting those of others.

All of these biological differences, in combination with cultural reinforcement and stereotyping, result in divergent ways of perceiving and approaching the world.[6] And it is *these* differences—not those of strength, reproductive function, etc.—that play the most significant role in male/female relationships, even among children. Studies show that girls are from a very young age more attracted to people than objects (the reverse is true of boys), and that girls have a talent for reading others' nonverbal clues. Boys, probably due to their higher levels of testosterone, are more physically aggressive, and more goal oriented.[7]

One has only to watch children at play to see the disparities: Boys tend to play competitively, in large, hierarchically structured groups, and their games have winners and losers. Girls tend to play cooperatively, in small, intimate groups, and their games less frequently require a specific outcome. Even their speech patterns are notably dissimilar. Researchers studying preschoolers at play have observed that little boys more frequently speak in commands ("Do this," and "Get that"), little girls in suggestions or proposals ("Let's do this," and "Why don't we get that?").[8]

These marked differences in interaction and communication reflect the divergent way in which males and females approach the world. Men approach it, as linguist Deborah Tanner puts it, "as an individual in a hierarchical social order in which he is either one-up or one-down. In this world, conversations are negotiations in which people try to achieve and maintain the upper hand if they can, and protect themselves from others' attempts to put them down and push them around. Life, then, is a contest, a struggle to preserve independence and avoid failure." Women, on the other hand, approach the world "as an individual in a network of connections. In this world, conversations are negotiations for closeness in which people try to seek and give confirmation and support, and to reach consensus. They try to protect themselves from others' attempts to push them away. Life, then, is a community, a struggle to preserve intimacy and avoid isolation."[9]

These differences in perception and approach intrude themselves on a daily basis into relationships between men and women, in particular in the area of communication. In my experience, most men communicate to give or receive information or to resolve problems. For women, conversation is more often a means of interacting and expressing their feelings.

A typical case in point is a couple I'll call George and Andrea. George comes home from work and Andrea regales him with the details of her day: the washing machine broke, the laundry room flooded, little George has a fever. George responds by going into action: "I'll call the plumber" and "Why didn't you call the doctor?" Andrea explains that the plumber has already fixed the washing machine, and she's already talked to the doctor about little George. But she is hurt because what she is really asking for is a sympathetic ear, and his concern and support. To her, it is important to vent her frustrations and let George know what her day was like. George is exasperated because he can't understand why she bothered him with these problems if she'd already resolved them; to him, she is rambling on about nothing.

George then sits down as usual to read the paper. Andrea, feeling shut out, continues to try to engage him in conversation. She wants to connect with him, to feel that they are in this together, by conversing with him. George doesn't see the point of conversation for conversation's sake. He becomes frustrated by what he perceives as unnecessary "interruptions"; she's frustrated by what she perceives as a lack of intimacy. This conflict demonstrates what Joe Tanenbaum, in *Male & Female Realities*,[10] calls men's "exclusive" orientation (they are able to focus on only one thing at a time), while women have an "inclusive" orientation (and would not find reading the paper while responding to questions or comments from their partners so disorienting).

Is Culture the Culprit?

To what extent are gender differences genetic (nature) and to what extent are they created by the culture in which men and women are nurtured and socialized? Watching young children is a marvelous entrée into the mysterious origins of gender-specific behavior. Have you ever noticed the flirtatiousness, the downcast eyes, the love of dressing up exhibited by very young girls? The louder voice, the hands-in-pocket swagger, the determination to complete a task in even a very young boy? And this regardless of their home ambience? Have you ever been a fly on the wall at a little girls' tea party, complete with the adult body language, table manners, and the verbatim "adult" conversation? Biology clearly lays the foundation, but its influence is inextricably linked with that of our cultural context.

The human brain evolved within the context of a hunter/gatherer society, in which men and women performed roles requiring distinctly different skills. Gathering and preparing food, tanning hides and fashioning clothing, nurturing and educating children, women regularly utilized left- and right-brain functions, juggling more than one task at a time, tuning in to and facilitating the needs of others. Men hunted in a more exclusive, objective, goal-oriented world, where strength, aggression, strategy, and nonverbal skills were required.

The industrial revolution, when fathers for the first time left home to work in factories while mothers stayed at home, powerfully defined gender roles. The message children received was not only that the mother (woman) had near-total responsibility for raising them, but that the father (man) needed to separate himself from the family in order to fulfill his responsibilities.

It may well be that if men had always shared the organization of the community and the child-rearing responsibilities traditionally shouldered by women, the size of their corpus callosum would be similar to that of women, and they too would have more access to their right-brain functions. In other words, cultural patterns become encoded in our genes over time, just as our upright posture and our ever-diminishing body hair evolved in adaptation to circumstance. Eventually culture is expressed biologically, as competitiveness in men or cooperation in women.

As contemporary men become more actively involved in child rearing, as their nurturing instincts are awakened, and as women become more comfortable with authority, assertiveness, and strategizing, it is possible that—over centuries of evolution—the *genetic* capabilities and traits of men and women will become more similar. Even short-term studies have demonstrated that when little boys take care of their siblings, they develop lasting nurturing skills.[11] It is likely that culture influences biology as much as biology influences culture. The way I see it, the perceived differences that are usually attributed to biology are in fact the legacy of evolution and culture.

Wherever it might be that biology leaves off and culture takes over is a moot point, however. What is clear is that this is where the trouble begins, for biological differences are reinforced by socialization, to the extent in our culture that little boys learn to deny their "female" aspects and little girls their "male" energies. Studies show, for example, that little girls are encouraged to care about the problems of others and discouraged from expressing anger. Boys, on the other hand, are exhorted to be tough and independent, and discouraged from crying. We are no longer hunter/gatherers—*we just behave that way.*

Even the most conscious and liberated parents cannot eliminate cultural influences, as every parent knows who's ever tried to dissuade a daughter from her desire for a Barbie doll, or a son from his determination to have a toy gun. Young children have a strong need to define and identify themselves by roles they see played out all around them. And the unconscious, archetypal aspects of our innate gender inheritance are not to be denied.

Moreover, we cannot discount the impact of the fact that most of us have been raised primarily by women. Girls understandably stay connected to and continue to identify with their primary caretaker, while boys must eventually break from the female and become independent, separate. This male necessity for psychic separation from the mother perpetuates the division between men and women. Again, the long-range effect of the sharing of child rearing might be to temper the polarization of gender roles and to obviate the need for boys to reject the feminine.

Playing Our Roles, Losing Our Selves

Culturally determined sex roles and stereotypes (and the value assigned to them)—not biological differences—unquestionably have the most destructive influence on individual growth and the relations between the sexes. In actuality, gender develops along a continuum. When we speak of "masculine" men (*real* men) or "feminine" women (*real* women)—or, for that matter, "masculine" women and "feminine" men—we are talking about the degree to which they display characteristics our culture—through the agencies of parenting and propaganda—has assigned to one gender or the other. As any cursory survey will corroborate, there is a broad range of characteristics *of all kinds,* not only those designated gender specific, among the members of the same sex. The spectrum of gender-designated characteristics within members of the same sex is no wider (or narrower) than the range of, say, intelligence, or weight.

Rigid sex roles or sexual stereotypes are damaging to the individual because they reinforce the cultural maintenance of the Lost and Denied Selves. Slavish adherence to role expectations necessitates dropping from our repertoire any gender-incorrect emotions or behavior. Roles tell us how to behave, and which parts of ourselves to change or cover over if we want to attract someone of the opposite sex; they influence how we present ourselves. Over time, these societally dictated ideas about gender become part of our Imago; they color the image of our perfect mate, and impose limitations and expectations on our dates. Thus we look at prospective partners not only from our differing biological perspectives, but also through the lens of culture and culturally imposed stereotypes. Role-playing is destructive to both the individual and the relationship.

Because women in recent history have made great strides in breaking out of stereotyped roles, they do not so strongly identify being "female" with specific roles or behavior. As women have moved into traditionally "male" roles and assumed "male" responsibilities, they have added male-designated skills to their own. Consequently they are generally more comfortable in a fluidly defined role, for they have learned that the role they play does not define who they are. (This is not to say that they are not subject to enormous cultural pressures, even disapproval, when they "step out," or that their role changes are without guilt or self-doubt.)

For men, this is not generally the case. Our patriarchal culture has so codified men's roles that many men have particular difficulty distinguishing their prescribed roles from "masculinity" itself. Men who are asked to step into what they view as a "female" role often feel emasculated and unsure of who they are. Because they are so identified with their role, they are more out of touch with their true selves, and so feel incomplete without the structure that the role imposes. In short, they suffer an identity crisis. Whereas women can give up changing diapers for running a business without feeling like they've lost their "woman-ness" (although, as I said before, not necessarily without disapproval or guilt), men think, "If I change this diaper I'm not a man."

As the feminine continues to emerge, the male identity crisis is bound to intensify. Men will be faced with the need to accept their female natures through having to accept the equality of those on whom they now project their recessive, denied female energy—women, their partners. It is a crisis that can lead to reintegration—or to disintegration and increased male-female antipathy.

The difference between the ability of men and women to function outside of their roles may have to do with the fact that women have been pushed by social and economic forces into the "man's" world and have had to adjust. It may have to do with the fact that the "male" skills being developed by women are valued and desirable in our society, while the "female" skills being avoided by men (nurturing, expressing emotions) are not. Or it may have to do with the fact that women's roles have traditionally kept them subservient (so they *want* out), while men's roles have empowered them, and they have a vested interest in maintaining the status quo. Roles have enthroned men, and the power of their roles, rather than personal power, has acted as the enforcer. It's hard to give up the throne—even though it separates the powerful from the less powerful in ways that are at least as psychically destructive to those in power as it is to those over whom power is wielded.

Historically, men and women have "annexed" the contrasexual energy they needed to be whole, since in most Western cultures there were few models, and little approval, for those whose polar aspects were developed. The Don Juan and the femme fatale paired up, the domineering man and the submissive woman, the breadwinner and the homemaker. But because they were psychic strangers to each other, and because they were dependent on each other for what was missing in themselves, such symbiotic matches eventually led to conflict, alienation, and criticism for what the other lacked. There's a vast difference between a stable marriage in which the polarities somehow compensate for each other, and a union of two *whole* people in which neither one has to carry the undeveloped or unrecognized parts of the other, but carry their own complete nature and relate to each other from that experience of wholeness. Two whole people can empathize with each other's experience; the experience of a polarized, symbiotic couple is in continual conflict.

Owning Your Contrasexual Self: Swimming Against the Tide

If you hope to break this pattern, and to feel complete in and of yourself, you must own and accept your own Contrasexual Self. And you must stop looking at culturally defined pictures when scanning the world for a partner. But barring overnight changes in our culture and perhaps consequential changes in our biology, how are men and women—who sometimes seem like fundamentally different species, raised in seemingly disparate cultures—to live in peace? 1) By becoming aware of both the genetic differences and the cultural biases that separate male and female; 2) By honoring the equal value of masculine and feminine energies; 3) By developing their own contrasexual energies, so that they are not dependent on their partners to provide what is lacking in themselves.

YOUR PARTNER IS NOT YOU!

Accepting the "other" seems simple and harmless enough. However, my experience is that people have difficulty accepting differences in their partners without making value judgments about those differences. There is something *wrong* with the difference, something that needs to be *changed*. "You mean you don't like opera?" "You don't like oral sex?" "What do you mean, you never eat oysters?" "You think that's funny?" Even the simplest differences in tastes are disparaged, let alone more fundamental differences in temperament or point of view.

It is difficult to recognize that others live in their own idiosyncratic worlds as well and that their way of seeing things has its own integrity and legitimacy, whether we agree with it or not. This perceptual tunnel vision leads to the judging and blaming that undermine communication and intimacy. If you hope to succeed in your partnership, you must first and foremost accept one shocking reality: *your partner is not you.* He or she is an equally valid and worthy "other." And one of the main reasons your partner is not you—that he (or she) views and interprets and interacts with the world from a different but equal perspective—is purely and simply that he (or she) is a man (or a woman) and you are not.

On the surface, this seems so obvious that it sounds foolish. But the point is this: all of us have our own inner world, our idiosyncratic way of seeing things, our particular history, that makes us unique. Most of us, however, do not think much about this as it applies to others. We assume that others think the way we do. When they don't, we assume they're wrong. One young woman I know was thunderstruck to realize that her boyfriend's opinions often differed radically from hers. "I thought that when I figured something out," she told me in all sincerity, "that meant that everyone else saw it that way, too." But there is no such thing as "objectivity." We are all embedded in our perceptions, which are the function of our own experience and the beliefs arising out of that experience. We are all biased; the most we can have is "consensual validation." However, it is essential in a relationship to cross the chasm of separate experience. Men and women experience the world differently. To understand your partner, you must stretch to see and validate his or her point of view. You must accept your partner's logic as equal to yours.

When I made this point to Oliver, he was irate that I was questioning his observation that his girlfriend, Alexandra, was too emotional and overinvolved with her work. I validated the reality of his perceptions, but pointed out that they represented his unique vantage point; they were not only personal opinions but value judgments. They did not describe Alexandra's experience. Oliver was still irate, and went on to insist that Alexandra was frigid, because she only wanted sex twice a week, expounding his theory that women are too emotional, sexually repressed, prone to exaggeration, and unreliable. Over the course of several visits, he finally admitted that he was describing his experience with his mother and the attitudes he had grown up with, rather than his actual experience. It took months for him to truly accept that Alexandra was a different person from his mother, and himself, that she lived in a different body and mind, and that he must accept the parity of her reality if they were to make progress toward a conscious, equitable relationship.

This sort of exclusionary thinking is, of course, the basis not only for gender wars but for bigotry, nationalism, and the kind of religious fervor that leads to war. It is narrow-minded provincialism. Unable to transcend debilitating stereotypes, we blame each other for having the effrontery to be different. Out of fear of and discomfort with what is strange to us, we build barriers against intimacy.

The fact is, we are egocentric creatures, each locked in our own idiosyncratic world. The mind is self-referential; we see ourselves at the center of the universe. To recognize the equal worth of another is to give up our egocentricity, to *share* the center.

DIALOGUE IS ALL WE CAN HAVE

Befriending and learning from the opposite sex is a primary means of getting in touch with our contrasexual energy. As science and theology each has only partial access to the truth, so it is with men and women. Our relationships with the opposite sex serve thus as training grounds for self-discovery and growth, if we are open to our partner's otherness and to the different perspective he or she brings to the world we also inhabit. By exploring that otherness we not only add to the store of information that we can draw upon, like a computer, but we enrich ourselves. We expand our horizons. By befriending the opposite sex, we befriend our shadow side, for the otherness in them is a mirror of the unknown, undeveloped, and rejected aspects of ourselves.

The most powerful tool—perhaps the only real tool—we have to make that connection is dialogue. Through dialogue with the other who is different we gain access to a larger truth than we can access alone or through same-sex relationships. Dialogue says to the other: I respect your otherness, I want to learn from it, I want to teach you about mine. Dialogue assumes equality, and equality calls for dialogue.

Dialogue's goal is not conversion of the ignorant, overpowering the other with the truth of your superior point of view. Its goal is understanding. Think of yourself as an adventurer in a strange new country that the opposite sex—your dates and mates—have lived in all their lives. To them it is ordinary, but to you it encompasses mysteries. "Show me how the world looks to you," dialogue asks. "Tell me what you thought about that movie; why did it make you cry?" "Do you ever worry about death?" "How do you feel when a friend criticizes you?" "What do you do when you're afraid?" "Let me in on your secrets."

Be alert, pay attention to details, to nuance. I remember going fishing with my brother-in-law, a man with a third-grade education and a magical way with fish. The circumference of a ripple on the water, the exact sound it made, conveyed volumes of information to him: it signified that a three-pound bass had just grabbed a grasshopper on the water's surface and would circle back in about twenty seconds. I sat next to him, used his bait and tackle, watched how he moved and breathed, how his hands moved in a certain way, but nothing happened. The only thing he ever told me directly was, "You're not holding your mouth right."

To see how observation and dialogue dissolve differences, let's go back to our story of George and Andrea (page 183). If George had been mining Andrea for her secrets, he would have a better understanding of the feminine. He would recognize that Andrea is just trying to connect with him when she tells him about her travails. If he didn't feel blamed, if he didn't feel like she expected him to *do* something, perhaps he could learn to give her the sympathetic ear and support she needs before he reads the paper. Perhaps he would learn that she would feel loved and respected if he were to fill her in on the inconsequential events of his day.

And if Andrea had tried to penetrate the mysteries of George's masculine orientation, she would realize that George assumed she needed his help, and would never bother talking to her about a problem that was already solved. She'd understand that he isn't trying to shut her out with the paper, and that he gets disoriented dealing with interruptions. Perhaps she could learn to enjoy the different kind of intimacy of just sitting and reading together without talking.

In doing so, they would be accepting each other on their own terms, without judging each other's behavior inadequate or trying to change it, rather than applying their own standards. Over time, it is likely that George would naturally want to confide more in Andrea, and Andrea would experience intimacy just sitting quietly with George in the evening.

Participants in dialogue come away feeling neither victorious nor defeated, but enriched, with a better understanding of both the other and themselves. The process has a supportive symmetry to it: the greater consciousness of the other leads to greater empathy for the other. Our opposite-sex partners provide the pole for the integration of our own split-off selves. Dialogue narrows the gap between us, reducing our fear, tempering our adversarial stance. Through dialogue we come together and heal each other. (An exercise for improving dialogue skills appears on page 282.)

Developing the "Other" in You

Dialogue teaches you about the opposite sex and makes you more comfortable with what is different. But equally important for relationships is recognizing and developing the "other" in you—that is, giving voice to the repressed "maleness" or "femaleness" that has been lost to you during the socialization process, and that you seek to regain vicariously through a relationship with a member of the opposite sex.

This is easier said than done, for society's taboos are strong, and our discomfort level when bucking the tide is high. Getting in touch with our repressed Contrasexual Self demands that we act in a consciously *transcultural* manner—refusing to buy into the stereo-types that society imposes on us as men and women. We are as blocked from the contrasexual energy within us as we are biased against it outside ourselves. Believe me, I do not minimize the strength of character and conviction required to say no to stereo-typed sex roles, nor do I underestimate the power our culture wields in our lives. Men and women who buck the cultural norm do so in the face of fearsome disapproval and pressure to conform. Behavior that is approved of or even admired in a man or a woman is often criticized when exhibited by the other. We've all heard an assertive or outspoken woman labeled a "bitch," or an emotional man a "wimp."

To behave in a transcultural way we must trade places with the "other," trying out new behavior that feels awkward, and trying on for size the different abilities and perceptions of the opposite sex. It means learning to separate *role* from *gender*. The payoff is that, as you awaken and exercise your creaky contrasexual energy, you will become more balanced, and you will be attracted to partners whose energies are not so polarized.

Going against the grain involves doing what comes *unnaturally*, overcoming resistance, anxiety, and discomfort. For a man, this might mean making himself vulnerable, talking about something that he's kept private, writing a poem, doing volunteer work with children. A woman might make an effort to be brave—hiking a mountain alone or river rafting. She might overcome her terror of numbers and learn to balance her checkbook, or speak up in a group where she's remained silent. (It's interesting that despite the stereo-type that "women talk too much," it is men who speak more often and for longer periods of time in public.)[12] If you are dating someone who likes football, try to learn something about its rules and strat-egy. Make a sincere attempt to see its attraction, instead of turning up your nose, or recoiling at the violence. Try watching the soap opera that your girlfriend likes, try writing the thank-you notes or shopping for the holiday gifts. In this way you waken dormant energies; you *enliven* yourself. (An exercise at the end of this chapter will help you to see how your gender energies are distributed, and what needs developing.)

Experimenting with the unfamiliar energies and behaviors of the opposite sex does not mean that you *identify* with them. You will always identify yourself as a man or woman, but you are expanding your horizons, stretching yourself back toward your original whole-ness. When women were first trying to get a foothold in corporate America (no easy task), the strategy was to bury their femininity, their vulnerability, and live behind a mask, even to the extent of wearing men's clothes—drab suits with tailored blouses and frilly "ties." As women gained more confidence in their abilities, and as their position became stronger, they learned that they didn't have to imitate men, and that their own strengths—intuition, cooperation— in combination with their newfound assertiveness and business savvy, were doubly powerful and attractive.

SHARING THE CARING

I want to address a delicate, volatile core issue between men and women. One area where role embeddedness is badly in need of change is in the areas of nurturing and caretaking within relationships. While both men and women need the nurturing they did not get in childhood, it is women who are *trained* to provide it. Insufficiently nurtured as adults, women typically transform their need to be nurtured into a need to nurture. It comes as no surprise that married men have significantly higher survival rates, and are more content, than unmarried men—while the same does not hold true for married as opposed to unmarried women.[13] Real love is not possible in such an unbalanced relationship. To correct this disparity, men must intentionally and consciously work on developing their nurturing skills, and women must allow for that development by leaving room for it—not rushing to fill all the gaps.

The necessity for parity carries over to the sharing of household responsibilities, especially in two-career relationships. Every recent study of couples reveals this to be a major issue of conflict between men and women now, and the frustration and anger inevitably filter down into all other aspects of a partnership.[14] Even men who consider themselves "helpful" around the house are often oblivious to the nature and extent of the demands on working mothers. While sometimes this is a feigned or contrived ignorance, it is sometimes a real lack of awareness. Recently, fathers left behind with their children while their wives served with the armed forces in the Persian Gulf (a remarkable reversal of roles!) said they had been unaware of how inequitably the child-rearing tasks had been divided and were overwhelmed by how hard it was to work and run a household at the same time. One said that the first thing he would do when his wife came home was "say thank-you."[15]

There is no reason, other than adherence to traditional power strictures, why women should be the primary housekeepers and caretakers, and why the word "wife" should be synonymous with the provision of those services. A friend of mine who was for several years juggling three small children and a full-time job with minimal participation from her husband, who often worked late or traveled, told me a story about her young son that was particularly revealing. One night after she had fed, bathed, read to, and tucked in her children, she was cleaning up the kitchen and doing laundry and other housework, as she often did at night. While folding laundry on her bed she dozed off and woke up a few hours later to find her five-year-old son standing by her bed. He had awakened to go to the bathroom and, seeing her light still on, came into her room and found her asleep in her clothes in the middle of a pile of laundry.

"What's the matter, Mommy?" he asked, concerned.

"Oh, nothing, honey, I was just tired and fell asleep, that's all."

He sat down next to her and put his little hand over hers. "You need a wife," he said. "We should get you a wife."

Curious as to what he meant she asked, "What's a wife?"

"Oh, you know," he told her. "Someone who will do all this work for you . . . and they like it!"

Out of the mouths of babes! The fact is, *everyone* wants a wife! It's a role, not a gender, and in a healing relationship, both parties are going to have to take turns playing the part. Single men will have to give up the prerogatives of their societally conferred power base. And women must be willing to risk insisting on sharing the responsibilities. They need to teach their partners how to help with the caretaking, and then be able to step back and let their partners do their share.

At my singles workshops, some irate bachelor would invariably jump up at this point and ask, "What's in this for me?" What kind of woman is that, he'd demand, who doesn't take care of her man? Why should I go out with one of those liberated types who expects me to cook dinner and take care of the laundry? I can find lots of women who will take care of me properly!

Understandably, many men are angry at the new rules and expectations, especially if they've been in traditional relationships. First I'd point out that those relationships haven't worked—that's why they are attending my workshop! Most of the time they admit that there were many fights, and a constant undercurrent of resentment, over the inequity of the caretaking. What I tell these men is that they are hurt, just as women are, but in less blatant ways, by their dominant roles. I tell them that there is no healing, no hope for wholeness in an unequal relationship, and that they will have to see for themselves the world that opens up to them—both in the response of their partners, and within themselves—in becoming a giver as well as a receiver of nurturing.

Women often have trouble giving up their role-based behavior, for they too are raised to believe that men are stronger, that men are uniquely qualified to lead, that women should be the caretakers and raise the children. Many a woman's sense of worth begins and ends with what she does or contributes *for others*. Even if she craves caring—or resents the caring she gives—she may be loath to relinquish her position as the provider of caring services, fearful that she is loved only for her instrumental function. Giving up care providing is scary, but sometimes the only way to find out if we are loved for ourselves is to *stop*.

As we are seeing in Russia and Eastern Europe, many people are skittish when given their freedom; they cling to the old ways. Fearful of an independence they haven't learned to handle, they continue to want to be provided for by the state, to be told what to do, to live by strict rules and guidelines. The Equal Rights Amendment did not pass in part because many women were scared to take on the freedom it implied. Marabel Morgan's book *Total Woman* sold like hotcakes during the most vociferous period of the women's movement, because it reassured women who didn't know how they would survive and be loved if they weren't meeting their mate at the door wearing a negligee and carrying a cold, dry martini.

MOVING TOWARD ANDROGYNY

Transcending cultural stereotypes to experience our whole selves moves us toward androgyny. We are inherently androgynous creatures, embodying both male and female energy, but the split in our culture is deep, and parts of ourselves are undernourished. Androgyny has become a loaded word, often misunderstood, so I want to clarify my terms. It does not mean asexual, bisexual, or hermaphroditic, and certainly not unmasculine or unfeminine. Androgyny is our natural state. It refers to an *inner* balance and wholeness that allows us to be strong or gentle, logical or emotional, as required, because we are comfortable with a full range of modes of being. An androgynous person is a man secure enough in his masculinity to permit the feminine aspects of his personality to emerge, or a woman secure enough in her femininity to permit the masculine aspects of her personality to blossom. As we confront and hold our contrasexual energies (without identifying with them), we become more integrated; debilitating stereotypes are eroded. A woman who identifies with the feminine and can access her masculine energy is very powerful. And there's something incredibly appealing about a masculine yet gentle man.[16]

The move toward androgyny will bring men and women back together on common ground. To achieve this within the cultural context in which we are socialized and live requires being *conscious* and *intentional* about who we are and how we behave, which is what this book is all about. As we practice new behaviors over time, we become aware of the evolution in ourselves that will lead us to whole partnerships. New experiences will create new internal images of each other, which in turn will create new experience that will further deepen intimacy and our drive to wholeness. Hard as it is to buck the tide, it is essential for personal growth. You have to choose to be a pioneer, to be at the forefront of change. As they say, if you're not part of the solution, you're part of the problem. The next chapter describes the conscious/androgynous relationship. But first I want to discuss how gender roles and stereotypes carry over into the area of sexuality and sabotage sexual intimacy.

Sexuality: Me Tarzan, You Jane

Our sexuality is a highly personal and central aspect of our identity, and it plays an unparalleled role in our relationships. We like to think of sex and our sexuality as so "natural" that we don't have to think about it, or work at it. But in fact sexuality, like gender, is largely a cultural construct. What we believe and do sexually is what we're taught to believe and allowed to do. What we do in bed— *that* we do it in bed—is learned. Pure, raw sexual pleasure—or any pure, raw emotion, for that matter—is all but impossible, except in fleeting, unguarded moments, so pigeonholed are our ideas about sexual behavior. As Jamake Highwater notes in *Myth & Sexuality*, even what we *feel* about sex is culturally determined.[17]

The fallout in relationships of the effects of our sex-negative, pleasure-negative culture would fill another book. The strongest influences on our attitudes toward sexuality have been transmitted through biblical epics and the theory of original sin attributed to St. Augustine. Rather than viewing human nature as essentially good, and sex as life affirming (as is the case in some Eastern cultures), our attitudes toward sex—the evils of the flesh—are based on the premise that human nature is essentially evil and sex the depraved act of an evil being. Even the product of sexual intercourse—the infant child—is born "of sin."[18] Thus we have the sex-prohibitive religious practices—celibacy, the proscription of sex other than for procreation, etc.—so prominent in our cultural history. More subtly, we have the fear, shame, guilt, sexual "acting out," and other psychological and political ramifications of these culturally transmitted values superimposed on our innate sexuality.

It was probably inevitable that our rigid sexual strictures would explode, in the form of the so-called sexual revolution and sexual liberation. But revolutions are also destructive. Nature has its own timetable, its own pace; hurricanes and volcanos wreak havoc. Certainly sex has come out of the closet in recent history: adolescents experiment at an ever-younger age, sex education is more widespread, birth control more accepted and readily available, and premarital sex is the norm rather than the exception. Some point to widespread pornography as indicative of our liberation from sexual repression. However, pornography *reflects* that repression; prurience is the flip side of puritanism. When a normal avenue of self-expression is blocked, that expression often surfaces in an exaggerated and distorted form in an effort to restore balance. This is dysfunctional, for it only reinforces negative attitudes; nevertheless it gives expression to something otherwise repressed. But orgies and sexual marathons are no more liberated than sex in the missionary position with the lights off. Even the seemingly innocuous romance novels to which many women are addicted, in which dastardly men force them to do their bidding or handsome princes come and carry them away from their dreary lives, are cultural distortions of sexual expression. They are a subset of pornography.

A culture that denies pleasure breeds the expression of pleasure in distorted ways: rampant drug and alcohol abuse, for example—and violence. Rape, in particular, has nothing to do with sexual pleasure, and everything to do with the lack of, or denial of, pleasure. The depersonalization of the other, in rape, is an expression of a split self, a desperate attempt to connect with the hated opposite in oneself. A rapist suffers from sensory deprivation, from the repression of *eros*, from a deep self-hatred acted out upon a hated object—the perfect formula for violence. Sexually permissive cultures are typically nonviolent.[19]

A telling indicator of the negative sexual programming widespread in our culture today, which has increased as we have supposedly become more "liberated," is the incidence of inhibited sexual desire (ISD). ISD is a complaint about which I and other therapists hear all too often. Now that we are permitted to have sexual pleasure, it seems that many people are having more sex, but enjoying it less. Pleasure has become a duty. Telling people who have grown up under the old rules that they should love sex, that they should feel "free" and "turned on," is like telling someone flying in the coach section that he has to land the plane. Without years of training, it produces tremendous performance anxiety.

It is no wonder that sexual pleasure is so elusive. How can we enjoy sex, which is nothing if not private and idiosyncratic, when our expectations, and those of our partners, are a function of the social bias? Sex should be loose and juicy, hard and heart-stopping— a sensual experience. But how can we enjoy sex when we've been told that pleasure is sinful, that our bodies are to be hidden, or that they must conform to a narrow interpretation of permissibility? We do not so easily shake off the bonds of repression. Sex in our culture is a means to many ends (physical release, amusement, power, debasement, control, connection), but rarely is pure sexual, bodily pleasure the goal.

THE SEX-LOVE TRADE-OFF

The culturally imposed sex roles and sexual stereotypes we have been discussing with respect to gender are particularly devastating in the sexual arena. The sexual repression of men and women takes quite different paths. Women in our society are cut off from enjoying the *physical* pleasure of sex; men are cut off from enjoying the *emotional* pleasure of sex. Women supposedly "give" their sexual favors; men "take" their pleasure. Women are in essence cut off from sex, men from sexuality.

We have all heard the stereotypes: Men want only sex, women want only love (or affection). Men enjoy sex; women don't. Furthermore, men *should* want only sex (only wimps fall in love and let a woman control them); women *should* want only love (women who enjoy sex are nymphomaniacs, or whores). Boys are raised to view sex as a conquest, girls to see it as something they do to get love. A learned emotional ignorance makes it difficult for some men to experience sex as a vehicle for and expression of a variety of feelings and needs. Socialized not to experience their feelings and emotions fully, those feelings become localized in the genitals. But there is a big gap between an ejaculation and a full-bodied orgasm.

Women, on the other hand, have been denied orgasmic pleasure by the insistence that they don't have orgasms, or shouldn't enjoy them. Physiologically, women are multiorgasmic, but women who openly express (or actively seek) their sexual pleasure are often degraded, referred to by derogatory terms such as "slut" or "tramp." Despite pornography and the media's promotion of the sexually assertive woman, and the fact that many men *say* they wish their partners were more aggressive in bed, most women who take the initiative sexually find themselves confronted with disapproval or impotence. Because sex has been an instrument of power for men, women's exercise of it is threatening.

For women particularly, sexuality is another area that cultural inequities have infiltrated and undermined. Much of the sexual language and practices in our culture are demeaning to women. Sex has become an expression of conquest and control over, even hostility and violence toward, women, rather than the expression of intimacy and connection they seek. (As Gloria Steinem replied when asked why she never married: "I can't mate in captivity.") It is hard to feel comfort, much less pleasure, in an atmosphere of subjugation or objectification, where sex is used as a weapon. Again, the conflict between men and women in the sexual area is not a "natural" by-product of biology or nature, but a reflection of patriarchal power. The subjugation of women is not cross-cultural, and in cultures where there is greater equality between men and women, there is less sexual tension. Sexual intimacy—like all intimacy—requires equality.

RECLAIMING SEXUAL PLEASURE

In order to become what we are supposed to be sexually, we have become what we are not. And what are we, sexually speaking? We are sexual beings, and our sexuality is a part of the pulsating energy of life, which we express through mind, body, and psyche. Our yearning for sexual union is a core manifestation of our drive to achieve union with the universe through our partners. True sexuality *is* "natural," and our goal is to return to a purer perception and experience of it—to its joys and pleasures. Sexuality is the spiritual center of partnership and the foundation on which trust and commitment rest. As Andrew Greeley, a Catholic theologian and novelist, writes:

> If a man and wife do not have fun with each other in bed, they will have neither the motivation nor the courage to tackle the more complex problems in a personality conflict. . . . When two people are trying to grow in their mutual lovemaking, a psychological tone develops in their relationship that greatly enhances their attractiveness to each other. . . . Familiarity breeds contempt only for those who have stopped growing. For faithful lovers, it breeds both heightened pleasure and even heightened mystery.[20]

To quote D. H. Lawrence, "The instinct of fidelity is perhaps the deepest instinct in the great complex we call sex. Where there is real sex, there is an underlying passion for fidelity."

We recapture our sexuality in the same way as we break down the barriers of gender roles and stereotypes: through becoming *conscious* and *transcultural*. It is an ethical and political as well as a personal quest. The true sexual revolution is the revolution for sexual justice between the sexes, and for legitimizing sexual pleasure for women and emotional expression for men. Since our attitudes toward sex are sociological rather than biological, they can be transcended.

To participate in the real sexual revolution, we must become what John Stoltenberg calls "erotic traitors," creating a new sexual identity by *how we decide to act.*[21] Identity is created by behavior, not vice versa. If single men view sex as a conquest, and single women view it as a way to get a man, they deny themselves the spiritual connection and full aliveness that true sexuality embraces. A relationship in which a man can't be tender and a woman can't be aggressive is a relationship in trouble—a limited partnership. Our goal is to be whole partners in whole partnerships.

What can you do while you are single to discover your own innate sexuality, and to increase the potential for sexual intimacy? We've already talked about one major step you can take: developing your Contrasexual Self. It is also important that you be aware of your sexual history, reviewing your past liaisons and relationships for what they reveal to you. (An exercise at the end of the chapter will help you with this.) You must become conscious of the impact of sexual myths and stereotypes on your behavior and feelings, and then refuse to behave in accordance with those stereotypes. For men, this means expressing the need for tenderness and being open to the *emotional* pleasure of sex. For women, it means expressing the need for sexual gratification and being open to the *physical* pleasure of sex. Technique, endurance, and acrobatics are not the point. It means finding partners with whom you feel safe, with whom you can express your vulnerabilities, desires, and fantasies, partners with whom you can both give and receive. It means reversing roles, trying what is unfamiliar or uncomfortable for you: being aggressive as a woman, perhaps; allowing yourself to be passive, to receive, as a male. It certainly means having a sense of humor and playfulness, not taking it all so seriously. Imagination helps, too. It means *allowing* pleasure, including the pleasure of expanding into the other's awareness.

And it means dialogue. Communication with your sexual partner is the key to *knowing*, to penetrating the mystery of the other who is different from you. Couples must talk about sex—*exactly* what they want, what they like and don't like. This dialogue serves a dual purpose: it expresses *your* needs and desires, and it allows and requires you to consider the needs and desires of the *other*. Sexual talk is itself erotic, and it breeds intimacy. As mentioned earlier, dialogue assumes equality; it requires recognition of and respect for the other's idiosyncratic sexual feelings and preferences.

What it boils down to is *safe sex*, sex that is truly consensual. No one should engage in sex that isn't mutually pleasurable. We have to learn to say no to sex that feels like conquest or submission, sex that expresses hostility or anger, or is manipulative. Sex can transform the ordinary, reaching far beyond the mere meeting of two bodies, the release of tension. To again quote Andrew Greeley:

> "When a man and a woman practice their mutual wiles on one another they are imitating the way God works on us . . . they are literally cooperating with God's gentle seductions. . . . It is disgraceful for [God's] followers to mate with each other in any but the most fervent, erotic way. The greater the pleasure that man and woman give to each other—in bed and in every other dimension of their relationship—the more God is present with them."[22]

Our sexuality can fuel the spiritual core of our relationships. With clear intention, we can drop labels like "masculinity" and "femininity" and talk instead about *"human-inity."*

EXERCISE 11A   ■   ■   ■   ■   ■

Your Gender Energy Balance

The purpose of this exercise is to get an impression of the balance (or imbalance) of your masculine and feminine energies. Listed in two columns below are traits that have a high level of acceptance in our culture as stereotypically masculine or feminine. There is general understanding that any item on the list could describe a characteristic in either sex, but the traits in the left column are generally ascribed as dominant in men, while the traits in the right column are recessive in men. The opposite holds true for women: the traits in the right column tend to be dominant in women and those in the left column recessive. All traits are situationally desirable in either sex. In an androgynous person, the traits are more or less in balance, and s/he can take on and put off any "gender" trait at will, without conflict or fear of losing his or her identity.

Rate each trait on a scale of 1 to 5, with five indicating the highest degree to which you perceive yourself possessing that trait. You may have two ratings on each line, meaning that you believe you possess both traits to some degree. Any trait that you believe does not describe you should be given a zero (0).

To determine your "masculine" score, add the total of your responses to the left of the zero. To determine your "feminine" score, total your responses to the right of the zero. To get an idea of the balance in your gender energies, look at the *difference* between the two scores. In an androgynous person there will be little difference between the two scores. If your scores are highly skewed in either direction, it is an indication that you need to work on awakening your contrasexual energies. Take note specifically of which traits might be desirable for you to develop. In Chapter 15, you will have a chance to look back at this exercise to aid you in making behavior changes that will alter your androgyny quotient. (NOTE: It might be illuminating for you to have a couple of friends or intimate partners evaluate you as well; feedback from others can be immensely valuable.)

	5	4	3	2	1	0	0	1	2	3	4	5	
aggressive													passive
independent													interdependent
rational													emotional
objective													subjective
dominant													submissive
competitive													cooperative
logical													intuitive
adventurous													cautious
decisive													ambivalent
ambitious													security oriented
worldly													domestic
leader													follower
assertive													tactful
analytical													integrative
strong													tender
sexual													sensual
philosophical													practical
thinking													feeling
good in math													good in the arts
good in science													good in literature
self-reliant													consults others
individualistic													interpersonal
goal oriented													process oriented
exclusive													inclusive
instrumental													expressive
disciplinarian													nurturing
pleases self													pleases others
takes initiative													receptive
likes time alone													likes time with others
sees parts													sees whole
masculine													feminine
rebellious													conformist
theological													religious
separative													affiliative

EXERCISE 11 B   ▪   ▪   ▪   ▪   ▪

Your Sexual Self

PART I: EARLY SEXUAL EXPERIENCES

Using a piece of paper divided into four columns, list your early sexual experiences from childhood through age twelve. These might include masturbation, playing doctor or other games, watching animal sex, sex-education class or other messages about sex, sex play with peers of the same or opposite sex, incestuous experiences, rape. List your experience, the feeling you had during the experience, your behavioral reaction, and the decision you made as a result of that experience. Use the examples and chart below as a model.

EXPERIENCE	FEELING	REACTION	DECISION
Getting an erection while taking a bath when I was five	Excitement	My mother was upset so I knew it was wrong	I kept my feelings to myself
Hiding and hugging under the covers with my cousin Sally, telling scary stories	Cozy, loving, happy	Sought nonsexual affection from women	It's good having women as friends
Masturbating with my best friend at our "clubhouse"	Excited, scared	Shame that what I was doing was forbidden	Don't get caught

Put a plus sign (+) by the experiences you consider positive and a minus sign (−) next to those you consider negative. Next fill in the blanks below.

1. As a result of my positive early sexual experiences, my feelings about sex are [summarize positive feelings above]

_____

_____, but because of

my negative sexual experiences, I also feel _____

_____.

2. This influences me to react in sexual situations at times by [summarize positive reactions above] _____

_____

and at other times by [summarize negative reactions above] _____

_____

_____.

3. As a result of my early sexual experiences I decided that sex was [summarize decisions above] _____

_____

_____.

PART II. ADOLESCENT/ADULT SEXUAL EXPERIENCES

Now list your memorable positive and negative sexual experiences from adolescence through adulthood, followed by the feeling generated by the experience, how you behaved in reaction, and the decision made or reinforced by the experience. A chart and a few examples are given below as a model.

EXPERIENCE	FEELING	REACTION	DECISION
Making out with Amy in back of Chuck's car	Wanted to go all the way	Purposely turned off	Sex is powerful, dangerous
Guy in men's room at bar exposed himself	Turned on, repulsed	Acted offended, macho	Homosexuals are disgusting
Impotence with first intercourse	Shame, feared I was gay	Avoided sex for two years	I'm sexually inadequate, not a real man
Lynn told me I was "hot" in bed	Relieved, thrilled	Became sexually promiscuous	Sex is fun, I am a great lover

Again, mark the positive experiences with a plus (+) sign and the negative experiences with a minus (−) sign. Then fill in the blanks below.

1. As a result of my positive sexual experiences, my feelings about sex are [summarize positive feelings above]

_____

_____

but my negative experiences make me feel [summarize negative feelings above] _____

_____.

2. As a result, sometimes in sexual situations I react by [summarize positive reactions] _____

_____

and at other times by [summarize negative reactions] _____

_____.

3. Because of these experiences, I believe that sex is

_____

_____.

Compare this with what you said about your childhood sexual experiences above. Then complete the sentence below:

The similarities between my childhood sexual experiences and my adult sexual frustrations are _____

_____

_____.

The main differences include _____

_____

_____.

The major thing that has changed is _____

_____

_____.

PART III: SEXUAL RELATIONSHIP VISION

Now it's time to think about your sexual desires. You do get to have a little fun with these exercises. Whatever trauma, embarrassment, fear, or shame we've experienced, we all have dreams, fantasies, and hopes for our sexual fulfillment. I want you to write down that vision below, in the form of a list, in as much detail as possible. There are several sources for you to draw on: the exercises above, your secret dreams and fantasies, your frustrations and pleasures with past partners and theirs with you. Several examples appear below. In Chapter 15, you will have a chance to convert these desires into action.

- "I would like to feel that I didn't have to be so aggressive in bed."
- "I'd like to make love surreptitiously in a public place without getting caught."
- "I'd like to be able to tell my lover how I feel while making love."
- "I'd like to feel free to make noise while making love."
- "I'd like to have my lover play with my feet."
- "I'd like to make love in the shower."
- "I'd like to make love for a long time and not feel like I have to have an orgasm."
- "I'd like to experiment with Tantric sex."
- "I'd like to have an erotic painting in my bedroom."
- "I'd like to live someplace where I could walk naked outdoors."
- "I'd like to be able to talk with my lover about my fear of impotence."
- "I'd like to feel less self-conscious about how hairy my body is."
- "I'd like to watch my lover masturbate."
- "I'd like my lover to tell me her fantasies."
- "I'd like my lover to be aggressive and seduce me and let me be passive."

Complete the following sentence:

1. If I could satisfy all my sexual desires, then I would feel

_____

2. and respond in sexual situations by _____

_____

3. because my fear of/that _____

_____would be gone.

4. Then I would think of sex as _____

_____

and would feel that I am a complete sexual being.

NOTE: It might be of interest to compare your answer to item 4 with your beliefs about sex from Exercise 9B, page 155. Are there any similarities?

PART
IV

The Journey of Partnership

12

The Imago: Recipe for Romance

But love is blind, and lovers cannot see
The pretty follies that they themselves
commit.

—WILLIAM SHAKESPEARE

Now that you have completed all this detective work, we can look at exactly how your childhood experiences will affect your choice of a partner, and the journey you will undertake after that fateful meeting. We are going to unmask your Imago: *your unconscious image of the person your childhood programmed you to fall in love with.*

Programmed to fall in love? We strenuously resist the idea, knowing all too well the pain and disillusionment of failed romance. Now we are armed with detailed checklists of qualities we want—and don't want—in our dream mates. But the notion that we have free choice in the matter of our partners is wishful thinking. The painful wounds of our early years, and our feeble adaptations to them, did not miraculously disappear when we "grew up." They are the "dowry" we bring to our adult relationships. To our horror, those partnerships have not delivered the love and healing we so trustingly sought; rather, they have echoed the pain of our past. It is our buried Imago that drives us to repeat ourselves, choosing over and over the angry, aloof workaholic, the smothering complainer, the secret drinker—facsimiles of our caretakers' worst traits. We must bring the Imago to light and change it if we hope to break the pattern.

The Imago: Distillation of Childhood Experience

Looking back at what we've learned about how we were nurtured and socialized, let's review the ingredients of the Imago.

1. *Your Imago match resembles your childhood caretakers.* The idea that we choose to be with someone like our parents—and react as we did as children or act toward them as our parents did toward us—is not an appealing one. This is especially distressing when we have gone out of our way to avoid repeating past problems.

My clients tell me chilling stories of disappointment and disillusionment. After several romantic evenings, one patient's date stalked out of a restaurant at the first whiff of an argument—an ominous reprise of her father descending to his basement workshop the moment her mother would ask him for something. Another patient's ex-husband became sullen when he drank, just as her mother had done. In response, she stalked around the house in a rage, a mirror of her dad's reaction. Mary's lover didn't drink (as her father had)—until they got married. Traumatized by the way her mother would fly off the handle at minor provocations, Elaine was reassured by Carl's calm, easygoing manner. But he "blew up" three times the day they moved in together. Shifting from the role of traumatized child to that of raging mother, Amanda angrily broke up with the critical, judgmental boyfriend who reminded her of her mother, only to find that the man she is now dating has started to find fault with her clothes and her reluctance to find a new apartment.

A history they'd hoped to forget is repeating itself. When you find yourself saying, "You're just like my mother (father)," you've met an Imago match. When your partner compares you to one or both of your parents, you have learned something about your Denied Self.

Though the Imago is a picture of both the positive and negative traits of our caretakers, the negative traits carry the most weight in our attraction. Because incidents of neglect, abuse, criticism, or indifference affect our survival, they are more deeply etched on our Imago template than our memories of caring and attention. They are the aching sores that we want healed. This is frustrating, because we consciously seek only the positive traits in a potential partner, so that we can get our needs gratified. But without the negative traits, we would not be attracted in the first place. There is a perverse logic here; the old brain is making sure that we find what we need to heal. Inevitably, the person you need in order to heal is similar to the person with whom you were wounded, because that is the only type of person from whom your unconscious will accept what you need.

You can see why people from dysfunctional homes have particularly powerful Imagos. They've been flooded with specific, repetitive, negative imagery, much of which is so traumatic that it is deeply buried. The compulsion to find the source of their hurt and shame is out of their control, and like a shell-shocked soldier, they over-respond to all cues.

2. *Your Imago match possesses some of your Denied Self traits.* As we saw in Chapter 10, many of our Denied Self traits are introjected negative traits from our parents that we cannot bear to recognize in our own behavior. So the negative traits of our caretakers that we find replicated in our Imago partners may *additionally* be traits we ourselves possess.

The anger that is so unsettling in your partner was unconsciously chosen by you not only because it reminds you of your mother, but to substitute for the anger you cannot admit to in yourself, and your perception of that anger is at least in part a projection onto your partner of your own inadmissible anger. When you accuse your partner of stinginess, what may truly be so infuriating is your own denied stinginess, however generous you may think you are. Your partner's accusations of overdependence may be a way of masking his own fears of abandonment and dependence. By choosing a partner with your Denied Self traits, you get to be "whole" without having to take responsibility for aspects of yourself that you find distasteful or uncomfortable.

3. *Your Imago match possesses some of the traits of your Lost Self.* Though the Imago primarily embodies the negative traits of your caretakers (and by extension, your own denied traits), it also possesses the positive traits you need to be whole. This is the "you're everything I always wanted" piece of the Imago. Though our False Self stands in for the invalidated, split-off parts of us, the loss is unforgettable. We are incomplete, and in our drive for wholeness we gravitate toward someone who has what is missing in action in ourselves. We saw in Chapter 10 how Earl recaptured his lost sensuality in Christine, while Christine recovered her buried intellect. We seek in the other what has been repressed and buried in ourselves. Looked at this way, our romantic attachments are a kind of self-love. Part of our Imago—and thus part of what we fall in love with—is our Lost Self.

4. Your Imago possesses some of the Contrasexual Self traits that you lack. Since the Imago is an image of the opposite-sex partner, it follows that our Imago partners will possess the contrasexual gender traits that our society denies us, as we saw in Chapter 11. Again, there is an overlap, in that our contrasexual traits are actually part of the Lost and Denied Selves.

To sum up, the Imago is your homing device in the search for someone who is like your caretakers, as well as someone who possesses some of the qualities of your Missing Self. It is an image assembled over time, bit by bit, in response to our perceptions of our childhood experience. An intricate, subtle blend of what our unconscious perceives as the source of healing for our discrete wounds, our Imago match is, in many ways, the last thing we consciously want.

Is there no escape from falling for an Imago match? Unless your mate is chosen by the village elder, or you send away for a mail-order bride, the answer, I'm afraid, is no. To understand the Imago, and its seeming stranglehold on our will, we have to return again to our original thesis: our goal in life is to return to that original state of relaxed joyfulness that we somehow remember, to feel alive and whole. In order to do that, we have to go back to the scene of the crime, to the place where we were wounded, in order to undo the damage and re-find what was lost. From the perspective of our old brain, we must get what we need from the person or persons from which it should have come in the first place—or, failing that, from a reasonable facsimile.

But childhood is over; we cannot run back to our parents to get what we missed. So we find the next best thing—a relationship that recapitulates in its vital aspects the complex, idiosyncratic pattern of our wounding and loss. The tool that our unconscious uses to perform this feat is the Imago.

HOW DOES THE IMAGO WORK IN PARTNER CHOICE?

You are a walking encyclopedia of everything that happened to you in childhood. Every look and deed, every meal and conversation, every hug or harangue is stored somewhere in your memory. You harbor information about your mother's slight lisp and the low, calm pitch of her voice, your big brother's crushing bear hugs, his ambling walk, and his habit of glancing over his shoulder. You recall what was said during arguments, and reconciliations. You've never forgotten Dad's distinctive scent and his characteristic sniffle; your mind can hear the music that played on Christmas morning. This may seem improbable, since we often can't remember what we ate for breakfast, or what it is we came into the hardware store to buy. But it's all neatly filed, waiting to connect with the appropriate stimulus. (Think of how a certain smell, or a scene from a movie, can trigger the memory of a friend, or a long-forgotten incident.)

Each byte of information is stored—each word, deed, or action that has trickled down into the unconscious. Your pattern-forming brain organizes these myriad bits into a complex, shadowy picture, very much like a computer-generated image in which each tiny pixel finds a place. Impressions are combined and superimposed, one upon another, into a shimmering apparition of "the person who will make me whole."

Out in the world, a part of us continually scans the environment for a mate. It is a task important to our survival, and the old brain is intensely interested in the outcome. We examine each new prospect for a fit, almost instantaneously computing how they stack up to our composite picture. Waves of incoming information are matched against the image. Each byte registers as a "hit" or a "miss"—either it finds a receptor site, and attaches to a matching byte in our internal grid, or it is discarded. Our scanner operates like a rule in/rule out screen: lopsided smile = yes; furrowed brow = yes; downcast eyes = no; running shoes = no; cigarette = yes; beer = no; slight nervousness = yes; narrow tie = yes. If you're like me, you probably form instant opinions of people you pass on the street: this one you'd like to know; that one is very intelligent; she has no idea how foolish she looks; he has a responsible job but would be boring; she's uptight about sex; he acts like an overgrown boy; they look like a happy couple.

If enough of those bytes find receptor sites in our internal grid, we are attracted. If not, our interest is not piqued, and that person, like countless thousands of others, is discarded as a potential mate, before we've even said hello. Maybe we begin to date someone who possesses many fine qualities, but if the chemistry isn't there (meaning we can't match up enough of our Imago pixels), it probably won't last beyond a few dates, and we'll wonder why nothing "clicked."

When I was single after my divorce, I consciously sought the ideal mate, foolishly thinking I was immune from the process to which others, lacking my knowledge, were fated. I made a list of the qualities I wanted: warmth, vitality, intelligence, laughter, emotional stability, sensuality and sexuality. I tracked down several potential mates who had all these qualities, but nothing was stirred in me.

They were all interesting people to be with, but I was bored. Each lacked the essential traits that corresponded with the depression of my mother; my abandonment fears were not activated.

You may be worried that you may never meet someone who "clicks" with your Imago picture. Let me reassure you that there are many potential partners out there who will be Imago matches for you. No matter how intent our search, we will never find an exact match for the inner image. After all, our caretakers and our home situation are unique in their myriad detail, which we have turned into a complex collage of infinite subtlety based on our own perceptions. Yet we need to create as best we can that original situation, so that we can behave toward, and in response to, our partner as we did with our childhood caretakers, in the hope of getting the desired response this time around.

Fortunately, the Imago itself is but a facsimile, more like an impressionistic painting than a photograph, of the original. Usually our Imago partner will bear a rough likeness to the original, embodying at least a few of the most critical negative traits. But in order to get a good enough match to enable us to complete our unfinished business, we rework the image, exaggerating the likenesses and diminishing the differences, embellishing and fine-tuning the truth of our partners to achieve the verisimilitude we seek.

THE ILLUSION OF LOVE

The Imago, then, is an image not only of the other, but of wholeness, combining the deficits of our nurturing and socialization into a picture of our Missing Selves. What we have here, embodied in the Imago match, are all the ingredients for romance. When we hear birds singing and violins playing, when our heart skips a beat and our brain dumps endorphins into our bloodstream, our powerful sensors have singled out someone whom we've identified as having the unique potential to restore us to wholeness, a potential lacking in others whom we've seen and rejected. Here is the person with whom we can finish our childhood business and reclaim what is lost.

No wonder nothing else feels quite so good. When we fall in love, we change, and the world changes. We're suddenly filled with energy and optimism; we are entranced, enthralled, uplifted. Once separate and defensive, we feel truly connected and involved in the world. My clients tell me about how their world was transformed by love. After Peter met Veronica, he had a hard time going to work, because what he did all day when he wasn't with her felt unreal.

Martha, who had barely noticed the beggar on her block, found herself giving money to every homeless person she encountered. I've had clients tell me their migraine headaches disappeared, their lifelong depression lifted, their creative blocks evaporated in the embrace of romance. Life energy vibrates at a higher frequency. All in all, the world seems a better place to be.

THE LANGUAGE OF LOVE

All lovers believe they have been lucky to find someone so special. "No one else has ever felt what I feel," they think, "no one has ever experienced love like this." In a way this is true, for every Imago match is an intricate dovetailing of two people's unconscious pictures. One man's Imago match is another man's "when will this be over?" blind date. "What does she see in him?" is exactly the point of the Imago.

To demonstrate how the romantic partner does in fact echo our childhood and fill in our lost pieces, we have only to look at the four phenomena which are embodied in what appears to be the universal language of love.

The first is *recognition*. This is the eerie feeling that lovers have, even on their first and second encounters, that "even though we've just met, I somehow feel as though I already know you." This sense of familiarity stems from the resemblance of their new love to the unconscious image of their caretakers.

Because Steve grew up with a depressed, emotionally unavailable mother, he was on the lookout for someone with a smile on her face, who liked to cuddle. But repeatedly he was drawn to one type: a serious woman with a faraway look in her eye. Then he would find himself constantly searching her face for clues to her feelings, waiting for a smile. When she did, he would instantly feel a relieved euphoria.

The second is *timelessness*. "I can't remember when I didn't know you," the lovers say, though they may have only been together for days or a few weeks. Their old brains have merged the image of the lover with the caretakers, binding the present to the past. They are back in the all-nurturing arms of their fantasy mother, and everything is going to be perfect.

I recall a client telling me how she would lose track of time when she was with her new love. Their evenings together seemed wrapped in a sense of eternity. She would lie in his arms for hours, blending with his body, fusing with his feelings as if they were one person, and it would seem as if only minutes had passed.

Third is *reunification*. As the lovers spend more and more time together, they say, "I no longer feel empty or alone; with you I feel whole and connected, at one with things." They have found in each other what was missing in themselves. Two incomplete people have been made whole—temporarily.

Alice told me that she had never felt fully herself before she met Alex. "He is a perfect balance to me. When we are on a trip, I never know where I am going, but Alex has it planned out in every detail. He's sort of like my right hand. It's just great having someone with whom I feel so compatible. Part of me was missing before Alex came along. It's like we are one person."

Finally, there is the feeling of *necessity*. This seems to be an almost universal experience. An obsessional quality creeps into the relationship, and the beloved becomes essential to one's feeling of safety and survival. "I can't imagine what it would be like to be without Jack," Melissa said. "I don't think I could live or would want to." This theme, central to countless love songs and the subject of much of the world's love poetry, reflects the unconscious connection of the lover to the original parents, who wielded the power of life or death. Having found the caretaker again, need satisfaction seems guaranteed, and the primal fear of death recedes. Now, they will live; they will get what they need to survive.

Though the exact words may not be expressed, what the lovers are saying is "I've found what I've always been looking for. You are everything that was missing in my life. You are going to meet my needs. I feel like myself again, and I'm no longer lonely. You will never abandon me. You have saved me, and I'm not going to die."

THE BENEFITS OF ILLUSION

For a while, all is wonderful between the lovers. Indeed, they *do* feel more alive. In the thrall of love, they *are* able to abandon some of their self-absorption, capable of giving up the destructive habits that they employed to compensate for their pain. He quits smoking and leaves the office by six every night; her eating binges are a thing of the past, and she's no longer spending most of her paycheck on makeup and shoes. In the safe cocoon of their new love, they are able to stretch themselves, to be more honest and intimate than ever before. In the cradle of love, sexual inhibitions melt away, wit bubbles to the surface, once-rigid bodies move to the music. Because their partners are supportive and sympathetic, they are able to share their pain, their guilt, their fears and hopes. Shameful secrets and tender wounds are revealed and accepted. The lovers spend more and more time together. They start to make plans for the future. And then . . . things just start to go wrong.

The illusion of romantic love is that it blinds us to the negative aspects of our Imago choice. Desperate to maintain our newfound sense of joy and salvation, we enlist every tactic of denial to keep the bad news about our partner at arm's length. When, as day follows night, reality pierces the smokescreen of denial, the illusion ruptures and we come face to face with the final and most devastating piece of the Imago puzzle. I will save the sad story of what happens when romance goes awry for the discussion of the unconscious relationship in Chapter 13. What I want to do here is to reframe our picture of romantic love from the perspective of the Imago match.

LOVE: NATURE'S ANESTHESIA

It is fashionable these days to be cynical about romance, but I in no way want to diminish or demean romantic love. Not only does it feel wonderful, it is the catalyst for healing and change. Nature would not invent anything so grand for trivial purposes. In blinding us to reality, romantic love performs a valuable service. We unwittingly choose someone like our caretakers, who we expect to love us as they never did. Paradoxically, our beloved is uniquely able to reopen our old wounds. It appears to be a recipe for disaster and heartbreak; if we were not in love's thrall, we would run screaming in the other direction. We have, in fact, chosen a person who will frustrate us as our caretakers did. But that person, when responsive to our needs, has what we need to heal. And no other person does, or at least no other type of person.

Even when love fails, it provides us with a glimpse of our better self and a reminder of our potential for wholeness. Though it holds out a premature promise, it reconnects us—if only briefly—to that lost state of relaxed joyfulness we experienced as infants and have longed for ever since. However crushed we've been by love, most of us have fond memories of the good times, and most of us want to feel that way again.

Romantic love bonds us to our Imago match so that we will stick around long enough to see if we can make it work. It gives us the strength for the long undertaking of self-repair and the arduous work of a conscious relationship. When we are in love, we have the feeling that we can do whatever it takes to work things out. Falling in love forces our hand; without it we would choose to stay in the safety, however unfulfilling, of our singleness, or of a safe "arrangement." *Romantic love is nature's anesthesia.*

THERE IS NO LOVE IN ROMANCE

The notion that we love other people for themselves, just as they are, with their peculiar needs and quirks, is an illusion. Romantic love is not at all what it appears to be. We are in love with the projection of our Missing Self, and the expectation of what our beloved can give us through our association with them.

The Imago bond creates a spurious wholeness. Our attempt to get through another what is missing in ourselves never works, for personal emptiness cannot be filled by a partner. If that fusion were successful, we would be aborting our own chances to deal with our issues of self-completion.

Romantic love is a time bomb; it carries within it the seeds of its own destruction. It is supposed to end. Inevitably, reality rudely shatters our illusion. I hate to say it, but *there is no love in romance.* Real love is something entirely different—and better—as we'll see in Chapters 13 and 16. But it only comes to couples who wrestle with their demons and stay the course during the power struggle.

WHY IS IT IMPORTANT TO UNDERSTAND, AND TO MODIFY, THE IMAGO?

We need an Imago partner in order to grow and heal. The issues of self paradoxically require relationship for resolution. The partnership itself is the process by which we reclaim what is missing. Aware of what our Imago looks like, we know the kind of person we must finish our business with. We understand the issues we will have to face. We recognize what is going on with us in our mate search, and come to terms with the fact that we cannot avoid facing the old wounds of our childhood by "choosing" a mate who matches some set of criteria that we hope will allow us to avoid pain. When we meet an Imago match, we are prepared for what's in store.

An Imago-match partner has the potential to hurt us more deeply, or to heal us. We cannot close our eyes to the Imago. We must cooperate and work in concert with it, so that we are not driven by it. Until we familiarize ourselves with the Imago, even befriend it, we are in a waking sleep, fated to repeat the same mistakes over and over. We get rid of the person who hurt us, but keep the problems.

Knowing the details of your Imago will show you clearly what your self-completion issues are. It will clue you in to what needs to be changed or modified, and pinpoint how you can accomplish that. If you are able to reclaim some of your split-off parts while you are single, you will not need to seek them in another. If you can begin to get some of the nurturing and validation you need to heal your childhood wounds while you are single—from friends and coworkers, from group therapy or casual dates—you will diminish the intensity and severity of your negative Imago traits. There will be less emptiness to fill up, fewer missing pieces to compensate for. The Imago will literally mutate, and will become a picture of someone who, like you, is more healthy and whole. You will fall in love with a healthier partner. A healthier partner will fall in love with you.

Unmasking the Imago

By now you've gone over your childhood with a fine-tooth comb, and have thought a great deal about how your family functioned and how you responded to your environment. You've looked at your past and current relationships. We are now going to produce a picture of your very own Imago, using the clues that you've amassed from your responses and reflections in the exercises you've done so far, and your awareness of the issues now current in your life.

You may be appalled by the picture that emerges after all this arduous detective work, discouraged by the seeming repetitious intractability of your relationship conflicts and disappointments. I can't stress enough that knowledge about your Imago is *redemptive* information. It has the power to heal you. The Imago is the key to your relationships, and the basis for self-integration. Think of it as a map showing where the buried treasure lies.

EXERCISE 12A   ▪   ▪   ▪   ▪   ▪

Unmasking the Imago

Most of the information that you need to fill in the blanks below is available in the exercises you have already done. The parenthetical phrases tell you where to find it.

1. In all likelihood, I will be attracted to someone who is

_____

_____(positive qualities of your caretakers, Exercise 9A, #1, left half of circle, page 152), as well as _____

_____

_____(negative traits of caretakers, Exercise 9A, #1, right half of circle, page 152).

2. My partner may also turn out to be _____
_____(positive qualities of anyone else who was a strong early influence in your life—a sibling or live-in grandparent or parental lover) and _____

_____
(negative qualities of the person or persons above).

3. I have already seen evidence of this in my past relationships, which were _____

_____
(positive traits from Exercise 2B, #7, page 31, top half of circle, which duplicate traits listed in #1 and #2 above) and _____

_____(negative traits from Exercise 2B, #7 bottom of circle, which duplicate traits above).

4. I should also be prepared for my partner to be _____

_____
(Denied Self traits, Exercise 10C, #4, lower right quarter of circle, page 173; these traits may duplicate negative parental traits above).

5. Like me, my partner will have been wounded at the stage of

_____(Exercise 7D, page 113), but s/he is a

_____(Minimizer or Maximizer, but *opposite*

of you), and a _____(*opposite* coping response in same stage as yours. Thus, if you are a Caretaker wounded at the Concern stage, your partner will probably be a Loner). Thus his/her growth challenge is _____

_____

(look this up under the pertinent stage).

6. My partner will also possess traits that are lacking in me. Thus s/he is likely to be strong in the areas of _____

_____(Exercise 10B, #3, page 172, Lost Self traits) and

lacking in the areas of _____

_____

(Exercise 10B, #3, page 172, areas where you have not been re-pressed) (you may want to draw a "Four Functions" circle for your theoretical partner, so that you end up with a diagram similar to that of Earl and Christine on page 164).

7. Since I have also chosen my partner to compensate for my buried contrasexual energies, s/he is also likely to be _____

_____

(opposite-sex gender energies where you are weakest, Exercise 11A, page 202, not already mentioned in #5).

Now you have a complete impression of your Imago—your inner image of the opposite sex. The positive traits will be of interest to your conscious mind. The negative ones will attract your unconscious. They are the traits that are connected to your frustrations. Although nature's anesthesia will keep you from seeing the negative traits in your chosen partner, they will be the traits that activate your deepest feelings when you meet, and that cause you the most difficulty later in the relationship.

Knowing the traits of your Imago partner, you can also infer the nature of his or her wound and the issues that s/he will present for healing. In Chapter 15, you will have the opportunity to engage in some exercises that will help you make personal changes that will, over time, soften the harsher aspects of your Imago picture and help you cope with the conflicts you will face.

EXERCISE 12B   ■   ■   ■   ■   ■

Childhood Frustrations

Take a sheet of paper and copy the following diagram.

A. MOTHER   B. FATHER   C. OTHER
1. FRUSTRATIONS

2. NEGATIVE FEELINGS

3. POSITIVE BEHAVIORS

4. POSITIVE FEELINGS

List under "MOTHER" all the frustrating behaviors you can recall from your childhood with your primary female caretaker. In the "FATHER" column list all the frustrating behaviors you can recall with your primary male caretaker. In the column labeled "OTHER" list all frustrating behaviors with any other older person/s who had a caretaking role with you. Now circle your three deepest frustrations. Under "NEGATIVE FEELINGS" write your worst feeling with each caretaker. Under "POSITIVE BEHAVIORS" list all the behaviors of your caretakers which you view as positive. Now underline the three most positive behaviors in the list. Under "POSITIVE FEELINGS," write your best feeling with each caretaker.

On another sheet of paper write out the following sentence fragments. Notice that at the end of each fragment there are parentheses with instructions as to where in the previous exercises you can find the information to complete the sentences. Fill in the blanks with the information you have already collected. Modify the information only enough to make a readable sentence; do not change the content.

EXERCISE 12C ▪ ▪ ▪ ▪ ▪

Your Unconscious Childhood Agenda

1. In my childhood I lived with caretakers who were (Exercise 9A, #1, left half of circle, page 152) _____

_____

2. with whom I often felt (Negative Feelings, #2 above)

_____

3. because they frustrated me (Frustrations, #1 above—list circled frustrations) _____

_____

4. and that influenced me to become (Denied Self traits from Exercise 10C, #5, lower-right quadrant of circle, page 173) _____

_____

5. and to inhibit or repress my (Lost Self traits from Exercise 10B, #3, page 172) _____

_____ .

6. If they had been more (Exercise 9A, #1, left half of circle, page 152) _____

_____

7. and given me (underlined items from #3 above) _____

_____

8. so that I could have always felt (items from #4 above) _____

_____

9. then I would be (positive qualities from 12A, #1, page 222)

_____

_____

10. and would express my (qualities possessed by partner, from Exercise 12A, #5, page 222) _____ _____.

This is an impression of the unconscious childhood agenda that you will bring to a partnership. I include it as a means of comparison with your Unconscious Relationship, Exercise 2D, page 33, so that you can see how your present situation connects with your childhood past.

13

Partnership: The Journey to Consciousness

> Throughout our lives opportunities for
> new integrations and adaptations present
> themselves.
>
> —HARRY STACK SULLIVAN

This book is about how to take advantage of the opportunity your current singleness provides to prepare you for the journey of a healthy, healing partnership, and the creation of real love. In the preceding chapters, we have looked at how the process of selection works, based on your childhood experiences. We uncovered the type of person you will be attracted to, and reviewed the issues that your Imago match will present. Now I want to talk about what your relationship journey is likely to look like. Knowing what to expect will prepare you for the challenges you will face. Knowing what to hope for will inspire you to take the journey.

It should be clear by now that you do not have much choice when it comes to selecting your mate. Marriage is, by default, the final catchall for the ravages of childhood. It shouldn't surprise us, therefore, that of all human enterprises marriage exhibits the starkest contrast between beginnings and outcomes. All too often the person

227

we idolized and were madly in love with becomes the person who "fails" us, the person we bitterly divorce in the end.

Although our unconscious selection process doesn't bode well for marriage as a way of life, I am convinced that the negative Imago traits of our partners are the catalyst for personal transformation at the deepest levels. A conscious relationship, in which partners call on each other to change those aspects of themselves, and in so doing unleash repressed potential, is in fact the most effective path to psychological and spiritual wholeness. Our other options—denying our unmet childhood needs, trying to fill them on our own, or through friendships, "live-in" relationships, or serial lovers—will never heal us. The love that is essential to our healing *must* come from an Imago match, and a partnership—committed, continuous, consistent—is the process through which we heal and regain our original wholeness and full aliveness.

Fortunately, we *do* have a choice about what kind of marriage we have. Most marriages fail because of the persistence of the unconscious aspects of the relationship. Any unfinished business we had with our caretakers becomes a compelling agenda with our partners. All too commonly, however, the partners never become aware of the hidden needs that drive their relationship and never learn the skills they need to successfully address those needs. As a single, part of your preparation is to understand and prepare for a *conscious* marriage in which you and your future partner can undo the damage of childhood and recover your true selves.

The Unconscious Relationship

As you contemplate marriage, you should be aware that marriage, like childhood, has a "natural history": it develops in identifiable stages that parallel those of childhood. The correlation between the issues of our childhood and the issues of our relationships is not as uncanny as it seems, since the relationship, like childhood, proceeds from attachment to independence, through identity and competence, to concern and intimacy, unconsciously re-creating the issues needed to resolve our unfinished business.

As with childhood, each stage arises out of the prior stage, but each new stage carries forward the achievement or failure of the preceding stage. Romantic love mirrors the stage of Attachment, as partners establish the bond that will enable them to weather the storm to follow: the power struggle. The power struggle recapitulates the issues and hard work of the stages of Exploration, Identity, and Competence. If the couple is aware of what's going on, each partner strives to become an integrated self, and together they achieve a well-functioning relationship with a unique identity, just as children find out who they are and become competent in the management of their environment. If this work is successful and the relationship moves beyond the power struggle, the relationship becomes one in which partners can move on to genuine concern for each other's welfare and a deep intimacy that evolves into real love, which fulfills the promise foreshadowed in the romantic-love stage. Such a union is a powerful entity in the world, expanding its boundaries of care and concern, recapitulating the emergence of "care for others" at the stages of Concern and Intimacy.

Relationship stages follow a cyclical, not a linear, progress. We may return to romance, to the power-struggle issues of Identity and Competence, and to reemergent caring many times throughout the life cycle in response to the circumstances and crises of each stage of life. A new cycle might be prompted by the birth of a child, a serious illness or financial setback, a child leaving home.[1]

WHEN ROMANCE DIES: THE TRAJECTORY OF THE UNCONSCIOUS RELATIONSHIP

When last we left our lovers back in Chapter 10, they were nibbling each other's ears and saying they couldn't live without each other. Lamentably, romantic love is the height of unconsciousness, sustained as it is by the idealization of our partner and our anticipation of fulfillment.

Romantic love can last for a few weeks or even a few years, but unfailingly the bubble will burst, the veil of illusion will be lifted, and we will see the disappointing truth of our partner. How does this happen? During the romantic-love stage of a relationship—buoyed by hope and endorphins—each partner is voluntarily providing what the other wants and needs, so there is some basis in reality for the anticipation that the relationship will be fulfilling. But commitment—often the wedding ceremony—changes that, and all hell breaks loose. Anticipation becomes expectation, and both partners tend to withdraw some of the unconditional giving that characterized the early relationship, at the same time that they begin to expect (or even demand or feel entitled) to have their own needs met. Since they have chosen partners with their caretakers' failings, it is likely that the partner will fail them as well, in the same devastating ways. Each is doomed to disappoint the other.

Every marriage moves inexorably from romantic illusion to the disillusionment that heralds the onset of the power struggle. This is just as nature intended it. Yet we are taught to believe that being in love is an indicator of the rightness of our partners. When the romance wanes, many take it as an indicator that the relationship has run its course. People who attend my workshops sometimes say to me, "My love has died; I'm just not in love anymore; I don't feel the same." It seems to be my unpleasant duty to give them the bad news. "It's supposed to die," I tell them.

If you get stuck at the stage of romantic love, you are stuck in the Attachment stage; in order for the relationship to go further, you have to move on to the stage of Exploration, and beyond. Romance is just the launching pad. To get real love, you have to knuckle down to the work of healing and consciousness. No one "works" on a relationship when the endorphins are rushing. This is a grave misunderstanding about the nature of love and romance that you, as a single person, would do well to understand ahead of time.

Romantic love is supposed to end. It is nature's glue, which brings two incompatible people together for the purpose of mutual growth, and enables them to survive the disillusionment that they did not marry perfect people. Though romantic love is a foretaste of the potential in the relationship, that potential can only be reached through the valley of despair that is the power struggle. If we do not use the relationship to finish childhood, our marriages will get bogged down in the same issues we were stuck in as children. When romantic love dies, it clears the way for real love.

The illusion of romantic love is dispelled when our partners fail to live up to our expectations and begin to exhibit familiar negative traits, the negative traits of our caretakers and of our Denied Selves that we were blind to in them at first. And even though our partners may embody only *some* of our caretakers' negative traits, and then only to *some* degree, we *project* the missing ones—especially those that we ourselves have but deny in ourselves—onto them and behave toward them as if they were carbon copies of our caretakers. In that way, we provoke the same response from them that we got from our caretakers. We begin to reenact our relationship with our primary caretakers within the context of our primary love relationship.

Remember that the negative traits of our Imago match are often denied traits in ourselves that are introjected traits from our parents. In other words, we ourselves possess the negative parental traits we criticize in our partners. During the power struggle, we shift from the child position to the parent position and treat our partners, when they fail to meet our needs, the way our parents treated us. Worse news, we tend to act with our partners like the parent with whom we had the most difficulty in childhood, because usually we saw this parent as the most powerful. We identify with this parent because, from the vantage point of our old brain, he or she had the most survival power. We may have hated our mother's whining and cowering, but it intimidated Dad, and he'd give up. Or, Dad's anger may have been brutal and scary, but he usually got his way. In behaving like our parent, we move our perception of our partner to the child mode. When our partner tells us we are "just like our mother (or father)" we are shocked. What is happening here is that we unconsciously identify with the negative traits in our parents, deny that we have done so, vehemently repudiate such a charge, but unconsciously reenact those old scenarios with our partner.

At other times, we feel like a child with our partner. After all, we see in him the shadow of our parents. It's no wonder that we respond to our partner's anger as we did to our mother's rage, however faint the resemblance between the two. If we got our father's attention with an endless barrage of stories about what went on at school, who we played with, what we watched on television, we are likely to think that we have to be an unrelentingly lively and entertaining partner to hold our mate's interest. In a matter of seconds, we may switch from feeling as we did as a child to acting like the parent we liked least. Here is the heart of the power struggle.

We also have to contend with the reappearance of the Lost Self. Remember that we have chosen a partner who fills in what is missing in ourselves. For a while that works out fine, and we revel in our ersatz wholeness. But sooner or later characteristics that partners originally found attractive about each other suddenly become annoying, as the Lost Self squirms in discomfort. What a husband saw through the rose-colored glasses of romance as his wife's independence he now sees as a lack of attention or commitment. What his wife saw as his fun-loving nature she now sees as self-indulgence. Suddenly our partner is *too* logical, *too* emotional, *too* sexy, *too* easygoing. The power struggle has begun in earnest.

THIS TOO SHALL PASS

Most marriages stall in the power struggle, but that is not the way nature intended it. The power struggle, like romantic love, is another way station en route to the real thing. It is supposed to happen, for it is necessary to make the potential hinted at in the romantic stage a reality. It is not even a negative indicator, but a sure sign that we are with the right person for our maximum potential growth—if we handle it correctly.

The power struggle is not supposed to last, either. It is a transient phenomenon, a conduit to the creation of selfhood in each partner and a relationship that has a unique identity, different and separate from that of our parents. To stay stuck in the stage of romance or the power struggle is to abort nature's process of attempting to finish the creation of a self that cares for others. Here again is the grand design of nature: that while the focus on the self may be a prerequisite for personal survival, moving beyond the self to the concern for, and intimacy with, others is essential to the survival of our species. The creation of real love is nature's way of repairing and completing itself—through you.[2]

But without awareness and the skills to transform their relationship, most couples will never move past the issues of Identity and Competence to achieve real love and the joy and wholeness it brings. *Consciousness* is the key.

David and Sarah

To show you how this convoluted theory works, and to give you a preview of the journey you will take after you marry, I'm going to use the example of a couple I counseled. David and Sarah seemed irretrievably locked in the power struggle when they first came to see me. Married twelve years, they had three children. Sarah worked part time in an art museum, but devoted herself primarily to the home and family. She was vociferous in her complaints about David: he was rarely home, he was preoccupied with his work, he wouldn't communicate, he was self-centered. David had recently left a management position in a mid-sized corporation to start his own consulting business, which was almost immediately successful. He seemed overwhelmed by Sarah's complaints and emotions, and professed not to understand them. His work was very demanding, he told me, but it provided well for Sarah and the children and he was careful not to bring his business problems home. When he was at home he just wanted to relax, but Sarah was always "on him"—to do things together or with the children, to talk. She was devoted and loving, he conceded, but not very interested in sex, which was frustrating for him.

It didn't take long to identify the traits that made David and Sarah an Imago match for each other. David's mother was an intense and indulgent woman, a loving but also a very smothering mother. David was her youngest child, and only son, and he felt particularly overwhelmed by her attention at times. His father was often unemployed, and although he was playful and fun to be with much of the time, he had a volatile temper. During long periods of unemployment he would vent his anger at his family, especially his children, and criticize them harshly. David remembers his father's outbursts as being particularly embarrassing during his teens. "I swore I would never be like him," he told me. Despite his father's problems, however, David's parents seemed mostly happy with each other. His mother tolerated his father's lapses, and they were openly physical with each other.

Sarah's parents divorced when she was quite young. Her father, a successful salesman, was away from home a lot even before the divorce. Sarah remembers him as smart and funny, but it wasn't easy to get his attention. She had seen him infrequently through her teens and young adulthood, and he had died of a heart attack within a year of our first session. Sarah was very close to her mother, who raised her and her two younger sisters alone. Sarah described her as self-sacrificing and devoted. Her mother was also vehemently angry toward and critical of Sarah's father—for working too much, for leaving them, and for remarrying. Sarah's mother never dated or remarried after the divorce, and she strongly disapproved of all of the women Sarah's father dated before he remarried.

Although it wasn't apparent to them when they first met, David and Sarah resemble each other's caretakers in a number of ways. Sarah is loving and devoted and emotional like David's mother, and she is playful as well as openly angry and critical like David's father. David is smart and funny and successful like Sarah's father, and similarly unavailable. Like Sarah's mother, he is loyal and providing, but also somewhat rigid. I deduced that David and Sarah's primary wounds occurred during the stage of Exploration, but in complementary ways: Sarah is a Pursuer and a Maximizer; David is an Isolator and a Minimizer. By the time they came to see me, they thought of themselves as oil and water, but they were in fact an almost perfect match.

David and Sarah met when they were standing in line for fall semester registration at college, where she was studying art and he was studying business, and discovered they were both signing up for Geology to fulfill their science requirement. They began getting together for study dates, and were both surprised at the immediate rapport they established. "We referred to ourselves as the Moon Unit," David revealed, "because we were off in our own little world, safe and self-contained. We sometimes felt sorry for our friends who didn't have the kind of love we'd found."

David says he was attracted to Sarah because she was lively and expressive and fun to be with. He admired the fact that she was devoted to her mother and sisters and did volunteer work with underprivileged children. He does not remember seeing any signs of her anger or criticism during the early years of their relationship, and thinks Sarah has "changed" since their children were born. At the time of our meeting, she had also lost interest in sex.

Sarah remembers David in college as quiet, but easygoing and funny. She admired his intellect and how hard he worked to put himself through school. He was very attentive to her throughout their courtship, especially physically, and, as she describes it, "I could be myself with him. I felt safe."

David and Sarah were married shortly after graduation, and Sarah worked for a few years as an art teacher while David went to graduate school. Those first few years of their marriage were relatively happy. Like most couples faced with hints or warnings that their romance is over, they ignored or rationalized away any signs that all was not as they had hoped. David ignored Sarah's emotional outbursts when he spent a lot of time at school or went out with his friends instead of coming home; he accepted the excuses she made for postponing sex. Sarah convinced herself that David's preoccupation with his work would diminish once he had obtained his degree; she hoped that he would be more expressive of his affection once the pressure was off.

Things did not come to a head for them until after David's graduation and the birth of their first child. Then David threw himself into his job in much the same way he had thrown himself into graduate school. Sarah felt abandoned, and her anger became hard to ignore. "You're never home," she complained. "All you care about is your work. You're so self-centered, you never think about me—except when you want to get laid." David, no doubt hearing in Sarah the echo of his father's ire, retreated even further into his work, and into his weekend hobbies. "Sarah is so critical," he complained to me. "I work hard, and she has everything she needs. I don't know what she's so angry about. She's never satisfied."

Blame and criticism are characteristic of the power struggle stage of a relationship. What we are seeing is the flip side of the coin of romance: same agenda, opposite tactics. We no longer try to woo our partners into meeting our needs and making us whole; we try to coerce them into it. For some reason—probably because as infants we learned that if we cried or complained our caretakers would attend to us—we think we can provoke our partner into giving us what we want. What we get instead is conflict, and an escalating fear that we're not going to get what we so desperately need.

What was happening in this case was that David, in an effort not to be like his father, was denying his own anger and projecting it onto and provoking it in Sarah. It's true that Sarah was capable of expressing anger, but she was not the angry person David began to see her as. But anger-phobic as he was, David retreated from Sarah's wrath, as he had from his father's anger and his mother's smothering attention.

Sarah, on the other hand, who had disowned her own career interests and ambitions, now disparaged and undermined David's success. She had seen how her father's ambition had destroyed their family and had learned from her mother to think of ambition as selfish. She projected this kind of self-centered ambition onto David, who was in fact hardworking and ambitious, but not particularly self-centered.

While David's sexuality had been left relatively untampered with, he had, like many men of his generation, been socialized to keep a tight rein on his emotions, especially by his father, who criticized emotional displays and sometimes called David a "sissy" when he cried. In Sarah's emotional nature David saw the reflection of his lost emotional self, which made him anxious and uncomfortable—another reason to retreat from Sarah's grasp. David's active and comfortable sexuality—while at first attractive to Sarah—eventually stirred up her own taboo sexuality. By criticizing David's "obsession" with sex, she deflected attention from her own inner conflict. They began to criticize in each other what had been criticized—and lost—in themselves. David found Sarah "too emotional" and "too demanding"; Sarah thought David was "only interested in money and sex."

THE DENOUEMENT OF THE POWER STRUGGLE

What happens next? Although most marriages get stuck in one of them, the power struggle potentially has six predictable phases similar to the stages of grief identified by Elisabeth Kübler-Ross in her well-known book *On Death and Dying*: shock, denial, anger, bargaining, despair, acceptance.[3] What we are grieving is the loss of the illusion, embedded in the experience of romantic love, that we are secure and that with our beloved we will be painlessly, miraculously healed of our childhood wound and recover our original aliveness.

First, as we have seen, comes the shock when the veil of illusion is torn by the discovery of imperfections in our partner; then the denial when we try to ignore or rationalize away the negative traits of our partner; then comes the anger when they persist in spite of our efforts to vaporize them. The existence of those traits means to us that our partner is not going to give us what we need, because he cannot. In the unconscious, the old brain sounds an alarm that we are in peril, that not only are our best hopes dashed, but our existence is in question. Prepared by aeons of evolutionary learning, our life force transmutes into negative energy and assaults the partner, now the source of danger and thus the enemy, with open aggression, acute withdrawal, or passive hostility. Fight, flee, submit, or freeze: we employ whichever adaptation we long ago decided would get the job done.

Many marriages fall apart in—or get stuck in—the anger stage of the power struggle. Often the marriage is sustained through the anger by bargaining, in which each partner tries to get what he wants by negotiating for it: if you do this, I'll do that. If you come home earlier from work, we'll have more sex. If you let me watch TV all evening without interruption, I'll take the kids to the park on Saturday. Traditional marital therapy unwittingly prolongs this stage by teaching partners bargaining skills and encouraging the forging of behavioral agreements or contracts without understanding or addressing the hidden childhood agenda. The result is what I call the "quid pro quo" marriage, and it works to some extent for many couples. But for most couples, bargaining leads to resignation and despair, the fifth stage of the power struggle. They stay married, and although they eventually give up hope of ever having the love they need, they settle for a tolerable working relationship—often a parallel marriage in which they go their separate ways—because they don't know what else to do. While some couples at this point resign themselves to unhappiness, others remain amicable, cordial, and caring—despite an unspoken longing for what is missing. They have reached the final stage of the power struggle: acceptance. What they have accepted is an unsatisfying but tolerable marriage.

At the stage of despair, many other couples leave the marriage and seek real love elsewhere. Unfortunately, since they never became conscious of their childhood wounds, much less resolved them, they get rid of the spouse and keep their problem, taking it with them into the next relationship—and begin the cycle again.

BREAKING THE IMPASSE: THE END OF BARGAINING

David and Sarah had been in traditional marital therapy for several years before they came to me, and they had developed the bargaining techniques with which they had sustained their relationship at a bearable subsistence level during most of that time. Their marriage relied on an intricate structure of agreements through which each of them ostensibly got what he wanted—Sarah more availability from David, David fewer demands and more sex from Sarah. They remained in the power struggle stage of their marriage, but the conflict was mostly kept under wraps.

Looking back on those years Sarah told me, "We were both basically living up to our agreements, but it just didn't seem to make either of us happy. I kept thinking, 'What's the matter with me, I'm not a kid anymore, I should give up wanting hearts and flowers. What am I angry about? Maybe David's right, maybe I am just an angry person.' " David recalls: "We'd go along fine for a while and then the smallest thing would set Sarah off. I'd come home a half hour later than promised, or forget to call if I was out of town, and she'd blow up like I'd been out all night with another woman. I felt like I had all these tests I had to pass every week if I wanted to have sex with my own wife over the weekend."

It was apparent to me that David and Sarah's relationship was sinking slowly into despair. Not only were their bargains breeding resentment on the part of the "giver," they did not even satisfy the "receiver." Both of them kept vigilant track of their gives and takes, but they derived little or no pleasure from them. "He only comes home for dinner because I make him," Sarah asserted. "And then he's still preoccupied, so what's the point?" "Our sex life," David grimaced, "is like the moon. It comes up regularly on the calendar— but it rarely surprises us."

By the time David and Sarah were referred to me, the lid had blown off their charade. David's new business was demanding much of his time and energy, and he was becoming more and more impatient with Sarah's demands. Their youngest child had started school, and Sarah had an opportunity to increase her part-time job at the art museum to full time, but she found herself strangely paralyzed. She insisted that David's unavailability made it impossible for her to commit any more time and energy to her job, and was afraid the children would suffer if she worked full time. Since her father's death, according to David, she was increasingly prone to emotional outbursts and angry attacks on him. "She's not much fun to come home to," he admitted.

Bargaining had prolonged the power struggle in David and Sarah's relationship, but it had not resolved it. They were still frustrated and angry and unsatisfied with their marriage, not because they couldn't make and keep bargains, but because the unconscious is singularly unimpressed with them. It needs and will be satisfied only with *unconditional* love—the kind we had as infants. David and Sarah were surprised when I told them that we would be working not on forging new bargains but on their "waking up" to what was really going on in their marriage and learning the skills they would need to heal each other.

Becoming Conscious: A Turning Point on the Journey

Most partners remain unconscious in their marriages. They never develop beyond the power struggle, remaining focused on childhood issues that were never resolved. They move through the stages of shock, denial, anger, bargaining, and despair like robots in a waking sleep, and eventually either end in divorce or in acceptance of an unsatisfying relationship. But despair can be a turning point for couples, as it was for David and Sarah. It can lead to acceptance of the truth of the Imago and of the underlying healing purpose of the relationship, and to a commitment to reframe the relationship so both partners' unfinished business can be completed.

In order to reach the stage of real love, our unconscious aim must become our conscious intention. We must enlist our "new" brain—our cognitive powers—to achieve the vital objectives of our "old" brain: healing our childhood wounds and achieving wholeness. This is why I urge singles to familiarize themselves with their Imago and self-completion issues. In beginning to reclaim the Lost and Denied Selves, singles lighten the load of baggage they carry into their relationships, which leads to an altered Imago and a healthier partner choice. Their skills and awareness will prove invaluable in recognizing and working through the inevitable power-struggle stage of future relationships, when still-unresolved issues will confront them.

Not having had the benefit of the awareness and skills that this book is intended to give you before marriage, David and Sarah became entrenched in their power struggle. Even the seemingly *conscious* efforts they made to "improve" their marriage—mostly bargains and concessions—were *without consciousness:* their negotiations addressed the symptoms of their conflicts without understanding or addressing their underlying cause. They had a lot of work to do to change their unconscious relationship into a conscious one. And first they had to change themselves.

One of the most difficult truths about relationships for most couples to accept is that *in order to be loved you must first become a lover.* You must be willing to grow and change and commit yourself first and foremost to healing your partner. *Being* the right partner is more important to a good relationship than *picking* the right partner.

This is easier said than done. As much as people think or say that they want to do what's necessary to meet their partners' needs, they are in fact resistant to change. The general wisdom on the subject has been: "People don't change, you just have to accept them as they are." This is such a nugget of pop wisdom that people don't even question it. But it is wrong, although it is a safe and comforting defense against the fear and anxiety that change provokes.

The hard truth of the matter is that *in order to have a healing marriage, we must change and become the kind of person that our partner needs in order to heal.* The kind of person your partner will need to finish childhood is someone different from his or her parents. You will need to "parent" your partner's inner child in a way his or her parents did not. In other words, you have to become the parent your partner's parents were not. That will require changing the part of you that is similar to the negative traits of your partner's parents.

This is a daunting task. It is not simply obstinacy that paralyzes marriages—although it often feels like it! It is fear. We are afraid of having our long unmet needs—those needs we learned to deny or disparage—finally satisfied. We are afraid to get in touch with our Lost Selves—the traits we were taught to think were unacceptable. We are afraid to own up to the denied traits we feel are "bad" or unlovable. We resist change because to change means facing our own internalized self-hatred and accepting the responsibility for feeling unlovable. Changing feels *dangerous.* Our Lost and Denied selves are survival mechanisms; we fear that if we reclaim what was unacceptable we will die. On top of our fear, we are hampered by lack of partnership and intimacy skills.

The changes required of us in order to become healing partners for our mates are often the changes that are most difficult for us to make. If you remember the four functions of the socialization circle (page 141), you will recall that our partner will inevitably ask for what is repressed in us—just as David wanted more sexuality from Sarah and she wanted more emotional availability from him. The paradox is: when we give our partner what he or she needs in order to heal his or her wounds, we have to call upon the parts of ourselves that have been suppressed. In pushing the limits of our habituated behavior to heal our partner, we heal ourselves, for we reactivate our own evolution toward wholeness. The wondrous part is that when we meet our partner's need, we discover that we have the same need, for we were similarly wounded. The gifts we give our partner, our old brain receives as gifts for itself. In order to give Sarah what she needed, David had to get back in touch with his emotions and admit to his denied anger; Sarah had to get back in touch with her repressed sexuality and own up to her ambition. There is a beautiful symmetry in this two-way healing.

OWNING OUR PROJECTIONS

Consciousness can be painful. It means that you have to become aware of what you don't want to be aware of, and you have to give up an automated self and behave in ways that seem unnatural for you. But to be whole, we must become aware of our Missing Selves, and discard the false veneer we present to the world. We must confess, to ourselves and to our partners, the unpleasant details of our Denied Selves, those negative aspects of ourselves that we reject, and integrate them into our self-concept.

Our partners are mirrors in which we see reflected those parts of ourselves that we disown. They are reflected in our partners' criticisms of the negative ways we treat them, in what we withhold from them, and in what they want from us that we claim does not exist. Their needs call out to our Lost Selves to come back into being. Their pain challenges us to thaw the frozen parts of our character adaptations so that we can recover our original selves—the selves we were before we adapted to become what our parents approved of.

In an unconscious relationship, we project our Denied Selves onto our partners—who usually exhibit the undesirable trait to some extent—then we provoke and criticize it in them. We deny accusations that we too are angry, or lazy, or stingy, or ambitious. In David and Sarah's case, *he* was the ambitious one, *she* was the angry one. "David's angry, too. He just disappears and punishes me with his silence," Sarah claimed, while David vigorously denied it. "Sarah resents my success," David said. "She would have liked to be the curator of the art museum by now instead of the part-time administrative assistant." "That's ridiculous!" was Sarah's response.

As our partners change, however, we find it harder and harder to maintain our projections, for there is no reality to anchor them. Since our partners will no longer fully carry or express our Denied Selves, we are forced to own and express them ourselves. It makes us very uncomfortable. "Now that David's around more, I'm not nearly as angry with him for being so involved in his work," Sarah told me after they had moved to a bigger house so David could run his consulting business out of a home office. "But *he's* angrier! If I stay late at the museum to hang an exhibit, he lets me have it!" Sarah seemed more amused than upset by this, and David admitted that it was true. "It galls me to think I'm acting like my father," he said sheepishly. As Sarah's anger diminished, it became harder for David to project his anger onto Sarah. Also, Sarah made use of a crucial skill we worked on together (and which you will learn on page 286). She learned to "hold" David's projections of anger. For instance, when David accused her of being angry, she learned to listen to what he was saying without becoming angry at his unfounded accusations. She *mirrored* what he was saying, *validated* his point of view, and showed *empathy* for his feelings. Instead of her habitual exasperation or sarcasm, she learned to say something like, "You feel that I am furious now, that I was expressing anger by not picking up your dry cleaning. I can see how you would think that, given my past behavior. It makes sense, and I can see how upset you are. It must feel awful to think that you live with an angry, vindictive person."

This kind of response is the behavioral opposite of the angry parent David was projecting. Over time, David's projections had no screen on which to play themselves out. It took him a while to recognize that he was using Sarah to mirror his anger, and that not all anger was "bad." Once he had *confessed* to his anger, however—once he owned it rather than projecting it onto Sarah—he was able to drop his pose of calm unflappability and express his anger appropriately and in nondestructive ways.

The process of reclaiming our Lost Selves and re-owning and integrating our Denied Selves can be disorienting, sometimes frightening. To see ourselves stripped bare, without our usual defenses, in the eyes of the person who we count on for survival and happiness is scary indeed. Even clients who know rationally that the changes they and their partners are making are healing often go to surprising lengths to maintain the status quo. The old conflicts are unpleasant, but they are comfortingly familiar—they are what we recognize as love.

When Sarah's angry criticism of David's preoccupation with his work was largely dissipated by his working at home, he found himself almost missing her outbursts. "I started working through dinner every once in a while just to get a rise out of her," he admitted. "It made me nervous that she wasn't complaining. I almost felt like she didn't love me as much as when she used to be upset with me more often. Not only that. A part of me was afraid that she was getting 'healthy' while I was still mired in my old patterns. I wanted to keep her at my level so I didn't have to grow."

His ploy didn't often work, however. Sarah, who had claimed and integrated her denied ambition, was more frequently spending extra hours at the art museum. Now that she was fulfilling her own ambitions, she was more sympathetic to the demands of David's work and didn't necessarily think he was deliberately avoiding her if he occasionally had to work through dinner. Once David realized he was trying to provoke the old conflict because of his discomfort with change, he let it go.

COMMITMENT TO HEALING

David and Sarah's journey was neither short nor always easy and pleasant. There was lots of discomfort, even pain, and almost as many setbacks as triumphs. It is difficult to transform an unconscious relationship once it has reached the stage of despair; the commitment to consciousness should be made before despair and ill will sap the energy required to do the necessary work. That is why singles who have read and learned from this book *before* marriage will have an easier row to hoe. But there is no avoiding the reality of a successful marriage: it takes work, lots of it. The fantasy of a good marriage as "natural" or easy is just that, a fantasy.

For David and Sarah, the journey started with three commitments on their part, prerequisites to beginning the process of transforming an unconscious relationship into a conscious one. They agreed to:

1. *Eliminate the blame and criticism* that so permeated their relationship. In a word: STOP. So much criticism of our partner is in fact a cryptic expression of our needs. Criticism is the adult version of crying, nature's built-in distress signal for getting our parents' attention. In adulthood we translate our screeching, pathetic, insistent cries into language, inflicting our partners with pain in a warped effort to get them to meet our needs. Embedded in all criticism is a wish or a desire, just as a need not met stimulated the childhood crying. In an unconscious relationship, we expect our partners to intuit our needs, as our parents did in childhood, and we fault them when they fail to meet them. In conscious relationships, partners identify the needs hidden in their criticism and express them to their partners as desires followed by a request that they be met. (Exercise 15J on page 288 will teach you how to do this.)

2. *Commit to the relationship and to the process.* This means giving up what I call "exits"—the escape hatches partners use to avoid each other and their conflicts. For David, this meant less time at work, fewer board commitments, less television, and cutting down his weekend time in the basement workshop. For Sarah, it meant no more threats of leaving, less time on the phone with her friends, and getting the children to bed earlier. For all couples, at the very least, the door must be closed against separation, divorce, and affairs. Addictions of all kinds are also highly damaging exits, and are difficult to break.

3. *Learn new skills and to change negative, unproductive behavior.* See Chapter 15.

The Conscious Marriage

As the unfolding stages of a relationship reflect, first we idealize our partners; then we devalue them and polarize; then we integrate the positive and negative in ourselves and in the relationship into a couplehood that is unique for us; then we develop confidence in managing the process of being married and express our newfound ability in care for others. The result is a transformed relationship that consciously fosters the psychological and spiritual growth of both partners and gives something to the world at large. In the process of this transformation we create and express real love.

Real love might also be called "reality love." It is not based on the illusion of romance or the fantasy that our partners will intuit our every wish and desire. Unlike romantic love, which is created by childhood needs hidden in romantic yearnings, reality love is based on awareness, respect, and commitment. Reality love is based on awareness of ourselves and of our partners, and of the healing purpose of our relationships; respect for our partners' needs and desires; and commitment to healing our partners through unconditional giving. Such love does not give birth to relationships. It is *created* in the relationship.

Unconditional love—or, more accurately, unconditional giving— has not been in vogue in recent times. Too often we tend to think in terms of a balance sheet, of *earning* someone's love, or having him or her earn ours—an *economic* model. Unconditional love sounds like a willingness to love someone no matter what he or she does, even if he or she neglects or abuses us. "I can't agree to that," we think. But loving your partner unconditionally simply means committing to giving him what he needs without asking for anything in return— without rendering a bill for your service. Instead of "I'll come home earlier if you'll have more sex with me," we say "I'll come home earlier because you need me to spend more time with you."

As we discussed before, our unconscious is not satisfied with a tit-for-tat relationship. Our old brain wants only love without strings, much like that which newborns receive from their caretakers—and it wants it only from our imperfect original caretakers or a reasonable facsimile. Only true gifts are truly healing. When David came home for dinner because Sarah demanded it, or because she promised him more sex, it didn't feel "loving" to her. But when he decided on his own to move his business into their home and sit down with the family for dinner every night, even if he had more work to do after dinner, she felt cared for. Her anger dissipated, and the power struggle eased.

"The funny thing is," David told me about six months after they had moved, "I *like* being home for dinner. Some days when I'm really busy Sarah offers to bring me something to eat at my desk, but I feel left out eating in there! Even doing the dishes with the kids has become a ritual we all love and hate!" In satisfying Sarah's need, David has awakened a lost part of himself, his own need to be close and nurturing. Not surprisingly, David and Sarah's sex life also improved dramatically when David understood that Sarah's discomfort with her sexuality was part of her childhood wound, and when making love became something Sarah did to express her love for David rather than to placate him or as her part of a bargain. With David's playful encouragement, Sarah reclaimed her sexual self in the course of her commitment to David's needs.

Most couples who, like David and Sarah, have become mired in the power struggle and have resorted to bargaining to keep their relationship afloat have to consciously re-romanticize their relationship. This requires identifying each other's needs and engaging in caring behaviors that are specifically targeted to meet those needs. It starts off easy: perhaps David rubs Sarah's feet, or fixes her a cup of tea, or calls her every day when he's away on business. Sarah may make it a point to tell David something she loves about him, or wear his favorite dress.

But the degree of difficulty and discomfort escalates, since your partner most needs what is hardest for you to give. Giving your partner what he wants often requires what I call "stretching"— extending yourself into behaviors that at first are difficult and uncomfortable for you. (Men often have to stretch to give nurturing, for example, and women to receive it.) Such stretching behaviors may require major, significant effort—like Sarah's initiating sex on a regular basis—but it must be specifically targeted to meet the *other's* need, not our own or what we think our partner should want, and it must be *unconditional*.

Once David and Sarah became aware of the underlying issues and purpose of their relationship, they were able to develop the skills and make the changes necessary to move their marriage out of the power struggle and into consciousness and real love. Over time, they were able to provide each other with a new set of experiences, which contradicted their childhood belief systems, and eventually their thick-headed old brains got the point. They were able to transform their unconscious relationship into a conscious one, and in the process heal themselves.

The fruits of David and Sarah's labor to transform their relationship was apparent to me by the time they left counseling. Not only had they worked out their own pains, but they were aware of a higher purpose to their connection, and much of their self-centeredness had been abandoned in favor of a genuine care for the other's well-being. When they founded an organization to help disadvantaged teenagers find summer jobs, I knew that they were putting feelers out into the world, and that their love would have an impact beyond the doors of their home. In their hard-won wholeness and security, they had the energy and love to spare for the larger community.

CHARACTERISTICS OF A CONSCIOUS RELATIONSHIP

What does a relationship based on real love—a *conscious* relationship—look like? We've already seen—and most of you have no doubt had—an unconscious relationship, in which partners remain oblivious to the needs and drives that fuel their conflicts. A conscious relationship differs from an unconscious one in innumerable and significant ways, but its primary characteristics are:

1. The partners in a conscious relationship recognize that the purpose of their relationship is to heal their childhood wounds. They are committed to identifying the drives and directives of their unconscious and to designing their relationship to cooperate with them. They recognize that their partners' needs are a blueprint for their own personal growth. They realize that following this map will involve arduous work, and they are committed to the process. *The basic principle of a conscious relationship is intentionality.*

2. The partners in a conscious relationship educate each other about their childhood wounds. They identify their partners' needs and desires, and they commit themselves to meeting them. They take inspiration from the romantic-love stage of their relationship and offer their partners unconditional love. That is, they specifically target their behavior to meet their partners' needs and heal their wounds, without asking for anything in return. *In a conscious relationship, partners exchange unconditional gifts.*

3. Partners in a conscious relationship accept each other's absolute separateness, their unique way of perceiving reality, the sacredness of each other's inner world; they consider themselves equals. They explore and mirror each other's worlds, validate each other's experience, and empathize with each other's feelings. *In a conscious relationship, partners are separate but equal. Dialogue is the core of communication.*

4. The partners in a conscious relationship keep all the energy

that belongs in the relationship within its bounds. When they feel uncomfortable or when their needs are not being met, they bring their concerns to their partners rather than withdrawing from the relationship or getting their needs met outside the relationship. Rather than acting out, they convert their feelings into constructive communication. *In a conscious relationship, there are no exits.*

5. The partners in a conscious relationship communicate their needs and desires to each other in constructive ways. They do not criticize or blame each other, and they do not use provocation or coercion to try to get their partners to fulfill those needs and desires. *In a conscious relationship there is no criticism.*

6. The partners in a conscious relationship accept all of each other's feelings, especially anger. They realize that anger is an expression of pain, and that pain usually has its roots in childhood. Conscious partners never express anger or frustration spontaneously, for they know that "dumping" negative feelings is destructive. They learn constructive ways of containing and expressing anger and other negative emotions, and they help their partners to do so in nonjudgmental ways as well. Expressing their anger in a contained way leads to its conversion into passion and deeper bonding. *In a conscious relationship, anger is expressed by appointment only.*

7. The partners in a conscious relationship learn to own their own negative traits (their Denied Selves) instead of projecting them onto and provoking them in their partners. They accept responsibility for those parts of themselves of which they are not proud, and learn to manage and integrate them. *In a conscious relationship both partners are responsible for and carry all aspects of themselves.*

8. The partners in a conscious relationship develop their own lost strengths and abilities instead of relying on their partners to make up for what is missing or lost in themselves. They are therefore more whole, and they foster wholeness in their partners. *In a conscious relationship each partner calls the other to wholeness.*

9. The partners in a conscious relationship develop their own contrasexual energy and encourage the development of their partners' contrasexual energy. They do not behave or expect their partners to behave in accordance with gender or sexual stereotypes. They share income responsibilities as well as household responsibilities, chores, and child care in accordance with each partner's interests, abilities, and schedules, rather than a code of social expectations. *In a conscious relationship each partner strives toward androgyny.*

10. The partners in a conscious relationship are whole and balanced and in touch with their sense of oneness with the world. Like

children who have successfully mastered the stages of development, they are powerful, competent, caring, and capable of intimacy. For this reason, they are able and willing to direct their excess energies to the world outside their relationship. They become more altruistic, contributive members of society. *In a conscious relationship partners care for others and the world.*

A conscious relationship is an ever-evolving journey, not a destination. David and Sarah's marriage is now a conscious one, but this does not mean that conflicts do not develop, or that they always handle them easily or appropriately. "We still have a lot to learn," Sarah says. "But now we have the tools to work with, and we never question our commitment to the work or to each other. It's a very comforting feeling knowing there is this person with whom you can be yourself and who will always be there for you."

"All of a sudden our wedding vows make sense," David adds. "They aren't just words anymore."

Unfortunately, " 'Til death do us part" are still just words to too many couples nowadays. They hope their marriage will last forever, but they know if they run into trouble they can always get divorced—and all too often they run into trouble. It is my hope and intention to convince singles that wedding vows must be honored—not for moral reasons, but for their emotional well-being, physical health, and spiritual evolution. (It is by now well documented that married people live longer and are happier.) This is a revolutionary view of marriage: that rather than *leaving* it to find yourself, you find yourself *through* it. *Marriage itself is in essence therapy,* and your partner's needs chart your path to psychological and spiritual wholeness.

BECOMING A CONSCIOUS SINGLE

14

From Insight to Integration: Basic Strategies for Change

Inflexible mentality remains the biggest
stumbling block to change.
—MIKHAIL GORBACHEV

In the preceding chapters we have discussed the unconscious purpose of relationships, the opportunity your current singleness provides for your becoming a "conscious single," the necessity of a relationship for your personal growth, and some methods of becoming aware of your growth challenges. You have taken a long journey in your thinking, from an understanding of your cosmic origins, your evolutionary legacy as it applies to relationships, to an in-depth look at the psychological and social factors that have shaped you into the person you are. You have had the opportunity to deepen your self-knowledge and get an impression of your Imago—a preview of the type of person to whom you will be attracted for an intimate relationship.

By now, you are well aware of the roots of your relationship woes. But while insight is valuable, it is not a cure; it is not transformation. It tells you only how much work you have to do. In order for change to occur, insight must be translated into action. Whatever

251

is created by experience must be corrected by experience rather than mere analysis. In order to integrate our insights, we have to put ourselves in new situations and learn and practice new behaviors, which, over time and through repetition, actually change our past behavior and beliefs. This section is about that change process. In the next chapter, you will learn dialogue skills and methods for changing unproductive behavior. But first I want to talk about some basic strategies and the change process itself.

START NOW

The time to take action is now, while you are single. You are in training for a lasting relationship. Your single years are an opportunity to try out new skills and behaviors in a relatively low-risk environment, before that all-important relationship comes along. By practicing uncomfortable behaviors with friends or casual dates, you are not taking the chance of turning off someone you really care about by saying the wrong thing or behaving contrary to expectations. Most important, everything you do now to become more whole, to awaken your sense of aliveness, will modify the harsh edges of your Imago and have a corresponding effect on the type of person you attract. You will automatically upgrade your pool of potential partners.

Now, I don't want to overstate what you can hope to accomplish outside of an intimate relationship. As you know, I feel that the idea of self-help or self-healing is, in a way, a misnomer; there are limits to what you can do on your own. But I also want to be clear that I am not suggesting that you wait until you are "perfect" before settling into a long-term relationship. Not at all—the deepest growth and change will *only* happen there, for in the final analysis, a conscious, continuous, caring relationship is the only truly effective healer.

Some of your problems are no doubt apparent in all your relationships: the chronic lateness, the defensiveness, the habit of putting up a cheerful front, the thin skin when it comes to criticism. But your deepest wounds will only be reopened in the enforced intimacy of a prolonged relationship. There simply is no substitute for the kind of growth triggered by the hourly, daily interaction of intimate partners, the constant rubbing of two stones. No one else really sees—and will tell you—the truth about yourself, outside the privacy of your partnership.

But you can begin the process of self-integration now, armed with the knowledge you have gathered thus far. You can identify the changes you want to make, begin practicing new behaviors and the skills of partner dialogue. If you get a good running start and deal with the issues of your own selfhood, there will be far less to deal with in your future partnership.

WHAT'S THE RUSH?

You may be champing at the bit to make some of the changes you feel are needed to attract the kind of partner you want. But I caution you against either expecting, or provoking, sudden change. In our quick-fix culture, we are addicted to fast, dramatic results, especially if we are frustrated and discouraged with our present situation. But change must be gradual and timely. It is a natural process, with its own timetable—and you are part of nature. Too much, too fast is destructive—like a volcano erupting. Rushing headlong into a dramatic makeover can cause tremendous upheaval in relationships—with friends, lovers, and family—as I have seen all too frequently when my clients, in a frenzied burst of newfound knowledge and enthusiasm, spring all their new tricks on their unwitting partners, with drastic, unsettling results.

Too, the plodding old brain can only assimilate slowly. Precipitous change will not "take"; the unconscious will not process it. When you force new behavior on an unready psyche, you are just going through the motions. It is sometimes shocking how dense the unconscious is when it comes to change. My clients often lament the repetition of old patterns, the seeming intractability of the issues they thought they'd changed. Typically, the story they tell me is that they've gotten out of a bad relationship, suffered through the pain and loss, had years of therapy, tried hard to understand what went wrong and to learn from their experience. They date, perhaps for years, and seem to have put some of their old problems behind them—until they get "serious" again. Then they run headlong into the same conflicts.

Andy, a rumpled university instructor, felt discouraged and angry at himself for his seemingly unerring ability to end up with depressed women. Two years earlier, he'd left an eight-year marriage, determined not to be involved with another woman like his wife. On his own and in therapy, he had come to understand the family history that made such women so appealing. Yet the cheerful, lively women he made it a point to date never 'grabbed' him and held his interest. And women who early on would seem to be upbeat and positive would, as the relationship progressed, turn out to be depressed. Then he'd be furious at himself for repeating the pattern.

Over time, as he worked on his own issues and his own need for, and attraction to, depressed women, and as he worked through this attraction over several years of dating, such women became much less seductive. When he did settle down again, it was with a woman who had already made great changes in her depressive history, and while he tolerated her depression and supported her in her attempts to change it, he no longer needed it, or wanted it, to sustain his attraction.

You must learn to tolerate the slow process. Remember the moratorium you've set for yourself. The behavior and patterns you are trying to change took a lifetime to accumulate; you can't change them overnight. Evolution is far more effective than revolution.

WAKING UP IS HARD TO DO

While the description of how to achieve change and integration is actually quite simple, the process itself is hard. It is not like losing weight or learning to chat at cocktail parties. It demands clear intention, sustained attention, and the conscientious day-by-day practice of new skills and unfamiliar, uncomfortable behavior.

There is no way around this process, however. The needs of the unconscious for wholeness and aliveness are nonnegotiable. The psyche is committed to its own completion. Every living thing wants to reach its full potential, whether it's a tree struggling and twisting its way to the sky through rocks and desert sand, or a man trying to survive a painful partnership. Anyone trying to bypass the hard work of self-integration is driving down a dead-end tunnel. It seems obvious to me that drugs, skydiving, weekend spiritual makeovers, fast cars, or serial relationships don't do the trick, but many people keep looking for that magic shortcut to nirvana.[1]

Resistance is natural; changing our character defenses and habituated behavior can be frightening. We are identified with our character, and our frozen behavior, even if they get in the way of our happiness. It is important to remember that your habituated patterns are *not you*. They are your defenses.

If you truly want change, you must work hard for it, and stick with it. It is only in facing the negative parts of ourselves, owning them, and integrating them, that we can be whole and fully alive. To attempt an end run around the hard work of self-disclosure and behavior change is a form of self-mutilation.

Most of us live our lives in a waking sleep, oblivious to our inner lives, doing whatever seems necessary to keep ourselves fed, clothed, and not in pain. But in order to be alive and whole, we must wake up. Waking up, though, is hard to do, when we've been drugged and somnambulant, out of touch with the parts of our minds that are driving our waking behavior. Waking up to reality feels threatening. Our old brains think it is dangerous to be ourselves—which is why we buried the parts of ourselves we now want to recover to begin with. The socialization process functions like a prison, a restraint more powerful than our inner drive to wholeness. In waking up, we recontact the Lost Self, and the desires and needs that we closed off. Waking up puts us in touch with our buried pain. And with pain comes fear: fear of having our wholeness, fear of having those desires satisfied which we thought would kill us. Those buried parts of ourselves seek throughout our lives to come back into being, but we block them because to own them is to threaten the status quo—and our survival. We are reluctant; we resist in subtle ways. We've come to believe that to exist we must not have all our needs met, and we've learned to live with our losses; why rock the boat?

SURRENDERING TO CHANGE

The crucial first step is to surrender to the process, to take courage in hand and to commit to self-change. We must cooperate with, rather than resist, our unconscious drive to be our whole, true selves, to feel fully alive.

Even as a young minister, I never liked the concept of surrender. It seemed dogmatic, an authoritarian rationalization for having to submit, in childhood, to the dictates of rules and a reality I neither liked nor could do anything about. Surrender seemed like a kind of death. As children, we build defenses against surrendering to what seems our inevitable annihilation, to the disappearance of the self.

But I now see the underlying psychological truth of these old religious dictates. I've become aware that the liturgy is wiser than I am. Acknowledging the awful in us, admitting our weaknesses and failings, and owning our denied, split-off parts, is the prerequisite first step to healing, to becoming *all* of ourselves. When we stop projecting our negative traits onto others, and own what we've denied and rejected, we've taken an important step.

The modern psychological term *ownership* is just a new word for *confession*. It is part of the healing—or salvation—process. Without owning the truth about ourselves, without confession, there can be no change. Just as it is axiomatic in prison-reform theory that the prisoner must have remorse if he is to be rehabilitated, so it is with us. (Repentance is another discarded religious word that now makes psychological sense.) In Chapter 8 I spoke of a woman whose husband had an affair with her best friend when he couldn't seem to get her love any other way. He was deeply sorry and apologetic, but because she could not own up to her part in what happened, she had no remorse. As far as she was concerned, there was nothing to confess. She was stuck, and their relationship was at a standstill. Change was not possible.

Confession is free of guilt or judgment. It is purely acknowledgment of the truth about ourselves. Our wounded, negative, distorted parts must be brought into consciousness and to the consciousness of another *without judgment* in order to be healed. You have to trust that you will be OK, that you will still be loved and accepted, when all of you is revealed.

Confronting the negative parts of ourselves, disclosing what is wrong with us, may seem contrary to the conventional psychological wisdom in these days of "unconditional positive regard." But let me explain my terms. It goes without saying that acknowledging and validating the positive parts of ourselves is necessary for wholeness. All too many people disparage themselves unmercifully. Perhaps in response to this, it is common today to address personal healing only from the positive side, with affirmations and self-love, pushing aside the hard-to-face negatives. This is potentially dangerous, for the denial of our shadow side encourages a furthering of the internal split.

We cannot rebuild ourselves until we clear away the shaky foundation of our self-hatred and denial. Painting over the denied, unacknowledged negatives with a brittle veneer of ersatz self-esteem only increases our anxiety. We have to see the negative *and* the positive, side by side, in order to be whole.

As confession, or ownership, is implied in the process of surrender, so is the concept of atonement. Again, the religious implication has been one of punishment, or making up for past wrongs, but its true meaning is that of *restoration* to wholeness—literally, *at-one-ment*. At-one-ment is the natural outcome of recognizing, accepting, and owning *all* of ourselves.

SELF-HATRED: THE STUMBLING BLOCK

All of the above is much easier said than done. I used to wonder why resistance to change and healing was so strong, why many people had such a hard time giving up their maladaptive defenses. They had so much trouble accepting that their partners truly loved them, so much suspicion of my concern for them. (I remember one client saying, "You care too much.")

The explanation is shocking, but it reveals a hard truth. We hate ourselves for having needs that we were told were excessive or inappropriate, and for having traits that were hated by our caretakers. We hate everything that was disapproved of: our needs, our sexuality, our feelings, our vulnerability, our competitiveness. Because of this *self-hatred*, we cannot believe that we are lovable. Which brings us to a harsher truth. *If your self-hatred makes it impossible for you to believe that you are lovable, it is impossible for the love of a partner to heal your wounds.*

In order to let love in, you must have compassion for yourself. You must see that your self-hatred was in the interest of your self-preservation, protecting you from a worse fate, the murder of your soul by your parents or society. The hatred and repulsion you feel is inside, not outside.

Self-hatred is behind all the defenses. Its source is the presence inside our minds of a "bad" object, the internalization of the negative, rejecting parent. We feel both loyalty and fear toward this "bad" parent. If we accept the parts of ourselves that they rejected, or if we let others love us as we weren't loved by them, we feel disloyal. At the same time, to change, to let love in, arouses our fear of their continuing rejection, behind which is the ominous specter of death. No wonder we resist the very changes that we need to make. Alas, we will encounter that same resistance in our future partners.

We defend ourselves from love because we are afraid of reactivating the punitive voices of the past, which told us to reject parts of ourselves. Already we hate our rejected self-aspects as our parents and society did. To reconnect with those depised traits exposes us to the original death threat implicit in our parents' rejection. Hating ourselves preempts our fear of others' hatred of us. To keep our parents' love in childhood, or our partners' love now, we have to leave our self-hatred intact. It's a self-destructive paradox.

In order to let love in, we have to love ourselves, which means that we have to love the parts of ourselves that were rejected, first by our caretakers and other significant people of our early years, and later by ourselves. As singles, *the best way to complete this task is to learn to love in others (including our partners) the hated parts of ourselves that we project onto them.* Self-love is possible only when we accept and love the projected parts of ourselves.[2] To love what we hate in others is a form of self-love because the simple-minded old brain accepts the love we give to others as self-love. *The wall to love is self-hatred; in order to let love in, the wall must come down.*

Creating an Environment for Change

Establishing a supportive environment in which healing can take place is an important task for a single person in the process of change. This support system can be composed of family members, friends, coworkers, current romantic partners, a twelve-step support group, a psychotherapy group, or a private therapist. Each of these contexts involves a different degree of risk—of shame, exposure, ridicule, fear. You may not feel comfortable confiding in a coworker, reluctant to try out new behavior on a date who, presumably, has been attracted to you for behaving in a certain way. The bond may be too fragile, the relationship too instrumental, the past history too painful or conflict ridden. You may feel vulnerable revealing your shortcomings, even to your best friend.

Change can be awkward; people around us tend to be uncomfortable when we behave out of character, when we step out of our roles or overstep the bounds of polite conversation. There is also the problem of reciprocity: you will have to learn to practice new dialogue skills and change exercises in a one-sided fashion, in some cases not even letting your coworker or lover know what you're up to, without involving them directly. Yet it is not possible to make these changes in the privacy of your own home. These are relationship skills, and they must be learned in context with others.

THE BENEFITS OF GROUP THERAPY

Because the process of confession and change is so fraught with anxiety, I especially recommend group therapy for singles. It puts you in a supportive environment with a peer group with mutual/reciprocal interests *over time*. (If there is a leader, his or her function is usually as a facilitator only.) It is an ideal forum for change, and support for that change, without the risk of losing a friend or lover in the process. Because you have no history with group members, they will see you with fresh eyes, without the prejudice of past beliefs or conflicts. You will get new feedback on your life and your behavior, a new point of view; a new self-image will emerge.

In a supportive group, you can actively "try out" new, unfamiliar, uncomfortable behaviors, and see how others respond. You can be a different person. Though there will be anxiety, it won't have the intensity of "real life."

Over time, as you bond with the group, it will be like a new, safe, surrogate family in which you see yourself anew, and get love and support along the way. When your issues are evoked, the group will respond supportively rather than defensively. Because they have come to care about you, they will be conscientious in their response. As you change under the safer, albeit critical, eyes of the group, you will gain confidence as well as insight. And you won't be rejected because you have changed and no longer play the role you are usually expected to fulfill. As you begin to believe the responses of the group, and to adjust your self-image accordingly, you will slowly stop acting out of your belief systems rather than firsthand experience. Group therapy is a resocialization experience.

If there are no therapy groups in your area, then I suggest individual therapy. Your therapist will become, over time, a "good" object whom you will see as a parental figure, and onto whom you will project your Denied Self. This is known as transference. Since a good therapist will remain neutral, nonjudgmental, and supportive, no matter what you feel, do, or say, eventually you will discover that the "bad" you and the "bad" object is inside, rather than outside, and you will be able to love the disowned parts of you which the therapist accepts, change the parts of you that do not "fit" the therapist, and come face to face with "all of you." You will not be able to heal your childhood wounds with your therapist—his or her personality is not an Imago figure for you, so he will not catalyze the deepest layers of your wound—but you will have a good grasp of the project you will take to your future partnership.

UTILITARIAN DATING

"Utilitarian dating" is my term for making use of your current relationships or dating situations as an opportunity to practice new skills and behaviors. Perhaps the term sounds cynical or detached, hardly loving and honest. But I suspect that there already is at times a utilitarian motive behind your dating: you want someone to go out with so you won't spend Saturday night at home alone. You hope that you will meet new people by going to a party with someone you're not crazy about. You're broke, so you're happy to have someone who pays for dinner. You haven't gotten laid in six months.

However, when I speak of utilitarian dating, I'm talking about something a bit different. I'm proposing a new model of dating, in which you actively use noncommitted dating situations as a training ground for your future partnership. I'm talking about practicing the skills of relationships and the new behaviors you've identified as lacking in your repertoire *with someone of the opposite sex who you're not madly in love with and afraid of losing*.

Let's look at how this can work. One obvious area to begin with is the gender issues discussed in Chapter 11. Rather than staying stuck in your gender-defined role, here is your chance to find out how the other half lives. Ask your date, "What is life like for you? How did you feel about that movie/party/baseball game/dirty joke?" Try some straightforward talk about sex—what it feels like, your hopes/insecurities/expectations/fantasies. This is not a make-or-break situation. Ask intimate questions. *Answer* intimate questions. Listen in order to learn, without judgment.

Dare to step out of your role. Break the mold. Think of what you're doing as an adventure. If you're a woman who has never called a man for a date before, *do it*, knowing that if you're turned down, it's not the end of the world. *Don't* cook him dinner, if it's not what you usually do. Try not dressing up or wearing full makeup every minute. Don't be afraid to let on that you can change a tire.

If you're a man who's uncomfortable when a woman wants to pay for dinner, relax and enjoy it. Try playing the passive role in bed. Fix breakfast. Don't be afraid to let on that you can't change a tire, that you hate football, that you've always run from fistfights.

Alison, the daughter of a friend and an itinerant photographer, with whom I'd discussed these ideas, wrote to me:

> This past fall, I had an ideal opportunity to try out your Utilitarian Dating ideas. I was on a three-month assignment in Minneapolis, of all places, and almost immediately met Joel, who, like me, was divorced two years ago. We were attracted to each other, and though there was no heavy Imago energy between us, it was apparent that we'd want each other's company during the duration of this project—but it was also true that we'd both be going off to other postings after our project was over. I made up my mind on our first date that I would make a concerted effort to learn from the relationship.
>
> At first it was kind of haphazard. I made it a point to practice Mirroring in our conversations, to use "I" language and clearly state my opinions—which was hard, because my usual thing is to try and please, and let others take the lead. I also realized that it was a real effort to truly listen to his opinions, to solicit his feelings and learn from them, rather than judging them, or devaluing them. We had very different views of the Persian Gulf war, for example, but I was able to see his point of view, where in the past I would have judged it—or him—as wrong. He introduced me to science fiction, one of his great loves, and I surprised myself by enjoying it. And we went camping—me, who *loves* room service! I began

to be more assertive sexually, and to tell him exactly what made me feel good. Joel even got me to wear some sexy lingerie, which I had qualms about, both personally and "politically." Because we were so supportive of each other, it felt right, even though I was nervous and uncomfortable at first. Joel and I became very close.

As I gained confidence, I got more serious about my "program." I made a list of behavior changes I wanted to work on—not changing my plans to accommodate him if he called to make a date, not "grilling" him about where he'd been, telling him things about myself I'd never told anyone—and I started trying them out one by one.

After about a month, I hesitantly told Joel about your workshop. He was intrigued by it—he'd already seen it at work—and from then on we did some of the exercises together, and practiced the dialogue stuff. We even did a couples workshop at a local church. I got a priceless education about myself, about men in general. I learned, finally, how to reveal myself without feeling like I would get hurt by it; and I was able to change some of my more "clingy" behavior. By changing my behavior, I ended up changing *me*.

Try and change the push/pull dynamic of your dating relationships. If you run from intimacy, force yourself to sit still when the conversation, or the loving, gets intense. If you know you're too needy, try allowing more distance, more space. If you're always giving, try taking, and vice versa. If you're used to being cared for, try being the caretaker. If you have a sharp tongue, hold your criticism. If you never stand up for what you think, get some opinions, fast. Instead of "Oh, I don't know, what do *you* want to do," try "I'd like to go to that new Indian restaurant." And stick to it. If you're used to giving the orders ("I'm taking you to Jamaica for Christmas"), try letting someone else make the plans, and the decision. The important thing is to do what's *un*natural, *un*comfortable, and keep doing it, through doubt and anxiety, until it feels right.

You can practice utilitarian dating on your own, but you don't have to keep it a secret. Actually, I propose that you make it a collaborative effort when appropriate. Tell your date about this book and what you are working on. In so doing, you'll automatically increase the intimacy of the relationship, and get a coconspirator. That way the growth is mutual. Some singles who have attended my workshops have made agreements to mutually work on their issues in their ongoing dating relationships—relationships that, because of their honesty and openness, sometimes turned into something more.

To show you what I mean about being honest about your intentions when it comes to utilitarian dating, I'll tell you the story of Douglas, who, after breaking up with his wife, attended one of my singles weekends. He had recently placed a personals ad and was inundated with responses—pictures included—of dozens of seemingly fabulous women, and he had started working his way through the list.

The problem was that many of these women were interested in serious relationships, not someone fresh from a broken marriage and just starting to play the field. Douglas was feeling a bit sheepish because to him, at that point, sex and companionship were his main objectives. And in fact, as he explained it to me, from the evasive wording of his ad, and the way he deflected questions about commitment from the women he was dating, he was at least being misleading, if not exploitive.

I urged him to tell his dates just what was going on for him. To tell them that he was looking for nurturing and company and sex, but definitely not commitment at this point. A couple of women, he reported, were shocked at his candor, but most seemed to respect his honesty, and it opened up more directness and understanding on both sides. As he established a dating pattern with a couple of these women, he was able to tell them about this work, to bring them in on what he was trying to accomplish.

One woman was particularly interested, and even though the relationship never moved beyond a deep friendship, they continued to use each other as a forum and training ground for their new skills. As Douglas told me, "Approaching my single life in this way made *all* my relationships more intimate and more comfortable for me. I feel like I got to know myself—to *be* myself—and to know women, a great deal better. And I learned, finally, to have women as friends."

WHEN YOU FALL IN LOVE . . .

Having talked about how you can learn and grow in casual "utilitarian" relationships, I want to summarize briefly what you can do when you meet your Imago partner and fall in love. I need to remind you that while you can make changes now that will affect your relationship choices, and the course of your journey later, no amount of knowledge or change will save you from the struggle with your partner once you are in a relationship. The bubble of romantic love *will* burst, and you *will* find yourself locked in a power struggle. But now you know yourself, and know what can be expected to happen. You are *prepared* for what is coming, and you have new coping skills.

Let me give you a few guidelines for the early stages of your relationship:

1. Be wary of making a commitment to someone who isn't aware of his or her own self-completion issues, and willing to grow and change. As you are by now well aware, you don't have much choice in who you are attracted to, but you *can* choose to be with someone who wants and values a conscious marriage. This is hard to determine in the early stages of a relationship, when we're blinded by love. At some point—when your head isn't in the clouds—you must assess your prospective mate's desire and ability to be conscious. I am not saying that a relationship in which only one person is willing to work and be conscious is impossible, and it is hard to be rational and practical when we are in love. Remember that the character defenses of your partner will prevent you from being healed until s/he changes, just as yours will have to change to heal your partner's wound. Everything is much harder when only one partner is willing to do the work, and you may not be able to achieve the wholeness and intimacy you dream of.

2. Apply the knowledge and skills you have learned in every possible situation. You are well aware of your own wounds, and you have some idea of what your future partner's wounds will be. You are now tuned in to the issues that are bound to arise, and you can respond with your new brain rather than your old brain.

For example, now you know that our tendency is to deny or ignore the first signs of our partners' negative traits until we become angry and disillusioned. Instead of being taken by surprise, and reacting by criticizing or retreating, you will not panic. You will have anticipated your partner's negative traits, you will know what issues in yourself are being activated, and you will be able to use the Intentional Dialogue process (Chapter 15) to talk with your partner about how to work things out. You will recognize your partner's projections, and be able to "hold" them until they dissipate.

3. Introduce your partner to this book, so that you are *both* prepared by the time you marry. When both of you have done the self-knowledge exercises, you can begin the journey of partnership together. Get to know as much as you can about each other. Share

the history of your home life as children and your parents' marriages. Tell each other how you were wounded, explore your belief systems and your hopes for wholeness and healing in marriage. Begin to use the skills you are learning in your everyday life.

4. A couple's ability to communicate and solve problems prior to and early in a marriage is the best predictor of its eventual success. I recommend that you attend singles workshops or seminars, and that you seek premarital counseling if you come up against conflicts you can't seem to solve on your own. My earlier book, *Getting the Love You Want: A Guide for Couples,* will tell you more about what to expect from marriage and will teach you some useful partnership skills. You will also find a series of exercises geared to couples.

"My, How You've Changed!"

Changing long-established patterns can be difficult and frustrating, and the results of all this effort and discomfort will not be immediately apparent—it is not like buying a new suit, or radically changing your hairstyle. In fact, it is hard to monitor change in oneself when it is happening in slow, day-to-day increments. From our personal point of view, it often seems as though the outside world has changed, rather than ourselves. We are mystified by our boss's seeming change of heart toward us, and speculate that her home life is happier, or she got a raise, when in fact it may be our more positive attitude toward the job, or our newly acquired skills at direct communication that have made the difference. I remember going back with a friend to the home where I'd grown up, and being shocked by how small it was. I walked all around the house to make sure there wasn't a wing that I couldn't see on the back. As a child, that house had looked big and spacious to me, the yard had stretched out as far as I wanted or needed to go. Now it was tiny, almost a shack, sitting on a postage stamp of land. It hadn't changed a bit, of course; I had.

The effects of change are cumulative. The more you accomplish, the faster the process will go, the more energy and wherewithal you will have to proceed to the next step. And you only have to do 51 percent of the work: at a certain point you will crest the hill and then change will proceed at a faster pace. Others will notice the change before you do, and you may see it first in their attitudes and actions toward you. When you realize that your efforts are paying off, and that you have changed, you are going to feel very good about yourself indeed.

What will happen as you make progress is that the energy that is now bound up in your defenses and adaptations, that you expend in protecting yourself from hurt, will start to be available to go back into the universe, into the energetic currents of the world, into *eros*, and you will naturally and effortlessly attract a healing partner.

15

New Skills, New Behavior: Steps to Self-Integration

A journey of a thousand miles begins with
a single step.

—OLD CHINESE PROVERB

This chapter consists of a series of exercises that will help you pull
together what you have learned so far into a working plan for self-
change. I want to begin by giving you a map to this chapter.

First, by going back to what you learned about yourself in the
earlier exercises, you are going to identify what needs changing.
Then you will learn a guided-imagery meditation, which will be of
continual use to you as you approach these changes. Next comes a
series of exercises aimed at restoring your feelings of aliveness,
followed by an exercise for altering your character defenses by
changing negative, unproductive behavior. In the last three exercises, you will learn valuable relationship skills: Intentional Dialogue, Holding Projections, and Behavior Change Requests.

Let me outline how I think you should go about doing this work.
I suggest that you do the first exercise on page 268, which identifies
what needs changing, and then read through the rest of the chapter.
As you will see, you are basically trying to accomplish three things:

enliven your inner core, change your character defenses, and learn valuable relationship skills. If you try to do everything at once, you will feel overwhelmed. Confused, bored, and frustrated, you will end up accomplishing very little. So you need to make a plan, and a timetable. This should be flexible and realistic, based on an evaluation of what you hope to accomplish and the time you can realistically give to this project.

As you do the exercises, you will be making lists of everything that you want to work on, and ranking the tasks according to their difficulty. I suggest you tackle one enlivenment activity, one behavior change, and one relationship skill together, beginning with the easiest in each category, with an intended time frame. For example, the plan for the first week might be: "I will do the belly-laughing exercise each evening" (enlivenment), "I will say 'hello' to the people at the bus stop in the morning" (behavior change), and "Whenever it is appropriate, I will mirror back what is said to me" (relationship skill).

Be aware of your reactions to what you are doing. Are you uncomfortable, tense, afraid? Elated, lighter, more at ease? At the end of the week, reevaluate what you have been doing. If you feel you would like to stay with what you are working on for a longer time, until it is grounded, integrated, and comfortable, do so. There is no rush, and too much change too quickly can be disruptive. Don't move on or add new changes until you are really at ease with what you are currently doing, until it becomes natural. Then, move on to the next step, the next changes.

All along the way, look for opportunities to bring others into the process, to share your thoughts, to confess your fears and shortcomings, to atone. The idea is to try your new skills and behavior in small doses, in increasingly "risky" situations. At first you might try them out with a supportive friend, or in your therapy group. As you gain confidence, move on to situations where you perceive the risk to be greater—with co-workers, then with dates who aren't "the one."

The more you can invite others' participation, the richer your experience will be, the faster your growth, and the more relational experience you will accumulate. Take advantage of "utilitarian dating"—this is as close to a "real life" couple situation as you will get without being in a committed relationship. Make the most of it. Keep in mind that behaving falsely in love relationships is precisely why they fail! The more you can become comfortable with new behaviors in low-risk arenas, the more you can be your true self when true love comes along.

You may find it useful during this process to keep a journal of your feelings, your reactions, and your progress. Be sure and give yourself credit for your gains; the more you are aware of change, the more fuel and encouragement you will have to go further. Tuning in to your dreams can also provide valuable insight during this process. Dreamwork is beyond our scope here, but there are many books available on working with your dreams.[1]

The secret to your success in this process is your diligence and intentionality. Change does not occur overnight; it comes about with effort, over time. The problems you are trying to remedy took a long time to lodge themselves in your character structure; they will not simply evaporate. You have to tackle each change conscientiously and diligently, repeating it over and over, in increasingly difficult and threatening situations. But each small increment of change fuels and supports the next one. And each one changes your Imago for the better, and vitalizes your stagnant energetic core. Each one brings you closer to your real, whole self, and to a healthy, healing relationship.

EXERCISE 15A   ▪   ▪   ▪   ▪   ▪

My Wholeness Agenda

Now we are going to itemize the tasks that you need to address in order to progress toward wholeness, and to increase your feelings of aliveness. Complete the following sentences, using the information you've already gathered.

1. From what I have learned about my childhood, I am a _____ _____ (Minimizer/Maximizer; all responses in this paragraph are from Exercise 7D, page 113) whose major wounding occurred at the stage of _____, and my wound consists of _____.
I also have issues related to the _____ stage/s, which means my wound also includes a fear of _____ _____.
My growth challenge, therefore, is _____ _____.

2. In looking at my Lost Self, I realize that my energy is restricted in the areas of _____ and _____ (Exercise 10B, #3, page 172). This has been confirmed by the complaints my intimate partners have expressed to me that I _____

_____

(partner frustrations with you, Exercise 10B, #2, page 172).

3. Also, in doing Exercise 11A, page 202, I learned that my gender energies are out of balance, and I need to develop my ____ _____ (masculine/feminine) side; specifically, the traits I would like to develop are _____ .
In Exercise 11B, on page 204, I discovered that in order to have a fuller, more exciting sexual life, I would like _____

_____

(desires listed in Part III, page 207).

4. From doing the Denied Self exercise, I recognize that I am _____ (Exercise 10C, #5, lower left quarter of circle, page 173); and I am now aware that others see me as _____

_____

(Exercise 10C, #5, lower right quadrant of circle, page 173).

As you do the following exercises, you will have a chance to reframe the above issues as positive behaviors that you can practice. The things you have identified as dysfunctional and life-hampering fall into two basic categories: "Behavior that I Want to Change" and "Areas Where I Want to Feel More Aliveness." Before we move on, though, I want to introduce the "Safe Haven" exercise, which will give you a valuable tool for working on these changes.

EXERCISE·15B   ■   ■   ■   ■   ■
_____

Creating a Safe Haven

You are well aware by now that your character structure is your adaptation to life, rather than your true self. Yet you identify this creaky edifice as "me." While it defines your habitual way of thinking and doing, however, it is a prison of your past that prevents you from experiencing full aliveness and estranges you from your authentic core self. What keeps you from changing, even when you are in pain, is fear.

To quiet the old brain you need to learn to create a sense of inner safety. This will require that you practice some mental training such as meditation, relaxation, or guided imagery. You may already have such a practice. Whether you do or not, the "Safe Haven" guided-imagery exercise below will help you relax into your old brain. Repeated practice of this exercise will foster a sense of safety in both your inner and outer worlds. When your fear abates, you will be more capable of examining and dismantling your character defenses so that your authentic self can emerge.

You need some relaxing music and a quiet spot; wear comfortable clothes. Since you will be using this exercise repeatedly, you may want to tape the instructions (while playing the music in the background). If you choose to do this, record the following instructions in a calm, soothing voice, pausing at the appropriate places, so that you allow enough time to follow the imagery. You may choose to have a friend read these instructions to you; it is also effective to do this exercise in a group setting.

Close your eyes . . . Breathe deeply, calmly . . . Relax . . . Let the music and your breathing be all that you are aware of . . . Take a deep breath, filling your diaphragm and then your chest . . . Hold to a count of four . . . Exhale slowly to the count of eight . . . Repeat this deep breath three more times . . . Let the music fill your consciousness . . . Be the music . . . Now let the word "safe" come to your mind. Repeat it . . . Safe . . . Safe . . . Let it lead you to a place that is a haven for you . . . Perhaps it is a place from childhood . . . An idyllic site from a dream . . . Or a photograph . . . Imagine a place where you feel protected and at home . . . Experience this haven with all your senses . . . Breathe the air, the fragrance, of safety . . . Hear its sounds . . . See its colors and forms . . . Touch the textures and temperatures of safety . . . Stay awhile, taking it in fully . . . Let it fill you with peace and comfort . . . Breathe the air of safety . . . Let it relax you completely. . . .

Now be aware that a light from above descends upon you, filling the space and enveloping you in a warm golden glow. It washes over your head and neck, relaxing . . . Moves across your shoulders, relaxing . . . Down your arms, relaxing your wrists and fingers . . . The warm golden light enters your chest, relaxing . . . Courses through your stomach, and your pelvis, relaxing . . . Your relaxation deepens as the light moves through your pelvis to your thighs . . . Down to your knees, relaxing . . . Your calves relax and then your ankles, in the warm golden light . . . It reaches your feet, and your toes, relaxing . . . You are completely relaxed . . . The pulsating warmth of the light matches your heartbeat . . . You are deeply relaxed . . . Safe. . . .

Now, into this safe haven, bring your mother . . . See her with the X-ray vision of a child . . . every detail of her dress, her expression . . . Tell her about your deepest hurt with her . . . She is listening to you . . . Now tell her about her most shining moment with you . . . Now bring your father to this place . . . You can see him very clearly . . . Tell him how he hurt you . . . He is listening to you . . . Tell him about your best memory of him. . . . [If there were any other significant figures in your childhood, do the same with them here.]

Now tell them that you have decided to complete your childhood and create a relationship in which your wounds can be healed . . . Say good-bye to each of them. [You may want to eliminate the instructions for this paragraph from your tape, since you will not repeat this section of the exercise each time.]

You now find yourself walking down a path through a meadow . . . You come to a stream . . . You sit down on the bank to rest . . . An animal appears beside you . . . And speaks to you . . . You tuck the message away in your memory . . . You stand up and cross the shallow stream . . . And continue on the path . . . Which leads into a forest . . . The ground is soft and fragrant . . . Birds are singing . . . There is a rustling of leaves . . . Deep in the forest you come to a clearing . . . Someone is sitting in the center . . . As you approach, you sense that this is a wise person . . . You ask a question . . . And there is a reply . . . You tuck the answer away in memory . . . And continue along the path through the forest . . . To the light beyond . . . And you are back in your safe haven. . . . [At this point, you can bring anyone into this safe place and have a conversation— your lover, boss, friend, sister.]

Relax again for a moment . . . Reflect on your journey . . . When you are ready, become aware of the music playing in the background . . . Move your hands and feet slowly . . . Count backward slowly: ten . . . nine . . . eight . . . seven . . . six . . . five . . . four . . . three . . . two . . . one . . . Open your eyes.

* * *

If you practice this exercise daily for three months, you will experience a deepening peace inside you. Guided by your instinctual animal wisdom and the wisdom of your higher nature, you will be better able to make the changes you need to become whole and improve your partner choice. You may want to keep a journal of these meditations. As you proceed with the exercises, remember to use this meditation as a way to relax and as a place in which to visualize and practice the changes you are making.

Recovering Your Aliveness

Every day in dozens of ways you refer to your aliveness. "I feel good," you might declare, or "I feel so depleted lately," "I have the Monday morning blues," "That orgasm blew me away," "I feel wide awake now," "My body feels like a lead weight," "I'm all fired up about . . . ," or "I've run out of steam." Such remarks are a running commentary on your continuous experiencing of aliveness.

Our need to feel and express our aliveness fully is second only to our drive to survive. The purpose of the next group of exercises is to rekindle the smoldering coals of your energetic core, to stir the flagging pulsation of your innate energy. They involve the broadening and intensification of your awareness of your own vitality. The goal is not ecstasy or "peak experiences," but the free flow of *eros*, your natural life energy. In doing these exercises, you decrease the rigidity of the defensive structure around your energetic core, the "Berlin Wall" you erected in childhood and probably reinforced in your intimate relationships, which keeps your core energy imprisoned and prevents outside energies from entering.

These exercises are the most important part of the process of your journey to wholeness as a single. But I caution you that they may well be the hardest part of the work you'll be asked to do here. Why? As a result of the oppression of *eros* in childhood, most of us fear our own life energy. We were told it was dangerous—even evil— to run, sing, shout, touch our bodies, act silly. Nothing is more difficult in therapy with couples than getting them to have fun. They will gladly work on their pathology and pay for it, but most resist the amplification of pleasure. So don't be discouraged if you resist this work, or if you find it anxiety provoking. Stay with it. It is your own life force that you are attempting to free from its cage. You will never feel fully alive until you break through your rigid defenses to your pulsating inner core.

We are going to start this process with an assessment of your Aliveness Quotient, and a look at your aliveness "stimulants." Following that, you will find a section on "enlivening" activities, after which you will create an "Enlivenment Agenda" which puts together a tailor-made list of activities to enhance your sense of aliveness.

EXERCISE 15C ■ ■ ■ ■ ■

Your Aliveness Quotient

Here you are going to run a "diagnostic" on your current feelings of aliveness: Just how good do you feel right now? Rate the comments below on a scale of one to five (five is the highest rating).

	1	2	3	4	5
I wake up feeling rested.					
I feel alert and awake.					
I am content.					
Life excites me.					
I enjoy a good meal.					
I laugh a lot.					
I am aware of pulsating energy in my body.					
I feel joyful.					
I am happy most of the time.					
Sometimes I sing spontaneously.					
I experience intense orgasms.					
I see colors vividly.					
I taste what I put in my mouth.					
I am relaxed.					
I enjoy dancing.					
I enjoy moving my body.					
I feel all my feelings intensely.					
I feel vitally alive.					
I have creative ideas.					
My memory is good.					
I live in the present.					
Music turns me on.					
Sometimes I feel ecstatic.					
My sex life is satisfying.					
Many things interest me.					

Add all the numbers of your responses together. Your highest score is 100. If you scored 75–100 you have a high aliveness quotient. If your score is 40–75, you have a medium aliveness quotient. A score below 40 means that you have a low aliveness score: your life energy is constricted.

E X E R C I S E   15 D   ■   ■   ■   ■   ■

Sources of Aliveness

In this exercise you are asked to identify the sources of your aliveness, the stimulants that make you "feel good" or jolt you into a "high." In the left-hand column below is a list of stimulants that many people use to stir their aliveness—to feel good. Add any others that you may use to the list. In Column 2 indicate the frequency (daily, twice a week, monthly) with which you turn to this source of stimulation. Column 3 asks you to rate the intensity of the feeling of aliveness you derive from this activity (five is the highest score). In Column 4, write down the "Outcome" ("I feel high," "I end up disgusted with myself," "It gives me energy throughout the day," "It makes me feel loved"). Then in Column 5 rate the activity as to whether it is "Healthy" (natural, life-affirming, beneficial) or "Unhealthy" (artificial, hurtful, life-denying).

Look back over your responses. Which of your "stimulants" are unhealthy, or leave you feeling bad or depleted? Which are healthy, and leave you feeling energized and alive? Which amplify the four areas of aliveness—thinking, feeling, acting, sensing—and which deplete them? Which areas are unenlivened? Which stimulants should you be avoiding or cutting back on, and which should you be increasing in your life?

Stimulant	Frequency	Intensity					Outcome	H	U
		1	2	3	4	5			
Caffeine									
Sugar									
Alcohol									
Cocaine									
Marijuana									
Other drugs									
Running									
Sex									
People									
Pornography/Phone sex									
Jokes/Comedy									
High-risk sports (skydiving, auto racing, etc.)									
Play with children									
Exercise									
Dancing									
Belly laughing									
Reading									
Work									
Gardening									
Masturbation									
Singing									
Anger									
Negative thoughts									
Meditation									
Massage									
Food									
Nicotine									
Games (cards, chess)									
Television									
Camping/Hiking									
Travel									
Sports (golf, bowling, fishing, etc.)									
Hobbies (photography, woodworking, etc.)									
Other									

EXERCISE 15E   ▪   ▪   ▪   ▪   ▪

Enlivening Activities

Recapturing your feelings of aliveness is often simply a matter of expressing stifled feelings and awakening blunted senses. What follows is a list of some things that work directly on your core energy. Many of them are simple, and many are frivolous, but that's the point. Simple, frivolous, sensual pleasures make us feel alive, and they are often sorely lacking in our busy, dutiful lives. Depending on what issues you are working on, you may choose to incorporate some of these activities into your Enlivenment Agenda, page 279.

HAVE FUN

The following activities are purely for fun; there are no rules; no skills are required: you cannot do them "wrong."

1. Jump-start belly laughing. Stand with your feet parallel and slightly apart, with your knees bent slightly. Begin to jar yourself by bouncing up and down gently, using your legs as springboards. Open your mouth and say "Ha" with each bounce. Increase the bouncing movement until your "Ha, ha" speed picks up and you are laughing. Continue for a full minute. Do this once each day. (This is even more silly and provocative if done standing face to face with a partner.)

2. Stand in front of a mirror and make faces at yourself until you laugh.

3. Learn several jokes or funny stories and tell them whenever you have an opportunity.

4. Speak in gibberish. Babble mindlessly. Do this in front of others, if you have a chance—kids, especially, love this.

5. Watch funny movies, comedy acts, stand-up comics. Let yourself laugh out loud, even if you're in a theater.

6. Spin around like a dervish until you're dizzy. Even better, do it with a partner. Hold your partner's hands, place your feet close together, and spin in a circle as fast as you can.

7. Go dancing. Move your body. Laugh.

8. Play games with children. Join in their laughter; run with them.

9. Listen to a canned-laughter tape and join in.

PARTNER GAMES:

10. Have a water-pistol fight or a shaving-cream fight. Wear a bathing suit or do it nude.

11. Have a wrestling match. Do it in the nude, coating each other with baby oil. Wrestle until you're exhausted.

12. Play tag. Chase each other until you're exhausted.

DEEPEN YOUR SENSUAL EXPERIENCE

1. Take a long bath in some fragrant oil.

2. Get a massage or have your lover give you one.

3. Have a meal of all your favorite foods. Serve it on beautiful dishes. Eat it with your hands if that appeals.

4. Take a long, bracing shower. Sing.

5. Play music when you're at home alone.

6. Have some fragrant oils or potpourri around the house.

7. Light candles in the bath, the bedroom, at dinner. Make it an everyday experience.

8. Wear silk or velvet next to your skin.

EXPRESS YOUR ANGER

Anger is the life force, *eros*, converted into negative energy. Some people do not experience their aliveness because they hold their anger in their muscles; others contain their anger in their emotions and do not experience it in their bodies. For many people, the shot of adrenaline they get from their rage is the only aliveness they feel. The first four exercises below will help you convert your bodily held anger into emotions. The final exercise will help you transfer your emotions into your body. Before you do these exercises, you should resolve not to hurt yourself or anyone else, or destroy any property.

A. You will need a tennis racket, a small baseball bat, or a Bataka (a foam bat made especially for this purpose) and a bed or other large soft surface. Standing close to the bed, take the bat or racket firmly in both hands. Open your mouth, take a deep breath, and raise your arms high over your head. Imagining the person or object with whom you are angry, pound the bed hard and repeatedly, making an "ah-h-h" sound as you make contact. Continue pounding the bed until you are exhausted or break into tears. If you do the latter, let yourself cry.

B. Stand on a carpeted floor, wearing tennis shoes or other shoes with soft soles. Imagining the person or issue that makes you angry, stomp around the floor until you are exhausted or break into tears. If you do the latter, let yourself cry.

C. Wearing loose clothing, lie on a large bed. Make your hands into fists. Raise your right fist and your left foot at the same time and pound the bed; then do the same with your left fist and your right foot, and continue pounding. Open your mouth and make a sound, allowing the sound to escalate as you speed up the pounding. You may want to experiment with shouting words such as "no, no, no," or "hate, hate, hate." Continue until you are exhausted or in tears. Let yourself cry.

D. Place a heavily upholstered chair opposite you. Make sure it is soft. Imagine the person with whom you are angry sitting in the chair. Start talking to the person about how s/he hurt you, and how angry you are about that. Let yourself go, raise your voice, shout, shout louder. If you feel the impulse, start pounding the chair (the imaginary person) until you feel exhausted. If you break into tears, let yourself cry.

E. If you tend to express your anger verbally, feeling it only in your throat and mouth, do the following. Let yourself see in your mind the person with whom you are angry. Bring up the angry scene. Then take a deep breath and exhale deeply several times, preventing yourself from expressing your anger out loud. Continue this exercise until you can feel the anger in every part of your body. Then let the angry scene go and feel the sensations of bodily aliveness.

(Note: the active exercises A–D will also help you feel the anger in your body, but if you tend to vocalize, you should refrain from doing so during the process. You may make nonsensical sounds, however. Always breathe deeply.)

EXPRESS YOUR SADNESS

Some people do not feel their aliveness because they have not grieved their losses. To see if this may apply to you, go back through your childhood, through adolescence and your adult life, and make a list of the losses you have sustained in your life. These might include a friend who moved away, a pet that died, a jilted romance, getting fired, learning that your parents were divorcing, a missed opportunity to travel, a career choice given up to raise children.

Take two chairs; place one in front of you and sit in the other. Place the "loss" in the chair and imagine it to be there. Begin speaking to the loss and put into words all your feelings about it. Include all the positive things it (they) meant to you, how your life has been affected by its absence, how you hurt because it is gone. Express any anger you may have that was not expressed when you had it or that you have about it being gone. Let your tears well up and let yourself grieve the loss. When you have finished, imagine that you are at a burial site and you are now going to say a final good-bye. In whatever way you choose, bury the person or object. Imagine the entire process. For instance, see the person you are grieving in the casket; see it lowered into the ground and covered with dirt; visualize the flowers and the weather. Then leave the scene in your imagination.

All past angers and ungrieved losses will follow you into any relationship. The more you complete any past experience, the less unconscious and archaic emotion will erupt as you search for and begin a relationship.

E X E R C I S E   15 F   ■   ■   ■   ■   ■

My Enlivenment Agenda

The task now is to put together a plan for awakening your dormant energies.

1. Look back at your response to #2 in Exercise 15A, page 269, in which you listed the areas in which your energies were dampened. You may want to go back to Exercise 10B, page 171, to recall the specific messages that you were given in each area. Also refer back to #3 in Exercise 15A, on page 269, where you were asked to see where your gender energies are out of balance, and what you want in order to have a satisfying sexual life. Again, you may want to refer back to Exercise 11A, page 202 and Exercise 11B, page 204 for the specifics.

2. Write at the top of a blank sheet of paper ALIVENESS AGENDA. Using the above sources, list all the ways you can think of to enhance/stimulate your feelings of aliveness in the areas where you have been deprived. I can't give you much more specific guidance here, since the program you develop will be highly individualized and responsive to your idiosyncratic needs. Keep in mind, though, that if you are a Minimizer, you want to do things that expand your energy and boundaries; if you are a Maximizer, you should move toward containing your energy by holding it in your body and feeling the sensations deeply. Don't worry at this point whether you have the nerve, or the wherewithal, to do these things. Just write them down. First, at the top of the paper write, "I give myself permission to feel fully alive by doing all the pleasurable and enlivening things on this list." Be specific and detailed. Don't

say, "I will do more things that help me to think" or "I will get more exercise" or "I'll express my anger more often." Here are some specific examples:

"I am going to take a course in basic auto repair."

"I am going to learn to use a computer."

"I am going to join the company volleyball team."

"I am going to take time to go to a museum or a show twice a month."

"I've never mourned having to leave medical school when Max was born. I want to do that exercise about expressing my sadness."

"I'm going to get a big bowl of sage and eucalyptus potpourri for my room."

"I'm going to speak up against the new dress code at work."

"I am going to buy myself a lacy camisole/silk boxer shorts."

"I'm going to let my boss know how angry I am that I didn't get that promotion."

"I'm going to tell my therapy group about _____."

"I'm going to figure out how to balance my checkbook."

"Next time Alice and I make love, I'm going to tell her that I want her to _____."

"I'm going to be sure and have soft-shell crabs while they're in season this year."

"I'm going to go for a long hike by myself to see the wildflowers."

"I'm going to plan and cook dinner for Marion's birthday."

"I'm going to do the belly-laugh exercise every day; maybe I'll try doing it with Andy/Susan."

"I'm going to do the exercise about expressing my anger with regard to _____."

"I am going to scream out loud when I feel like it."

"I'm going to sing loud."

"I'm going to do the weekend movement-therapy workshop at the Y."

3. Rank all the statements on your list according to how easy they are for you to do; the easiest should be ranked #1.

4. Begin to practice behavior #1 on your list. Do it as often as is possible or practical. It is natural for you to feel fearful, anxious, and uncomfortable at first. Some tasks will be difficult—asking for what you want sexually, confronting the boss. Some—hosting a dinner party, learning to use a computer—will involve a great deal of planning and extended effort. Try and stay with it through the discomfort; the more you practice it, the more natural it will seem. Use the Safe Haven exercise (page 270) when you get stuck. Visu-

alize an imaginary person acting out the new behavior. When the image is clear and comfortable, substitute yourself for that person. See yourself doing it. Continue on your journey and see what the animal by the stream and the wise person of the clearing have to say.

5. Stay with this behavior as long as is necessary to feel comfortable with it, and to feel that it is an integral part of you. Then move on to the next hardest behavior, #2 on the list, and so on.

6. Remember to enlist the help and support of friends and lovers where possible.

EXERCISE 15G   ■   ■   ■   ■   ■

Owning and Changing Negative Behaviors

In this exercise, we are going to take the negative traits that you identified in Exercise 15A and convert them into positive behaviors that you can practice.

1. Divide a blank sheet of paper into three vertical columns. Label the left-hand column NEGATIVE TRAITS; call the middle column POSITIVE TRAITS; label the right-hand column POSITIVE BEHAVIORS. In the left-hand column list all the negative traits from Exercise 15A, #4, page 269. For example, the column might read, "stinginess," "aloofness," "cynicism," "opinionatedness."

Now go back to #1 of the same exercise, page 268, and look at your growth challenge. Are any negative behaviors implied here that have not been covered above? For example, if you are a Controller, your growth challenge suggests that you might be "rigid," and "insensitive." Add these traits.

2. Now ask yourself what the positive opposite of each trait would be, and enter it in the middle column. The above traits might transform as "generosity," "warmth," "faith in others," "open-mindedness," "flexibility," and "sensitivity."

3. In the third column, list behaviors that you can try which would demonstrate the positive traits in action. Try and think of several behaviors for each negative trait. For "generosity," for example, you might list "I will give money to the panhandlers at the mall." "I will set aside $_____ per month to give to charity." "I will set aside more money for Christmas presents, and not use the excuse that I'm broke." "I will give Elinor my silver pin that she's so fond of." "I will be more tolerant of Jane's extravagance." Next to "warmth" you might list "I will say hello to the people at

the bus stop in the morning." "I will chat with the waitress in the coffee shop." "I will eat lunch in the faculty cafeteria twice a week instead of at my desk." "I'll join the Thursday-night book discussion group at the library." "I will call a friend just to chat at least once a week." "I'll talk to my friend Jake about what happened to Vera and me last summer." "I'll volunteer for the Boy Scouts." "I will tell my sister Anne how much I love her."

4. Now rank all the new behaviors according to how difficult they will be for you to do; the easiest behavior should be #1.

5. Begin to practice behavior #1 on your list. Do it as often as is possible or practical. It is natural for you to feel fearful, anxious, and uncomfortable at first. Try and stay with it through the discomfort; the more you practice it, the more natural it will seem. Use the Safe Haven exercise when you get stuck. Visualize an imaginary person acting out the new behavior. When the image is clear and comfortable, substitute yourself for that person. See yourself doing it. Continue on your journey and see what the animal by the stream and the wise person of the clearing have to say.

6. Stay with this behavior as long as is necessary to feel comfortable with it, and to feel that it is an integral part of you. Then move on to the next hardest behavior, #2 on the list, and so on.

7. Remember that the more you can involve others, especially intimate others, the faster and deeper the change will be. Be open to feedback from others; invite it. By "confessing" and accepting as part of yourself these undesirable traits—which your confidant probably knows about anyway—and seeing that he or she still cares about you, you will realize that you can be yourself, warts and all, and still be loved. And you will be less prone to disowning these traits and projecting them onto your friends, family, and partners, creating conflict.

E X E R C I S E   15 H   ▪   ▪   ▪   ▪   ▪

The Art of Intentional Dialogue

Dialogue separates us from other species, which are locked in unwavering old-brain patterns of stimulus/response in the face of danger and conflict. It is a crucial relationship skill. Without it you cannot relate to another person's internal reality; you only relate to your version of it, which means that you are relating to yourself. Without dialogue, you can count on distortion and the conflict that ensues. With it, any problem can be contained and resolved. Often, when dialogue is used well, the problem or issue dissolves in the process.

Dialogue is also a growth process. It is the process of transiently suspending your own consciousness and allowing the reality of another person's mind to enter yours without evaluation. This stretching of your mind to include the subjectivity of another opens you to new information that is essential for your growth. If you are to relate successfully to anyone and to evolve personally, dialogue is essential. Since it requires an intentional rather than a reactive response to another person's communication, I think it is trans-instinctual, thus nondefensive. That is what makes it so difficult.

Intentional Dialogue, therefore, is simply conscious communication, that is, communication that clarifies, confirms, and develops appreciation, respect for, and acceptance of the inner worlds of others. It consists of three parts: Mirroring, Validation, and Empathy. A demonstration follows. Remember that in most cases you will not have an aware partner with whom to practice these skills (though I urge you to enlist a friend or partner in this learning process). But you can practice on your own, mirroring or validating what is said to you whether or not the person you're speaking to is aware of what you're up to.

1. *Mirroring*. Mirroring is a reflective process that reassures the other that we accurately hear the factual content of messages sent. A useful metaphor is to imagine yourself a flat mirror, neither convex nor concave. A flat mirror reflects an exact image, while the other two distort it. Distorted communication is interpretation rather than reflection. Since an interpretation is what you understood or what you think rather than what your partner meant, it often results in conflict and judgment.

Here is how mirroring looks:

Sender: "I thought we had a date for Friday night, but you never came and you didn't even call. I hate that. I don't know what to think. Did you forget? Did I misunderstand? It makes me so furious when I get stood up. I felt abandoned and I don't like it."

Mirroring Response: "So if I am hearing you accurately, you thought we had a date Friday, and when I did not call or come, you were confused about our plans, and you felt abandoned and angry."

Now the sender evaluates the accuracy of the communication, and responds: "Yes, that is right; also I was confused, and I hate being stood up." (The sending partner must be sure that all of the communication was heard accurately. The mirroring process should be repeated until the sender agrees that it is fully correct.)

Nonmirroring response: (criticizing) "You always get so upset about little things. And you are constantly blaming me." Or (defending, denying) "What do you mean? We didn't have a date," or (rationalizing, explaining) "Yeah, well, I had to work so late that when I finished, I just went home. I didn't think it was a definite date, anyway." Or (distorting) "Well, you had it all wrong (you distort reality). I don't see how you could have thought that (you are crazy)." All these comments devalue another person's experience and communicate indirectly that he or she is wrong.

2. *Validation*. Validation is the recognition that the inner experience of the person you're speaking with makes sense from his or her perspective, that what he or she says is "true" for them and has its own logic. To validate another person means that you put yourself in his place, behind his eyeballs, and look at the situation from his point of view. It is essentially an act of self-transcendence. Here is how validation would look in the conversation above:

Validator: "Well, I can see what you are saying. From your point of view, we had a date, and I didn't show up or call. I can understand why you were confused and angry. That makes sense."

Invalidating response (after an accurate mirroring response): "I don't see what you are so upset about" (you have no right to your feelings—they are not valid). Or "You're always making mountains out of molehills" (you are hysterical—devaluation).

Validation does not mean that you agree with the other person. You do not have to surrender your experience or your point of view. It simply means that you recognize and accept that the other person has also had an experience, and that his point of view, while it may be different from yours, has equal validity. Remember that *others are not you*. Until that is learned, you cannot relate to others; you can relate only to yourself. The dialogue process establishes the facticity of the other and creates equity in the relationship.

3. *Empathy*. There are different levels of empathy. First-level empathy is the communication to another person that you hear and understand his or her *feelings* and that they make sense. Second-level empathy is a communication that you hear the other's feelings, that his feelings make sense, and that you are experiencing his emotion inside yourself. This second level requires a transcendence of self that is difficult for most of us. I recommend that you strive for the first level to begin with; that is difficult enough. When you have mastered the first, then you should attempt the second level. It is a deeply healing process. Here's how it would look:

Empathizer: "I understand what you are saying and I can imagine that my not calling or coming made you feel abandoned and angry."

Nonempathic response (usually there is no recognition of feelings; if they are recognized, they are devalued): "I can't imagine why you would feel abandoned by not getting a phone call, or why you would be angry about that (your feelings are not rational or justifiable). I would have just gone about my business (the way I respond is the only correct way)."

4. *Putting it all together.* These three processes, Mirroring, Validating, and Empathy, add up to a complete response: "So, if I hear you correctly, you were under the impression that we had a date on Friday, and when I didn't call or come you felt confused, abandoned, and angry. Do I hear that correctly? Well, given your understanding of the situation, I can see why you were confused and upset. It makes sense, and I can imagine that you felt abandoned and angry (and with deeper-level empathy) and I am feeling how scared and furious you must have been right now. And it's an awful feeling."

You can practice this type of response with someone whether or not he is conscious of what you are doing. It will have a profound effect. When you have finished the third step, Empathy, you can communicate your response to the original message sent. Then, if the Sender is familiar with the dialogue process, s/he becomes the receiving partner and responds with the three processes. The dialogue continues with alternation until the issue is dissolved. I suggest you try this in a variety of contexts.

If your experience matches that of many others to whom I've taught this process, you're complaining by now about how much this slows you down, and how hard it is. Your frustration is valid. It *is* hard and it *does* slow conversation. It makes sense that you do not want to do it. But, believe me, this tedious process is much faster than the time it takes most of us to work through the fallout of our distorted communications, and it eliminates the pain occasioned by misunderstanding, judgment, and interpretation. With practice, Intentional Dialogue becomes habitual, and it doesn't feel stilted. You will soon get the hang of it, and experience both its efficiency and the intimacy it creates. After all, it is merely a form of decency to treat others this way.

I suggest that you practice Intentional Dialogue at every appropriate opportunity, especially in situations where there is conflict, confusion, frustration, or anger.

EXERCISE 15I   ▪   ▪   ▪   ▪   ▪

Holding Projections

Projection involves assigning a denied negative aspect of oneself to another person and then responding to that person as if that trait belonged to him or her. For instance, if you are angry or stingy, but your self-concept does not include your being angry or stingy, then you will "see" anger and stinginess in others and relate to them, usually critically, as if they possessed those characteristics. It's like watching a movie. The images you see look like they are on the screen, but they are really in you, the projector. Of course, projection is an unconscious process, so you do not realize you are doing it. As far as you are concerned, your criticism and blame are perceptions.

In relationships, projections are the culprit in many conflicts. Dealing with them is a real challenge, for they are tricky. The fact is that most of the time, when someone projects his or her denied traits onto you, you *do* possess the trait, although perhaps not to the degree the projector sees, which is the degree to which s/he possesses the denied trait. In this case, the projector metaphor breaks down, because the image in the projector is *also* on the screen. But, since the traits are unacceptable to you, for the same reasons they are unacceptable to the other person, you deny having them, and usually respond with a rebuttal or with a counter-accusation.

This is the heart of the problem. The way you respond to the projection confirms for the projector that it is true: you give evidence that you really are as s/he claims. It is natural to get angry when someone accuses you of being angry or to become withholding if s/he says you are. In this case, the projection is attracted by a valid perception.

In other cases, the projector metaphor is accurate. The image is *only* in the projector and it is attracted by something in you that is perceived incorrectly. Your frown, for example, may mean you are thinking, but it is interpreted by the other as anger. The interpretation, however, arouses anger in you that was not there until you were accused of it. Attacked, you confirm the projection by behaving in the way you are accused of acting. This dynamic is called *projective identification*. You identify with the projection and become it.

There are two ways of dealing with either one of these situations. One is typical, but ineffective; the other is unusual, but highly effective. The first is to deny the projection and reassign it to the projector: "What do you mean, I'm stingy. *You're* the stingy one!" The effective—but rarely encountered—response is to *hold* the projection and not reflect it back to the other person. This is done through Intentional Dialogue. Instead of denying the accusation or identifying with it, you mirror it back, validate the other person's experience, and express empathy with his feelings. You neither agree with it nor reject it. When you do this, the projection does not get confirmed; it has nothing to grab on to and cannot stick. Eventually, if you continue to hold and accept the projection, it has no screen on which to display itself. Your failure to corroborate the projection disconfirms it and the other person has to drop it, reexamine it, or withdraw it. Its energy fizzles.

Here is the way such a transaction might look:

Example 1:
Sender: "I feel so alone. You are just not there for me. You don't want to be with me. You don't listen. I think you just don't want me to feel cared about."

Receiver (Mirroring): "So, right now you are feeling so alone, like I am not here for you, and that I don't listen. And you think I don't care about you and that I don't want you to feel cared about.

(Validating) "I can understand how you would feel that way. I can see that, since I realize that sometimes I don't listen to you with full attention or act in a caring way.

(Empathizing) "And I can imagine that makes you feel terrible. You must feel angry and afraid."

Example 2 (This an example that demonstrates possible projective identification, with the sender basing the criticism on the *appearance* of the other):
Sender: "Why are you always angry with me? I can see it in that look on your face. You just don't seem to like me. I don't know what I have done to deserve your anger."

Receiver (Mirroring): "If I am hearing you correctly, you are saying that I always seem angry with you, that I don't like you and that you don't deserve it. Is that correct?

(Validating) "Well, I hear you loud and clear, and, given the fact that sometimes I *am* angry at what seems like nothing, I can understand your saying you don't deserve it.

(Empathizing) "And I can imagine that you must feel really mad."

Here's how it would look if the receiver identified with the projection and was unable to hold it: "What do you mean, I am always angry (loudly, with anger)? You are always doing that (globalizing the sender to disempower him or her). I can't even look at you without you thinking I am angry. You are the angry one (projecting the aroused anger back on the sender)."

As you can see, the *response* of holding the other's projection, not criticizing in return or withdrawing or becoming angry, is *itself* proof that you care, and that you are in fact present and available. When you hold the projection through dialogue and do not become defensive or counteraccusatory, the energy in the projection dissipates over time and allows the other to withdraw the accusation and look at the possibility that the anger is coming from him or her. If you defend yourself, the projection will stick like glue, and the sender will be able to continue disavowing his or her part in the problem. Try this out the next time someone is upset with you. You will be amazed at how constructive this process is.

E X E R C I S E   1 5 J   ▪   ▪   ▪   ▪   ▪

Behavior Change Requests

Criticism is the most common reaction to frustration in a relationship, and it is the most destructive, a perverse and counterproductive attempt to get one's needs met or to correct an uncomfortable situation. Its misguided premise is that if we inflict pain on another person, we can get him or her to relieve our pain, to be sorry for the hurt s/he caused us, or force him or her to give us the pleasure or attention s/he denies us. Criticism is the frozen cry of childhood, now put into language; it doesn't work, but our hardwired old brain lamely persists.

There is a simple, highly effective, and easily learned alternative to criticism. Since every criticism is a desire expressed with negative energy, the effective strategy is to identify the desire and express it directly, and then concretize the desire by describing the behavior you want to replace the behavior that you are getting.

The example below illustrates the distinction between frustrations, criticisms, and desires, and it describes an effective way of responding to others' frustrations with you. It also suggests how to reframe your criticism positively when *you* are frustrated. Again, it essentially involves using the Intentional Dialogue process in contexts where change is desired in response to frustration, anger, and criticism. Whether the other person is aware of the process or not, you will greatly deescalate the emotions, and the other will learn from the way you use it with him.

The example here expresses a typical frustration. It is broken down into the *feeling* connected to the frustration, the *fear* behind it, the *critical form* it usually takes, the *desire* embedded in it, and the *desired behavior change*.

Frustration: "You did not call and tell me you were going to be late. I am frustrated because I was ready to go at 7:00 and now we are going to be late for the play. It's so embarrassing to be seated late and have to disturb everybody."

Feeling: Anger and embarrassment

Fear: Abandonment by partner; being ashamed by others

Criticism: "You are always late. You have no concern for my feelings. You are so tied up in your work that I don't matter. I can't count on you."

Desire: "I need you to be reliable and to do what you say you are going to do."

Desired behavior change: "In the future, when you see you are going to be late, please call me at least thirty minutes in advance so we can make alternate plans. Maybe I can meet you at the theater."

The statement of the frustration above is an ineffective communication. Here is an example of a frustration converted into an *effective communication:* "When you are late, I feel angry because I get afraid something has happened to you or that you don't want to be with me, and I get embarrassed at the thought of going late to the theater. I need you to be reliable for me. In the future, when you see that you are going to be late, please call me at least thirty minutes in advance, and let me know when you will be here, so we can make alternate plans."

Notice that the *behavior* (being late) is stated, followed by the *feeling* (anger) and the *fear* (something has happened or you don't want to be with me, and anticipated embarrassment). Next come the *desire* and the *desired behavior*.

An *effective response* to this communication might look like this: "If I am hearing you correctly, when I am late you get worried that I might not come at all, or that if I do, we will be late to the theater and you will be embarrassed. So, when I am going to be late, you want me to call thirty minutes before our appointment and reassure you that I will be there and make alternate plans. Am I hearing you correctly?"

Sender: "Yes, that is correct. Thanks for hearing me."

Validating response: "Well, I see your point of view, and it makes sense to me that you want me to be on time or to restructure things when I am going to be late."

Empathic response: "And I can imagine that when I don't it angers and frightens you and in this event threatened you with embarrassment. I am sensing how awful that feels."

The Behavior Change process works both ways. When you are frustrated with someone, I suggest that you forgo criticism altogether. Instead, identify your frustration and communicate it along with the embedded desire, followed by a request for the behavior you want. When you become proficient at this, you may omit the communication of the frustration. Simply describe the frustrating *behavior*, state your desire, and then state your behavior change request. You will be amazed at the efficiency of this process, and your friends and lovers will feel safer with you.

On the other hand, when someone is frustrated with you and/ or criticizes you, rather than react with a counterfrustration or criticism, as we are all wont to do, respond by Mirroring, Validating, and Empathizing. It does wonders to detoxify the situation. Then ask the other to state his or her desire and the behavior s/he wants. It might look like this:

Mirroring response: "So you are telling me that you get frustrated when I do _____ (describe the behavior that frustrated the other)."

Validating response: "That makes sense to me. I can see that you would be frustrated by that."

Empathic response: "And I can imagine that you feel———"

Request for the embedded desire: "Would you be willing to tell me what you really want in place of what I did?"

Request for desired behavior: "OK. I understand what you want. Now will you tell me just what you want me to do instead?" (Ask your partner/friend/work associate/child to be specific and positive, and to quantify just how much, when, and where. This will help you develop a target response that will exactly satisfy his or her need.)

If you experiment with this process in your current relationships, intimate or otherwise, you will be well on your way to mastering an essential skill for making your future relationships work. I can assure you that, without this skill, your new relationships will mirror your old ones.

One last note: In my study of partner criticisms, I have found that a frustration or a criticism not only contains a desire; it also contains an accurate description of a Denied Self trait or an aspect of the Lost Self. In other words, when others are frustrated with us or criticize us, they are telling us about a part of ourselves we don't want to acknowledge. The prime indicator of the accuracy of the match between a criticism and a disowned part of the self is the degree of negative emotional response you have to it. I have also found that your criticism of others, especially if it is emotionally charged, is usually a projection of Denied Self traits in you, the criticizer. Therefore, others' criticisms of you and your criticisms of them contain valuable information, which if you listen to them and alter your behavior accordingly, will facilitate your progress toward wholeness. You may want to make a list of criticisms—those you make of others, and those that others make of you—and compare them with the traits of your Denied Self (Exercise 10C, page 173) and your Lost Self (Exercise 10B, page 171). When you change your behavior in response to others' requests, you begin to change hidden aspects of your character.

Now that you've done all this hard work, I will introduce you to the prize that is available in your future relationships when you become proficient in these skills: real love.

16

Real Love: Paradise Regained

Yet there be some that by due steps aspire
to lay their just hands on that golden key
that opens the palace of eternity.

—JOHN MILTON

Having journeyed from romantic love through the labyrinth of self-confrontation and toured the characterological terrain that must be restructured, we have come to the heart of the matter—real love. Throughout the preceding chapters I have referred to real love without defining it, but we are now in a position to preview the prize that lies ahead. I want to describe its core features so you can know what's ahead for you if you choose it.

In a way we have come full circle. But we are not at the place we began. Paradise regained is simultaneously the same and a different reality from the paradise lost in the power struggle. So what we shall see is both familiar and new, for while real love reflects the ambience of romantic love—its qualities, tones, and sensations—there is a profound difference. Substance has replaced fluff, surface yields to depth, and transience is replaced by stability.

Romantic love comes easily, but it is fleeting, nature's gift from

292

the unconscious to lure us on the journey to our full potential. It is a *state* of being created by the deep forces of the psyche. But real love is an achievement of consciousness and intentionality, a *way* of being, a hard-won prize granted only to those who persevere. The process of transforming romantic love into real love can be compared to the journey of a child of inherited wealth who squanders it all in foolish spending. To return home and recover his birthright, he must dirty his hands in the world of work, learn his trade, develop discipline, shed the fat gained through opulence, and surrender the illusion of entitlement. Only then, with newfound skills and his inherent potential developed, can he maintain his wealth and enjoy the fruit of his own labors.

Romantic love is a preview of the possible. It is an illusion only in the sense that it is unstable; given the person you are now, you cannot hold it. Nature knows it has to lure us with ecstasy—romance—to the portals of transformation. But nature does not leave us with the dregs of disillusionment—failed romance—nor does it have any interest in pain and suffering as our existential condition. These are the by-products of the journey. The euphoria of romantic love, the sense of wholeness, the feelings of connection and communion can become a constant in your relationship; such qualities are the prevailing tone of real love. But they are available only on the other side of the valley of conflict and fear.

Conflict, endemic to all intimate relationships, is the alchemical soup that transforms raw emotion and instinct into pure gold. It is the chemistry of growth which is a precondition for entering the paradise of real love. Deep, profound changes must occur, but they do not include your becoming someone else; you are already not yourself. You sacrificed yourself on the altar of fear many years ago. Now you must make another sacrifice, this time on the altar of love. You must surrender your fear of being yourself and sacrifice the false self you constructed to replace your authentic self. If you continue to journey's end you will rediscover that stranger within and befriend him—thus becoming whole.

Like romantic love, the power struggle is supposed to end. What do you get when you have paid your dues? Those who hang in through the power struggle emerge with real love's trophy—a passionate friendship. Passion, that chemistry that makes romance so intoxicating, is the most striking feature of real love. The Greeks call this passion *eros*. It refers to our life force, a pulsating energy that, under conditions of safety, undisturbed by fear, is experienced as a feeling of "full aliveness." When released from its imprisonment behind the walls of rigid character defenses and the fear that maintains the necessity of these walls, *eros* courses through the channels of the wounded self, healing the hurt places, restoring the body to its full capacity for sensate experience, softening held muscles, enriching feelings, and spurring creativity of thought and action. The experience is not one of ecstasy, although there are many moments of ecstatic highs, but rather an immense sense of well-being, a "relaxed joyfulness"—another gift of real love. The world is altogether a better place in which to live. The compulsive search for meaning, a yearning that seems to be a compensation for the absence of vibrant aliveness—is replaced by an almost mystical *experiencing*. I am reminded of the comment by Carl Jung, the great psychoanalyst who founded Analytical Psychology, who, when asked if he believed in God, said, "I do not believe, I know." Or St. Thomas Aquinas, who, after his experience of mystical illumination, referred to his previous voluminous writings about the nature of God as "straw." Such is the certainty and transformative power of the transition from romantic to real love. Vivid experiencing replaces the search, but unlike mystical knowing, which is often ephemeral, real love lasts. It is built upon the rock of character change, which makes it possible to hold the experience and maintain it when the storms come. Fear is the enemy of love.

SAFETY FIRST

The secret to entering this earthly paradise is letting go of fear. But you must not only surrender your own fear, you must cease being an object of fear for your partner and create an environment of safety. To achieve that, you must redirect *eros*, your life force, away from the self and its self-preservation toward the emotional, physical, and spiritual welfare of the partner. This trans-instinctual act changes *eros* into *agape*, an unconditional concern for the other that elevates the partner's emotional and spiritual welfare to a condition of absolute priority—thus guaranteeing your partner's safety and, paradoxically, your own. (Safety, it seems, is the necessary precondition for optimal life throughout nature.) In a relationship, safety means the end of criticism and all other forms of abuse.

Here we find a paradox: commitment to your partner's evolution toward wholeness stirs the chemistry of your own. Unfaltering attendance to your partner's needs; focusing upon healing his or her wounds; stretching beyond the comfortable boundaries of your self-concept and your accustomed ways of doing things; the activation of behaviors that feel distinctly alien to the defended self; and sharing of the most private of thoughts, feelings, and desires—all custom-tailored to your partner's needs—stir the chemistry of your own evolution. The gift of this paradox is that in directing *eros* toward your partner rather than holding your life energy for yourself—focusing only upon your own needs and your own security—parts of yourself that atrophied in childhood are returned to you. It is a two-way healing: you become whole in the process of healing your partner. Long-buried needs, which are similar to the needs you must meet in your partner, surface when you meet your partner's needs. You are reintroduced to hidden parts of yourself.

To stay calm in the maelstrom of change that attends these trans-instinctual acts requires commitment. But no journey's end is ever reached without continuing on the way, focusing on the task, bearing the pain, staying the course regardless of the shifting winds, avoiding tempting distractions to jump ship for the nearest island.

Which brings us to another key to opening the doors of paradise: *self-integration*. All aspects of your disowned self must be welcomed and restored to their original place in the house of the self. It's not a very romantic or exotic idea, certainly not new, but our resistance to it is enshrined in our institutions. We expend our life energy searching outside ourselves for what we seek, and keeping our Missing Selves hidden from consciousness, while our knowledge of the truth is unveiled in every mythology from the grail search to *The Velveteen Rabbit*. That which we need, and for which we search, is inside us all the while, but its awakening requires the care of another.

What is new is the concept that the parts we most need, to quench our parched thirst for wholeness, are inevitably mirrored to us by a committed partner, and that we can recover those parts only by meeting the mirroring partner's needs. When all our missing parts are reunited, we can have freedom from conflict, rest from our search, and the cessation of our yearning. To risk the self in the service of the other is to save the self.

NO STRINGS ATTACHED

However, this must be a reciprocal and unconditional gifting if the partners are to become passionate friends. The unconscious is not interested in bartering. Unconditional love of the other turns out to be the highest form of self-interest and the key to one's personal welfare. But the catch is that if you do it for the outcome, paradise will elude you. You must do it because it *should* be done, because your partner needs it. Then the doors of paradise open.

The term *agape*, which I equate with this process of "stretching" to meet the other's needs, was coined by the Greeks to differentiate between the forms of love. (In English we use adjectives to parse love's meaning.) *Agape* refers to the self-transformational act of caring absolutely and unconditionally for another in the exact way they need to be cared for. I want to elaborate on the fascinating etymology of *agape*, for it is both an ingenious and instructive concept.

When recently I returned to my study of Greek to search for the origins of the concept of *agape*, I was astonished to discover that the idea seems to have originated in the period of Greek tribal wars preceding the golden age of Pericles. As best I can piece it together from an etymological dictionary, the concept of *agape* arose in a time when the Greeks were musing about the best means to end tribal conflict. Pondering this eternal dilemma of how to end war, they came to the conclusion that war was a function of the *perception* of the "other"—i.e., the "enemy"—as a "nonperson," or someone who is not human. Such a perception justified killing the men, raping the women, and carting them and their children off to slavery, destroying their villages and laying waste their lands. A classic example of destruction being rationalized when the enemy is dehumanized is Rome's revenge against Carthage. After pillaging the town, the Romans poured salt on the land so that nothing would grow. There are parallels to our recent war with Iraq, and to the current practices of the Dani tribe, a cannibalistic people in Irian Jayah, which I visited a few years ago. Speaking through an interpreter to the elders of one of the warring tribes, we learned that they ate their enemies to ingest their strength, but the ritual was possible because they perceive their enemy as "not human."

Well, the Greek generals, as philosophically oriented as they were warlike, developed the idea that they could prevent war if they reconceived the enemy as human—as "like us." Further, they argued that the "other" who was the enemy should be redefined as "kin." That makes him "one of us." This expanded concept required that the privileges of kinship be extended to the enemy. What were those privileges? A guarantee that he would not be attacked without reason. His existence would not be considered a threat. Furthermore, the former enemies who are now kin should be allowed to "cross our lands" without paying a "toll." And "while they are in our lands, they will be protected from our aggression and that of others." To this new code of international behavior they gave the word *agape*—meaning unconditional acceptance of the other who is now "one of us," a "no strings" commitment to their welfare. This seems to be the origin of the idea of "unconditionality" in the granting of a privilege or the giving of a gift. *Agape* is not an economic barter or a "trade agreement" in which one or both racks up deficits in the exchange of goods. It is a reciprocal exchange without anyone keeping score.

The resulting relationship between the Greeks and their former enemies was called *philia*, or care and love of the other as "friend." Later, a word of Latin origin, *caritas*, was added to the permutations of love; this is the extension of care and kindness and a commitment to the welfare of those who are "not kin." From this historical reconstruction of the Greek (and Roman) understanding of love, the most practical relationship one can have with another is to *"agape"* them. That creates *philia*, or abiding friendship. The outcome is that the "other" will not attack you; the guarantee of safety to the other is the best guarantee of one's own safety.[1]

I see the emergence of this kind of love when couples complete their work. In the beginning, *eros* is held or directed as anger toward partners. Eventually, they transcend their defenses, become concerned and empathic toward their partners' wounds, and actively engage in healing behaviors. This transformation of *eros* into *agape* transforms their relationship into *philia*, making them passionate friends. This ultimately transmutes into *caritas*, a concern about the larger world of social ills.

That we humans have had to learn over the centuries that the care of the other is in our own best interests is suggested by Helen Fisher in her marvelous book *The Sex Contract*.[2] In it she suggests the origins of love in an imaginative reconstruction of the discovery of the value of "sharing" in prehistoric times. Our prehuman ancestors who learned to share survived and flourished, passing on this practical knowledge to their progeny. But even the learning of elementary sharing required a momentary transcendence of the survival drive, of the fear of the other, and the reframing of the other as an ally. Nature selected the "sharers" for survival, but the instinct to share competes with many other powerful ones in the genetic code.[3]

What I get from the Greek concept of *agape*, and from Fisher's book, is that love has to be learned; it is not a genetic legacy of the race. Our energy, part and parcel of the cosmos, is neutral. We become altruistic or selfish in response to the quality of our experience during our journey of development and socialization. If we are deprived of our essence, we turn against ourselves and others. But what we are learning—what religion, philosophy, and mythology have always recognized—is that obsessive self-interest is destructive of the self. Care of the other serves our own survival directive.[4] When in the developmental process we move from ego development to interest in others, that interest is in the service of the survival directive. If we survive that passage without hurt and fear, our natural interest in others emerges as altruistic; but if we do not, our interest in others is motivated by pain and fear, and we behave accordingly.

In my work with couples, I see that the Greek story of the origins of *agape* is eminently applicable to intimate love relationships. The partner, when the romantic illusion fades, becomes a stranger and can take on the character of the enemy. Ask any couple in the throes of conflict! Real love is both a process and a goal. It is born in the midst of battle when one partner decides to view the importance of the other's welfare as equal to his own. Then the offending partner's behavior is viewed as arising out of his or her fears and hurts; he or she is wounded and in need of healing. This reframing of the partner makes it possible to extend succor, empathy, care, and eventually love, which requires a healing of your own perception of the other. You guarantee that your partner is always safe in your presence. He or she can "live in your land" without fear of harm from you. If there are disagreements or conflict or needs, they will be expressed as desires for certain changes in behavior and not criticized under the magical belief that if you punish your partner (as if he or she were an enemy) he or she will care for your needs.

GOOD INTENTIONS

Beyond the doors of paradise is the promised land for which your psyche yearns. But it will be waiting for you only if you persevere along the way. Real love is both a cause and a consequence of your intentions, both an action and a state of being, an achievement that becomes a gift. This gift of grace is the fruit of discipline. You cannot create it, but it will come to you if you meet the conditions. The passion that is its character is a result of creating safety for the partner, which is done by meeting the partner's childhood needs.

I call the work that is the precondition of grace *intentional reciprocity*. Each partner intends the outcome he or she wants and acts to bring it into being. This requires the extinction of unconscious reactivity, a legacy of evolution resident in the old brain, and its replacement by conscious intentionality, a potential housed in the forebrain of the cortex. This is the part of the brain that observes itself and can redirect the ancient survival program. It will take time. We learn slowly and change more slowly still. Only when the new brain's revised program secures the organism's safety does the old brain turn off its alarm and surrender its ancient protective strategy. How long that process takes depends upon the degree of childhood injury and the steady commitment of both partners to the healing process. For some couples, it requires six months to a year; others need not expect to arrive at their destination in less than two to five years. It took Helen and me seven years.

But there is some good news. You only have to go a little more than *half* the distance. Kurt Lewin, the late, great social scientist, discovered in studying social systems that when 51 percent of the variables in any system change, the remainder of the system re-organizes itself at a higher level of functioning. Grace arrives, but only if you change the majority of your character traits and meet just more than half of your partner's needs. Then nature rewards you with a gift, and the rest falls into place.

You will know you are almost to the gates of paradise when you feel like you are falling into the pits of hell. The demons, those voices from the past, arrive to frighten you away from the prize. Your defenses are crumbling, your character structure is changing. Your worst fears surface as you violate the injunctions of childhood. The issues between you and your partner become more intense and your relationship goes into chaos. Despair sets in. You regret embarking on the journey and try to return down the path or, better yet, get off the path and get rid of your partner, as many couples do. Or fire your therapist, if you have one. But the gates are barred. Your psyche is reorganizing itself, returning to its original wholeness: it is hard to reverse the process once you have tasted the nectar of your original self. The breakdown is a breakthrough. Now is not the time for any decision; you must continue the journey, stay with the process. From these ashes will arise the phoenix of paradise.

I can testify to what happened to Helen and me. During the course of our eight years of marriage, we have felt the shackles of our character armor melt under our commitment to each other and to the process of mutual healing of our childhood wounds. We have gone through the throes of despair, hating each other and the process. Before we were far along, I arrogantly thought that since I had figured out the process and had taught it to thousands of people, I might be immune from the requirements and consequences of change. But I was wrong. Our only hope and salvation, when we hit the rapids, was that we knew what lay ahead. Dreading it as we did, we nevertheless struggled long and mightily. The rewards have been incalculable, and it is still not over. We have to integrate our experience, get used to this new reality, and grow toward our potential. There will be other hurdles along the way, but we are joined in our effort. It is a lifelong process, but the portals have been breached. I can add the testimony of hundreds of couples to our own experience, and can report the sorrier fate of those who refused to begin or complete the journey.

Life after this meltdown is quite miraculous. A change occurs, which I call *spontaneous oscillation*. What was an effort before becomes a desire. Spontaneous behaviors replace intentional efforts. It is not necessary to remember what your partner needs, because you are motivated out of joy to express your care in target-specific behaviors. And the most remarkable thing is this: *the core issues dissolve.* Your partner's needs actually dissipate, along with your own, and you find yourself in a relationship that feels like the horn of plenty. Laughter is abundant, the humdrum dailiness of life takes on deeper meaning, pillow talk is intimate, orgasms easy and plentiful. There's no more walking on eggshells, because your house finally feels like *home.* It feels, as it should be, as it can be, like full aliveness. Expectations of pleasure give way to *experiencing* pleasure, and time seems to be an eternal now. Living in the moment replaces imprisonment in the past and preoccupations with visions of a hoped-for future. The future has arrived, and with it the end of yearning and thus the end of striving. I call this phenomenon *desireless valuing.* No longer is your partner of value because he or she meets your desires; he or she is desirable because you value him or her. In fact, in the paradoxical reality of real love, your partner is of no value to you, yet is valued absolutely. A natural high alternates with plateaus of pleasure, and there are few descents into the valley of the fear of death. Along the journey to wholeness, compulsions give way to preferences, yearnings decrease—nothing is missing. You have you, and that ends the journey, for paradise has been regained.

NATURE'S GRAND DESIGN

Something wonderful is happening here that is far greater than our personal healing and wholeness. Through our healing and growth, nature is completing itself. We are a node of consciousness in a field of consciousness—the tapestry of being. What happens to one node affects the whole. When we are in pain, our woundedness is felt throughout nature. When we are healed, Nature's pain is assuaged.

But nature is in travail. The collective pain of the human species is externalized in all life forms, human and nonhuman, and to the planet itself. All life forms, fish and fowl, the animals in the forest, the forests themselves, the land, the sea, the air we breathe, and the remote ozone layer, are all victims of our insensitivity and the lack of empathy born of pain. We are the victims of centuries of failed parenting and loveless marriages. Wounded ourselves, we are nature's wounders. If we do not reverse the tide, we will be nature's victims.

Given no change in our affliction of the planet, optimistic scientists give us another hundred years (pessimists give us fifty) before the earth gets rid of us to save itself. The same survival instinct that expresses itself in us is indigenous to Nature on a global scale. Nature has always dispensed with any species that could not adapt to its changes, but we seem to expect the planet to adapt to ours. It will not; we are dispensable.

I think we have hope, but there isn't much time. Our hope lies in the fact that we are not only a thread in the tapestry of Nature, we are nature's apex. Because nature has equipped us with a frontal lobe, and with it the capacity for self-awareness and self-knowledge, we have as well the potential for self-correction. We are that part of nature through which it knows itself, can study and fix itself. But we must use our capacity for knowing and self-correction to consciously cooperate with Nature's impulse for self-repair and self-completion. Through its reflective consciousness—science, psychology, sociology, theology, and other disciplines—nature is revealing the tears we have made in the tapestry of being, and seeking to enlist our participation in the healing of our species and the planet. To cooperate with this fantastic project is to participate in the healing of the universe.

There is no way to salvation but the way of love. It is not in seeking love or in finding love, but in loving, that Nature's pain will be assuaged and we will survive. That is the lesson of evolution and history. We must learn it well. We have not learned it yet. It is my belief that love between intimate partners is nature's attempt to heal itself. The growth required—the completion of our own developmental journey—is nature's attempt to complete itself. The consciousness required is nature's attempt to become self-conscious through us.

When you meet your incompatible partner, nature has arranged for a biochemical reaction to occur, which transmutes the chemistry of attraction into the chemistry of growth. Through the knowledge from recent human sciences, we now have some of the instructions about how to cooperate with the process. So let your heart lead you. Go with the partner choice your unconscious presents—the person you fall in love with. It is wiser than your conscious mind, and its purposes are grander than your need to avoid discomfort. Stretch to meet your partner's needs, not giving the love *you* want to give, but the love your partner needs to be healed. Nature does not care if you are comfortable, only that you evolve. A part of its travail lies in your incompleteness. Your defenses disrupt its pulsation and partially block the flow of energy in the universe. Learning to love is the challenge. When through loving you become whole, Nature will reward you with the end of craving. You will no longer fall prey to the life-deadening enticements offered by society, because you will be reconnected to nature's enlivening elixirs.

If after reading this book and doing the exercises, you decide to marry and take the journey to wholeness with your partner, you will not only contribute to nature's healing itself, you will contribute to the prevention of its future injuries—especially if you have children. Someone said that adulthood consists of attempts to get over childhood. That seems to be the case for most of us. But children born to a couple who have learned to love sustain fewer injuries. They internalize a model of being that does not require them to separate from parts of themselves or deaden their sensitivities to their environment. They develop empathy for all living things. They understand that care for themselves includes care of the planet. Nature does not become their victim, or vice versa.

Mine is an idealized vision, to be sure. But just imagine it. Such children, unencumbered by fear, their caring instincts intact, become adults who care for others and the planet. The few social programs that exist are for those who are victims of circumstances that have nothing to do with ineffective parenting, for that has been eliminated by the proliferation of healthy, loving marriages. The medical establishment has been reduced by 80 percent and deals only with anomalies of nature. Stress-related illnesses are unknown, and no stress-reduction programs exist, because there are no customers. There is no drug war because there are no drugs. People get "high" on feeling the aliveness at their core. War has been eliminated because there is no dehumanization of the "other." The planet is nourished because everyone feels connected to it and consciously realizes and experiences the interconnectedness of all things. A society has emerged in which everyone retains his and her original wholeness and relaxed joyfulness, pulsating with the rhythm of Nature.

I believe this is our potential and our birthright. But we have lost it. I hope it is not too late to recover it. Nature has revealed the secret: love heals all wounds and makes the lover whole. It is simple, but the process is arduous; it may take a thousand years. There is an old proverb that says, "A journey of a thousand miles begins with the first step." You can help the process by healing the wound in Nature which your present or future partner bears, and in turn, recover your wholeness and sense of oneness with yourself and all things. That will make you an ally in the grand project of Nature's self-repair and completion. And paradise will be regained!

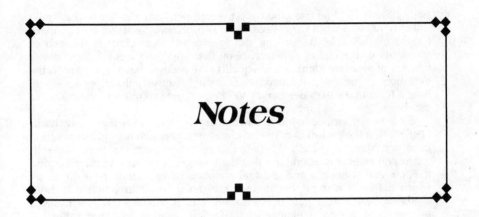

Notes

CHAPTER ONE

■

1. Mary Anne Meyer, "Success and the Single Woman," *The New York Times*, March 22, 1990.
2. Erik Erikson, *Childhood and Society*, W. W. Norton and Co., New York, 1950. See Chapter 8, "The Eight Ages of Man."
3. Robert Karen, "Becoming Attached," *Atlantic Monthly*, February 1990, p. 35 ff.

CHAPTER TWO

■

1. On a recent trip to Irian Jaya, I saw a Stone Age version of the practice of arranged marriage, the relics of which persisted in Western marriages until the nineteenth century. The Dani people have lived in the highlands of Irian Jaya for at least seven thousand years. Wives are bought—and can be resold—for five pigs, unless they are pregnant, or exceptional workers: then they cost more. Attraction is not a factor of choice; strong bodies and fertility are the prime virtues.

   Variations of spousal ownership have existed for thousands of years. In many parts of Europe, wives came with a dowry. All arranged marriages are based on social and economic factors such as wealth, social status, and fertility. Love plays little, if any, part. This has changed in most modern societies, most visibly in those which have moved toward a democratic political system which allows free choice regarding one's personal destiny, which encompasses the selection of a marital partner.
2. It is my belief that this evolution in marriage parallels the evolution of the collective psyche, which in turn follows the same path as the individual's psychic development—from fusion with the mother (the connection of the individual to the collective), to differentiation from the mother (differentia-

tion of the individual from the collective), to personal identity in the family (identity of self within the collective), to competence, concern, and intimacy (stages in the collective psyche still to evolve). Democracy is the end of monarchy or the end of dependence on the collective parent and the development of separate identity and equality. We seem to be at this point in the evolution of the collective psyche. Therefore, future political systems will have a form other than democracy to "house" the evolution of the collective psyche.

Since we are embedded in nature and are, in fact, nature expressing itself, I believe that the evolution of the psyche is an expression of psychic evolution in nature. More specifically, I believe that nature is committed to its own self-repair and self-completion, and that the emergence of the love marriage and the potential of healing and spiritual evolution inherent in it is the means by which nature is working out its own self-repair and completion. For thousands of years, in a patriarchal society and a monarchical government, marriages were devoid of love and affection, women were not valued as equals, and children were property. The result was much emotional pain and warped character that expressed itself in group conflict, and, finally, in our time, in damage to the planet itself.

Nature, from my perspective, is in travail because of our collective pain, and is seeking to heal itself through our healing. Working through our unconscious, it created democracy to "house" the emergent collective psyche, and through this political system freed the unconscious to select a marital partner so that a system of healing could be created that would ultimately result in the healing of nature.

3. The first national organization of marital therapists did not emerge until 1942 when the now defunct American Association of Marital Therapy was organized. Prior to that, a handful of marriage counseling centers had existed: the Marriage Consultation Center, founded by Abraham and Hannah Stone; the Marriage Council of Philadelphia, founded by Emily Mudd; and the American Institute of Family Relations, founded by Paul Popenoe. Supportive literature on marriage therapy did not appear until 1938, with a paper by Obenforf on the psychoanalysis of married couples, followed in 1948 by a paper by Mittleman on "the concurrent analysis of married couples."

Even so, marriage counseling focused on helping individuals with their personal pathologies, not on the marriage itself, and most counseling was based on psychoanalysis, a psychology of the individual. Focus on the couple and the marriage did not appear until the early 1970s, with the rise of a method called "conjoint marital therapy," a structure of counseling in which the partners were seen together. This was a radical innovation, the impetus for which was the breakup of so many young marriages after World War II.

4. Judith S. Wallerstein and Sandra Blakeslee, *Second Chances: Men, Women, and Children After Divorce*, Ticknor and Fields, New York, 1989. In this significant study, Wallerstein failed to find any instances of divorce that did *not* create emotional injuries in children that affected their adult adjustment to life and their intimate relationships.

CHAPTER THREE
■

1. William James, *The Varieties of Religious Experience: A Study in Human Nature*, Modern Library, New York, 1936, p. 469.
2. New York University neuroscientist Joseph LeDoux and his colleagues have identified in animals a nerve pathway that carries impulses directly between

the thalamus—an early processing station for sensory input—and the amygdala in the old brain. Information sent along this pathway arrives at the amygdala two to three times faster than that sent first to the cortex. This allows the amygdala to make an almost instantaneous analysis of whether a sound is something to be afraid of even before it is consciously heard or identified. This contrasts with the previous, more traditional view that sensory information traveled first to the cerebral cortex where the sound is consciously perceived, and the cortex then sent signals to subcortical areas of the brain, like the amygdala, which evaluated the emotional significance of the stimulus. These "lower regions" then sent return messages back up to the cortex and fired up the autonomous nervous system, producing, if the message was "danger," the pounding heart, rapid breathing, and rising blood pressure that usually accompany fear. *U.S. News & World Report*, June 24, 1991, p. 56.

3. In most discussions of our evolutionary heritage, little mention is made of play. This omission was brought home to me at the Bronx Zoo, where I watched two snow leopards play with each other for two hours. Play is often observed by students of monkeys and apes, and can be seen in any home where there are new puppies or kittens. It is most evident in the lives of children. I am convinced that play is a basic evolutionary adaption. It is perhaps omitted in the study of adult human behavior (historical and evolutionary) because of our Appollonian mind-set, our cultural rejection of Dionysian myths as a result of their debasement by Bacchian orgies, the suffering motifs of religious traditions, and the work ethic of a puritan civilization. Play remains the domain of children, not grown-ups. Too, the notion that play is a part of our human heritage is curiously missing not only from the history of our evolution, but from classical literatures on love, in which the most frequently mentioned association is between love and death. In fact, the message of these literatures is that the aliveness and wonders of love are meant to end, not in a transformation to a stage of sustainable bliss, but in catastrophe. See Tristan and Isolde as the prototypical story of love in the Western world.

4. This illusion is supported by the mental-health profession, in the orthodoxy that the separate, autonomous, self-sufficient individual exists, and that we must correct intrapsychic conflicts before we can expect to function well in a relationship. Although the influence and importance of intimate relationships on and to individual healing are beginning to appear in scientific literature, the main focus is still on lonely self-repair.

CHAPTER FOUR
■

1. This duality between mind and body is known as Cartesian dualism, after French philosopher René Descartes. The mind/body split, from my perspective, is a function of thought, rather than a reality. Mind and body are a continuum, as is being demonstrated by new findings in neuropsychobiology and psychoneuroimmunology, which find correlations between mental states and body functions, such as the correlations between the immune system and stress.

2. The developmental task of each stage is not confined to the age in which it appears but rather reappears, in different forms and circumstances, in cycles throughout life. We always need secure attachments, we are always differentiating and exploring, our identity changes with new experiences and mirrors from the world. Achieving competence is a lifelong task, and opportunities

to develop concern and intimacy crop up in new contexts throughout life. The point of saying this is that a focus on a particular task in later life does not necessarily mean regression to that childhood stage (although in some instances it is that), but a further evolution of that life task in response to a new challenge or context.

3. Margaret Mahler, *On Human Symbiosis and the Vicissitudes of Individuation: Infantile Psychosis*, International Universities Press, New York, 1968; Erik Erikson, *Childhood and Society*, W. W. Norton Company, New York, 1963; see especially Chapter 8, "The Eight Ages of Man." The view that childhood influences adulthood is a common theme of developmental psychology, psychoanalysis, object relations theory, and self-psychology.

CHAPTER FIVE
■

1. Most developmental theories posit an "autistic" stage in the early months of life. Margaret Mahler, the most influential object-relations theorist, places it in the first three months. However, there are counterviews that interpret so-called "autism" as a nonessential aspect of environmental influences on the pre-birth and birth experience. I am in sympathy with this approach. Therefore, I see the newborn's first cry as an impulse to reach out and reconnect with the mother from whom it has been separated. This would not occur if the child were still psychically fused with the mother: i.e., there is actually no autistic stage and the separation of birth is what activates the attachment drive. When autism occurs, from my perspective, it is induced by trauma at or prior to birth.

2. New research suggests that life in the womb is not always idyllic. Some unfortunate children arrive on earth already wounded. We are discovering the repercussions of the mother's prenatal depression, alcoholism, and drug abuse, as well as the fallout of overdrugged births and other physical and psychological problems. Such natal wounding may explain some features of temperament, character disorders, and autism.

3. Harry Harlow, *Learning to Love*, Jason Aronson, New York, 1974.

4. The time sequences of the developmental stages outlined here (see Figure A, page 58) are a composite of general agreement among developmental psychologists, but they conform to no particular theory. Perhaps the most influential theorist is Margaret Mahler, whose sequences are as follows: birth to six months is the stage of autism; six to ten months begins the stage of differentiation; ten to fifteen months she calls practicing; fifteen to twenty-four months is called rapprochement; twenty-two to thirty months the age of object constancy. Combining her observations with other theorists, mainly John Bowlby and Mary Ainsworth, Sigmund Freud, and Erik Erikson, I place the Attachment process between zero and eighteen months; Differentiation and Exploration between eighteen and thirty-six months; Individuation and Identity between age three and four; Competence from ages four through seven; Concern from ages seven through thirteen; and Intimacy from age thirteen through nineteen. Since little research has been done on the post-Oedipal stage of Concern, there are few guidelines in the discipline to document the emergence of this task. From the work of Harry Stack Sullivan and my own observations, it appears to emerge between the ages of seven and twelve, the so-called latency period identified by Freud. He considered these years a hiatus between the Oedipal obsession and the onset of puberty,

and since he was convinced of sexual motivation as the basis of behavior, he found nothing of interest there. However, he overlooked the most important development of the child's life: the movement from egocentricity to caring for others.

5. These terms and the position expressed here is based on the attachment studies by John Bowlby and Mary Ainsworth. It is integrated also with the developmental studies of Margaret Mahler and David Stern. The synthesis of these studies enlarges the view of the child as driven mainly by intrapsychic aims countered first by external inhibitions, which later become internalized prohibitions, an essentially closed system, and includes what I consider, following Bowlby/Ainsworth/Stern, the essential component of interpersonal experience as jointly formative of the infant's world and determinative of later attachments, especially to significant and/or intimate others. In other words, I view the human organism as an open system, essentially interpersonal rather than intrapsychic; thus early experiences are selective and edited memories, rather than fantasies. Emotional problems are thus not the result only of inhibited aims or instinctual striving, but of deficient nurturing and overrestrictive or laissez-faire socialization. John Bowlby, *A Secure Base: Parent-Child Attachment and Healthy Human Development*, Basic Books, Inc., New York 1988; David N. Stern, *The Interpersonal World of the Infant*, Basic Books, Inc., New York 1985; M. D. Ainsworth, M. C. Blehar, E. Waters, and S. Wall, *Patterns of Attachment: assessed in the strange situation and at home*, Lawrence Erlbaum, Hillsdale, N. J., 1978.

6. Studying detached/avoidant children, Ainsworth observed that when the caretaker enters a room where her child is playing, the child consistently fails to make eye contact with the parent and never runs to the parent for comfort even under stress, whereas the healthy child will notice her arrival and seem glad to see her and, if he is not too involved, will stop his playing and go to her within a short time. In contrast, the clinging child often breaks into tears and flees to his mother's arms to be consoled. Instead, the detached child continues what he is doing, as if he was not aware of the mother's absence or did not need reassurance, and does not take notice when the caretaker leaves the room. These behaviors give the child the appearance of independence and self-sufficiency. Although they look good and seem secure, they are actually "avoidant" behaviors, which protect the child from the negative feelings of rejection aroused by the coldness of the caretaker when present, and by his/her frequent physical absence. M. D. Ainsworth, above.

7. The Maximizer/Minimizer polarity is a complementary adaptation that seems to characterize couples with unresolved issues across all developmental stages. The Minimizer exhibits avoidant or schizoid behavior in the Attachment stage, distancing or narcissistic behavior in the differentiation or Exploration stage, obsessive/compulsive or rigid behavior in the Identity stage, and competitive or aggressive behavior in the Competence stage. At the Concern stage he tends to be a loner or a compulsive caretaker, and at the Intimacy stage he is usually a rebel or a conformist. The Maximizer exhibits clinging or symbiotic behavior in the Attachment stage, fusion or borderline behavior in the Exploration stage, diffuse/submissive or hysteric behavior in the Identity stage, manipulative or passive-aggressive behavior in the Competence stage, gregarious or compulsive caretaking behavior at the Concern stage, adaptive or conformist behavior at the Intimacy stage of adolescence. Given complementarity of adaptation in partner choice, we find the Avoider (schizoid)/Clinger (symbiotic) couple dealing with Attachment issues, the Isolator (narcissistic)/Fuser (borderline) couple dealing with issues of differentiation, the Rigid (obsessive/compulsive)/Diffuse (hysteric) couple dealing

with issues of individuation, the Competitive (aggressive)/Compromiser (passive-aggressive) couple dealing with issues of competence and power, the Loner (underinvolved)/Caretaker (overinvolved) dealing with issues of caring, and the Rebel (aggressive)/Conformist (passive-aggressive) couple dealing with the issues of intimacy and responsibility.

CHAPTER SIX
■

1. Freud saw all neurosis as originating in this Oedipal stage; pre-Oedipal stuff he labeled "primitive" and thus presumably untreatable. Along with most therapists, I agree that Oedipal fixation, or the failure of little boys to identify with their fathers and little girls to identify with their mothers, is the core of the neuroses, but I disagree that this struggle is confined to competition with the same-sex parent for the attention of the opposite-sex parent. I also disagree that such cases represent most therapy patients. I rarely see a patient with an Oedipal issue, unless there has been an affair. In primary love relationships, it is almost all "primitive" stuff, in my view, and it is treatable.

CHAPTER SEVEN
■

1. Harry Stack Sullivan, *The Interpersonal Theory of Psychiatry*, W. W. Norton Inc., New York 1953, pp. 245ff.

CHAPTER EIGHT
■

1. Patricia Love, *The Emotional Incest Syndrome: What to Do When a Parent's Love Rules Your Life*, Bantam Books, New York, 1990.
2. Daniel Goleman, "A Key to Post-Traumatic Stress Lies in Brain Chemistry, Scientists Find," *The New York Times*, June 12, 1990, p. C1.
3. Ivor Browne, "Psychological Trauma, or Unexperienced Experience," *Re-Vision*, Vol. 12, No. 4, Spring 1990, pp. 21ff.
4. Judith S. Wallerstein and Sandra Blakeslee, *Second Chances: Men, Women, and Children a Decade After Divorce*, Ticknor & Fields, New York, 1989.
5. Judith Hooper and Dick Teresi, "Sex and Violence," *Penthouse*, February 1987, pp. 41ff.
   Many studies have established the relationship between pleasure deprivation and violence, with the concomitant suggestion that pleasure enhancement or need satisfaction will decrease violence. While it is certainly true that need frustration often leads to violence, there are few studies that demonstrate the correlation between pleasure deprivation and apathy/despair. The pleasure deprivation/violence correlation is the polarity to the pleasure deprivation/apathy correlation. Again we see the two responses to deficit: the Maximizer who responds by turning inward, with illness and depression; the Minimizer who explodes with violence and rebellion. We don't hear as much about the deprivation/apathy correlation because violence gets more headlines, and wreaks more obvious havoc, while apathy and

despair are easier to ignore. I see this as unfortunate because, statistically, the pleasure deprivation/apathy correlation affects many more people, involves many more institutions, and has a greater economic impact than its polarity.

Too, I disagree with the premise that pleasure/need satisfaction is the cure for violence or apathy. Why is that? From my studies with couples, I have learned that there is no simple correlation between need deprivation that occurred in childhood and its satisfaction in adulthood. The reason for this is that when a need has long been frustrated, *the need itself*, not the deprivation, becomes a psychic danger to the individual. Now he only knows how to live *without* the need. Consequently, the psyche defends itself through violence or apathy in reaction to the need frustration. Perversely, the violence or apathy serves as the psyche's protection against gratification of the needs it views as dangerous or abhorrent.

These defenses become part of the character structure, designed to maintain system homeostasis. The need itself, if it remains conscious at all, becomes aversive and hated; or it may be entirely denied, banished from consciousness. In either case, its direct gratification is avoided and sabotaged. (See reference on page 256 to *self-hatred*.)

Additionally, both violence and apathy may be reactions modeled after observed behaviors of significant persons in childhood and thus incorporated into the character structure as learned responses. Whether they have a dynamic base or are learned from others, they are adaptive mechanisms that can be changed only by conscious awareness and intentionality. They do not yield to the stimulus/response paradigm.

CHAPTER NINE
∎

1. Most of the personal and collective malaise of the human race, which most of our remedial programs and organizations are designed to ameliorate, are the result of centuries of failed parenting. The survival demands which attended our pre-hominoid ancestors as they emerged from the forests into the woodlands and grasslands became even more complicated as early humans organized into settlements, villages, and finally into towns and cities. To the rules that made survival in nature possible were added yet more complex rules and strictures, and finally laws necessitated by the emergence of civilization. More and more of the self was sacrificed as the collective became more organized. We have not yet learned how to nurture and integrate the young into the collective without psychic injury.
2. Robert Ornstein, *The Healing Brain*, Simon & Schuster, New York, 1987, page 36.

CHAPTER ELEVEN
∎

1. Daniel Goleman, "Study Defines Major Sources of Conflict Between Sexes," *The New York Times*, June 13, 1989, page C1.
2. Gabriel Trip, "Call of the Wildmen," *The New York Times Magazine*, October 14, 1990, p. 37ff. Both Bly's *Iron John* (Robert Bly, *Iron John: A Book About Men*, Addison Wesley Publishing Co. Inc. 1990) and Robert Moore and Douglas Gillette's *King, Warrior, Magician, Lover* (Harper/San Francisco, 1990)

are provocative, revealing discussions of the price men have paid for their imprisonment in the roles patriarchy has assigned them. Whatever value the patriarchy has had in establishing order, science, and technology, it has done so at the price of wholeness for both men and women. In the authors' view, patriarchy is a "boy" psychology that keeps men from full maturity and self-integration. I personally see little distinction between their description of the "deep masculine" and the integration of the feminine, which is what I propose. And I do not support the redefining of the masculine via a return to the archaic symbols of the King, Warrior, Magician, and Lover, however archetypal (and convenient) they may be. Archetypes are predispositions informed by the collective, universal experience of the *past*. As a reflection of hierarchal patriarchal culture, they serve poorly to envision the future. The only archetype I value is the Lover, which I see as an emergent, not an archaic form, but we are not there yet. We have to complete this passage through the emergence of the individual to the development of Identity—a society of individuated, equal persons—and then develop competence with this new identity, before we can move on to a society of universal concern, caring, and love. Along the way, all the old archetypes will slowly mutate into representations of our evolved psyche. In the interim, we would be better served to look not backward, but to the brighter future we envision.

3. "Men vs. Women," *U.S. News & World Report*, August 8, 1988; "Guns and Dolls," *Newsweek*, May 28, 1990.

4. "Guns and Dolls," above.

5. "Guns and Dolls," "Men vs. Women," above.

6. Carol Gilligan, in her wonderful book, *In a Different Voice: Psychological Theory and Women's Development* (Harvard University Press, Cambridge, Mass. 1982), clearly and poignantly distinguishes the female mode of perception from that of the male.

7. "Guns and Dolls," "Men vs. Women," above.

8. Gilligan, above; and Deborah Tannen, *You Just Don't Understand*, William Morrow & Company, New York 1990.

9. Tannen, above, pp. 24–25.

10. Joe Tanenbaum, *Male and Female Realities: Understanding the Opposite Sex*, Candle Publishing, Texas 1989.

11. "Guns and Dolls," above.

12. Tannen, above.

13. Natalie Angier, "Marriage is Lifesaver for Men after 45," *The New York Times*, October 16, 1990, p. C1.

14. "How to Stay Married in the 90s," *Brides*, December 1980/January 1990, p. 126ff; "The Way We'll Be: Marriage in the 90s," *New Woman*, December 1989, p. 36ff; "Back Off, Buddy," *Time*, October 12, 1987, p. 68ff.

15. Jane Gross, "New Home Front Developing as Women Hear Call to Arms," *The New York Times*, September 18, 1990, p. 1.

16. June Singer, *Androgyny: Toward a New Theory of Sexuality*, Anchor Press/ Doubleday, Garden City, N.Y., 1976.

17. Jamake Highwater, *Myth & Sexuality*, New American Library, New York 1990.

18. Elaine Pagels, *Adam, Eve, and the Serpent*, Random House, New York 1988: This theological position, which has its roots in St. Augustine, has had a detrimental, permeating influence on Western culture. It counters the opposite romantic view that children, as Wordsworth put it, "come into the world trailing clouds of glory." From my perspective, children are neither

angelic nor demonic, but neutral bundles of energy with innate predispositions that are shaped in the cultural mill.

19. Judith Hooper and Dick Teresi, "Sex and Violence," *Penthouse*, February
1987, p. 41ff.
20. Andrew Greeley, *Sexual Intimacy: Love and Play*, Warner Books, New York
1988, pp. 178–179.
21. John Stoltenberg, *Refusing to Be a Man: Essays on Sex and Justice*, Meridian
Books/Penguin, New York 1990.
22. Greeley, above, pp. 190–191.

CHAPTER THIRTEEN

■

1. The birth of a child may retrigger the romantic stage, only to replace it with
a new power struggle around parenting, nurturing, and child care. This
contributes to the development of a new identity, which requires new
competence that gives the relationship added power and leads to the expression of care for the new infant or others. Other life cycles that reinvent the
process are children reaching adolescence, the mid-life crisis, aging, etc.
There is no end point, but a series of cycles that move in a linear direction.

2. I have come to believe that nature has a relentless purpose: to heal and
complete itself. Its goal is a grand unity in which all its disparate parts are
connected in one pulsating whole. I see this purpose recapitulated in the
human developmental journey, in which the individual organism moves
from self-care (survival) to care for others. Before the organism can move on
to care for others, it must develop the ego. This can be seen in the shift from
ego concern that caps the Oedipal failure at about age six, to peer involvement and concern, the love affair with the "chum" at around eight or nine,
to the adolescent obsession with the opposite sex. This process seems to be
not only a preview, but a preparation, for the emergence of adult love,
moving on to marriage, the care of children, and, finally, an altruistic care of
others beyond the nuclear family.

All developmental tasks appear to be present in the neonate; therefore,
real love arises out of our innate potential for caring (the nurturing adaptation
of our evolutionary journey), at the proper age and in the proper environment. The emergence of care at age seven or so must be a precursor of the
evolution of love in later life, for surely nothing could evolve in nature that
was not preexistent. Love must therefore be viewed as an indigenous potential in the human psyche which could (and may eventually) create a political
structure in which to house itself. We are still far from that, but I believe the
process of creating political structures in which the psyche can house itself at
its current state of development is an explanation of previous political
structures. Monarchy, for instance, the rule of the many by the one, recapitulates the dependency phase of the parent-and-child relationship. The emergence of democracy (envisioned by the Greeks and Hebrews) in America in
the eighteenth century is the rebellion of the many (children) against the
parent (monarch), a product of psychic evolution in the direction of individual autonomy and freedom that reprises the differentiating, exploratory stage
of the psyche. We have several more stages to pass through, but the direction
seems to be toward universal equality, care, and love.

Our essence, however, is not love; love is our potential. Our essence is
pulsating energy operating under the primal directive of survival and full
aliveness. To respond to that directive, the energy, under threat, may take

other forms to protect itself—forms that are oppressive, that we call evil. Such mutations of the life force will continue to plague us until we have created universal safety, equality, and respect.

I believe we are moving, fitfully, in that direction, but we have to cooperate with our own evolution. From my perspective, the core structure through which this impulse in nature is expressing itself is intimate, committed relationships. The healing of each psyche heals the pain in nature, and the continued development of every person facilitates nature's evolution toward self-completion. Beyond that, only in a safe, loving environment will children be born who can retain their innate wholeness. These children nature will select to complete its project of healing and universal harmony.

3. Elisabeth Kübler-Ross, *On Death and Dying,* The Macmillan Company, Collier-Macmillan Ltd., London 1969.

CHAPTER FOURTEEN
∎

1. I don't mean to imply that there is no benefit to many of the New Age/self-help offerings—Natural Child workshops, men's and women's retreats, spas, exercise ranches, etc. I offer weekend workshops myself, but they are clearly meant as introductions to a lifelong process of change that can occur only in a context. What I am dismayed about is the persistence of you-can-do-it-all-by-yourself-ism, with its glorification of individualism, autonomy, and independence, as if we do not live in a context. The fact that most self-help offerings are group processes, with a leader, contradicts this "individualism."

Guided imagery, visualization, and meditation work with the imagination, and are valuable forms of mental training, which I practice and recommend. But changes in primal imagery, instinctual reactivity, and character defenses—which we are addressing—must be rooted in concrete experience. What most people avoid by becoming change junkies, hopping from seminar to workshop to retreat, is addressing the necessary change in character structure, facing their shadow, the Lost and Denied Self. Happiness arises out of wholeness, and peace of mind comes with the integration of conflicting self aspects, and that is ultimately possible only in a committed relationship.

The Natural Child is reborn in a relationship, not in returning to nature, or singing songs, or exercising the imagination. I am not opposed to such activities; in fact, I enjoy them. The massive participation in these activities reflects our longing for reconnection to something primal. What I am opposed to is that idea that what we desire can be recovered in an "experience." The outcome we seek occurs naturally when the childhood wounds are healed, and that comes about in the struggle of relationship.

2. Jeffrey Seinfeld, *The Bad Object: Handling the Negative Therapeutic Reaction in Psychotherapy,* Jason Aronson, Inc., Northvale, New Jersey, 1990; Jerold J. Kriesman and Hal Straus, *I Hate You, Don't Leave Me: Understanding the Borderline Personality,* The Body Press, Los Angeles, 1989.

CHAPTER FIFTEEN
∎

1. A dreamwork book that I recommend is *Night and Day: Use the Power of Your Dreams to Transform Your Life,* by Jack Maguire, Fireside Books, New York 1989.

CHAPTER SIXTEEN
∎

1. This is reminiscent of the Old Testament promise that "if you cast your bread upon the waters, it will not return to you void," and its dictum, "Do good to your enemy, return love to them that hate you." Later, these words, especially *agape* and *philia*, became the cornerstone of religious language and were raised to the level of descriptions of God's behavior and attitude toward humans. Only God could express *agape*. But there is an opposing view in the same context. Some writers quote Jesus as saying, "God is love, and they that love dwell in God and God in them," which returns agape to the human sphere.
2. Helen E. Fisher, *The Sex Contract: The Evolution of Human Behavior,* Quill Books, New York, 1983.
3. The impulse for care and bonding does appear in the developmental evolution of each individual, but it is connected to survival. That the probability of our survival is increased by transcendence of the survival directive expressed as altruistic concern for the other must be learned in each individual life. That practical outcome is the canon and aim of most religious teachings.
4. The same message is now coming from studies of mind/brain interaction, the new discipline called psychoneuroimmunology. The consistent reports from this emergent discipline are that caring for others relaxes the nervous system and improves the immune system. When you are thinking of the welfare of others, you reframe them as objects of care rather than sources of danger. That produces endorphins, with consequent relaxation, rather than adrenaline, which activates the evolutionary defense mechanisms. (See Ornstein and Sobel, *The Healing Brain;* James Lynch, *The Broken Heart,* Basic Books, New York, 1977, for further reading.)

Bibliography

Abbott, Franklin, Ed. *Men & Intimacy: Personal Accounts Exploring the Dilemmas of Modern Male Sexuality*, The Crossing Press, Calif., 1990.

Ainsworth, M. D., M. C. Blehar, E. Waters, and S. Wall. *Patterns of Attachment: Assessed in the Strange Situation and at Home*, Lawrence Erlbaum, Hillsdale, N. J., 1978.

Beattie, Melody. *Beyond Codependency*, Harper & Row, New York, 1989.

Bellah, Robert N.; Madsen, Richard; Sullivan, William M.; Swidler, Ann; Tipton, Steven. *Habits of the Heart*, University of California Press, Berkeley, 1985.

Bly, Robert. *Iron John: A Book About Men*, Addison Wesley Publishing Co., Inc., 1990.

Bowlby, John. *A Secure Base: Parent-Child Attachment and Healthy Human Development*, Basic Books, Inc., New York, 1988.

Branden, Nathaniel, Ph.D. *The Psychology of Romantic Love.* J. D. Tarcher, Inc., Los Angeles, 1980.

Csikszentmihalyi, Mihaly. *Flow*, Harper & Row, New York, 1990.

DeRougemont, Denis. *Love in the Western World*, Pantheon Books, New York, 1940.

Durden-Smith, Jo; Desimone, Diane. *Sex and the Brain*, Arbor House, New York, 1983.

Erikson, Erik. *Childhood and Society*, W. W. Norton and Co., New York, 1950.

Fisher, Helen E. *The Sex Contract: The Evolution of Human Behavior*, Quill Books, New York, 1983.

Gilligan, Carol. *In a Different Voice: Psychological Theory and Women's Development*, Harvard University Press, Cambridge, Mass. 1982.

Greeley, Andrew. *Sexual Intimacy: Love and Play*, Warner Books, New York, 1988.

Harlow, Harry. *Learning to Love*, Jason Aronson, New York, 1974.

Highwater, Jamake. *Myth & Sexuality*, New American Library, New York, 1990.

Johnson, Robert A. *Femininity Lost and Regained*, Harper & Row, New York, 1990.

———. *Ecstasy: Understanding the Psychology of Joy.* Harper & Row, San Francisco, 1987.

Keen, Sam. *Fire in the Belly: On Being a Man*, Bantam Books, New York, 1991.

Kotre, John, and Elizabeth Hall. *Seasons of Life: Our Dramatic Journey from Birth to Death*, Little, Brown & Co., Boston, 1990.

Kriesman, Jerold J., and Hal Straus. *I Hate You, Don't Leave Me: Understanding the Borderline Personality*, The Body Press, Los Angeles, 1989.

Kübler-Ross, Elisabeth. *On Death and Dying*, The Macmillan Company, Collier-Macmillan Ltd., London, 1969.

Leonard, Linda Schierse. *On the Way to the Wedding*, Shambhala Publications, Inc., Boston, Mass., 1986.

Liebowitz, Michael R., M.D. *The Chemistry of Love*, Little, Brown & Co., Boston, 1983.

Love, Patricia. *The Emotional Incest Syndrome: What to Do When a Parent's Love Rules Your Life*, Bantam Books, New York, 1990.

Lowen, Alexander, M.D. *The Spirituality of the Body*, Macmillan Publishing Company, New York, 1990.

Lynch, James. *The Broken Heart*, Basic Books, New York, 1977.

———. *The Language of the Heart*, Basic Books, New York, 1985.

Maguire, Jack. *Night and Day: Use the Power of Your Dreams to Transform Your Life*, Fireside Books, New York, 1989.

Mahler, Margaret. *On Human Symbiosis and the Vicissitudes of Individuation: Infantile Psychosis*, International Universities Press, New York, 1968.

May, Rollo. *The Art of Loving*.

McDonough, Yona Zeldis; Yahm, Howard. *Tying the Knot*, Penguin Books, New York, 1990.

Mellody, Pia; Miller, Andrea Wells; Miller, J. Keith. *Facing Codependence: What It Is, Where It Comes From, How It Sabotages Our Lives*, Harper & Row, New York, 1989.

Miller, Alice. *Banished Knowledge*, Doubleday, New York, 1990.

Miller, Jean Baker. *Toward a New Psychology of Women*, Beacon Press, Boston, Mass., 1976.

Moore, Robert, and Douglas Gillette. *King, Warrior, Magician, Lover*, Harper, San Francisco, 1990.

Ornstein, Robert, and David Sobel. *The Healing Brain*, Simon & Schuster, New York, 1987.

Pagels, Elaine. *Adam, Eve, and the Serpent*, Random House, New York, 1988.

Person, Ethel S. *Dreams of Love and Fateful Encounters*, W. W. Norton & Co., Inc., 1988.

Rubin, Lillian B. *Intimate Strangers*, Harper & Row, New York, 1983.

Schoenewolf, Gerald. *Sexual Animosity Between Men and Women*, Jason Aronson, Inc., Northvale, New Jersey, 1989.

Seinfeld, Jeffrey, *The Bad Object: Handling the Negative Therapeutic Reaction in Psychotherapy*, Jason Aronson, Inc., Northvale, New Jersey, 1990.

Shengold, Leonard, M.D. *Soul Murder: The Effects of Childhood Abuse and Deprivation*, Yale University Press, New Haven, 1989.

Singer, June. *Androgyny: Toward a New Theory of Sexuality*, Anchor Press/Doubleday, Garden City, N.Y., 1976.

Solomon, Marion F. *Narcissism and Intimacy: Love and Marriage in an Age of Confusion*, W. W. Norton and Co., Inc., New York, 1989.

Stern, David N. *The Interpersonal World of the Infant*, Basic Books, Inc., New York, 1985.

Stoltenberg, John. *Refusing to be a Man: Essays on Sex and Justice*, Meridian Books/Penguin, New York, 1990.

Sullivan, Harry Stack. *The Interpersonal Theory of Psychiatry*, W. W. Norton Inc., New York 1953, pp 245ff.

Tanenbaum, Joe. *Male and Female Realities: Understanding the Opposite Sex*, Candle Publishing, Texas, 1989.

Tannahill, Reay. *Sex In History*, Stein and Day Publishers, New York, 1980.

Tannen, Deborah, Ph.D. *You Just Don't Understand*, William Morrow & Company, New York, 1990.

Wallerstein, Judith S., and Sandra Blakeslee. *Second Chances: Men, Women, and Children After Divorce*, Ticknor and Fields, New York, 1989.

Welwood, John, Ph.D. *Journey of the Heart: Intimate Relationship and the Path of Love*, HarperCollins Publishers, New York, 1990.

Index

About the Author

HARVILLE HENDRIX, Ph.D., began his career as a pastoral counselor in 1965, working mainly as a psychotherapist with individuals. After his divorce in 1975, he began a study of marriage, with a focus on marital therapy, that led to the development of Imago Relationship Therapy, first presented in *Getting the Love You Want: A Guide for Couples,* which has sold over half a million copies.

Dr. Hendrix was a faculty member at the Perkins Divinity School of Southern Methodist University for nine years prior to his transition to private practice in 1979. A graduate of Mercer University, which has awarded him an honorary Doctorate of Humane Letters, and Union Theological Seminary in New York, he earned his M.A. and Ph.D. degrees from the Divinity School, University of Chicago. He is a diplomate in the American Association of Pastoral Counselors, a clinical member of the International Transactional Analysis Association, a member of the American Group Psychotherapy Association, and a member of the Association for Imago Relationship Therapy.

Dr. Hendrix lives in New York City with his wife, Helen, who is involved nationally in the women's empowerment movement. Between them they have six children, a changing number of hamsters and turtles, and a dog. The family loves adventure travel, which they usually do in a motor home.

The Institute for Relationship Therapy

The Institute for Relationship Therapy was founded by Harville Hendrix, Ph.D., in 1984. Its purpose is to support the improvement of adult love relationships as a resource for emotional healing and spiritual evolution. The Institute offers workshops for couples who want to improve their relationship, singles who want to prepare for a successful marriage, and training for clinicians. To date, three hundred clinicians have been certified to practice Imago Relationship Therapy; they have recently formed the Association for Imago Relationship Therapy.

If you wish information on:

Nationwide 2-Day Workshops for Singles

Public lectures and 1-day workshops on relationships

2-Day and 4-Day couples' workshops

Study guides and audio cassettes for singles and couples

Clinical training and workshop leadership training in Imago Relationship Therapy for therapists

Please call or write The Institute for an information packet and workshop and training schedules.

The Institute for Relationship Therapy
1255 Fifth Avenue, Suite C2
New York, NY 10029
800-729-1121

Please send me information on your programs. I am most interested in:

☐ Singles
   Workshops
   and Audio
   Cassettes

☐ Couples
   Workshops,
   Study Guides
   and Tapes

☐ Professional
   Training Program
   and Schedules

Name: _____

Address: _____

_____

City: _____ State: _____ Zip Code: _____

Tele. No. (Day): _____
                   (Area Code)
Tele. No. (Eve.): _____
                   (Area Code)
Best Time to Call: _____

_____